ENDANGERED
PEOPLES
of the Arctic

Used by permission of MAGELLAN Geographix, Inc.

ENDANGERED PEOPLES
of the Arctic

Struggles to Survive and Thrive

Edited by Milton M. R. Freeman

The Greenwood Press
"Endangered Peoples of the World" Series
Barbara Rose Johnston, Series Editor

GREENWOOD PRESS
Westport, Connecticut • London

Library of Congress Cataloging-in-Publication Data

Endangered peoples of the Arctic : struggles to survive and thrive
/ edited by Milton M. R. Freeman.
    p.   cm.—(The Greenwood Press "Endangered peoples of the
world" series, ISSN 1525–1233)
  Includes bibliographical references and index.
  ISBN 0–313–30649–4 (alk. paper)
  1. Arctic peoples. 2. Acculturation—Arctic Regions. 3. Arctic
Regions—Economic conditions. I. Freeman, Milton M. R., 1934– II.
Series.
  GN673 .E72 2000
  306'.08'0911—dc21   99–31577

British Library Cataloguing in Publication Data is available.

Copyright © 2000 by Milton M. R. Freeman

Library of Congress Catalog Card Number: 99–31577
ISBN: 0–313–30649–4
ISSN: 1525–1233

First published in 2000

Greenwood Press, 88 Post Road West, Westport, CT 06881
An imprint of Greenwood Publishing Group, Inc.
www.greenwood.com

Printed in the United States of America

The paper used in this book complies with the
Permanent Paper Standard issued by the National
Information Standards Organization (Z39.48–1984).

10 9 8 7 6 5 4 3 2 1

Contents

Contents

Series Foreword

Barbara Rose Johnston

Two hundred thousand years ago our human ancestors gathered plants and hunted animals in the forests and savannas of Africa. By forty thousand years ago, *Homo sapiens sapiens* had developed ways to survive and thrive in every major ecosystem on this planet. Unlike other creatures, whose response to harsh or varied conditions prompted biological change, humans generally relied upon their ingenuity to survive. They fashioned clothing from skins and plant fiber rather than growing thick coats of protective hair. They created innovative ways to live and communicate and thus passed knowledge down to their children. This knowledge, by ten thousand years ago, included the means to cultivate and store food. The ability to provide for lean times allowed humans to settle in larger numbers in villages, towns, and cities where their ideas, values, ways of living, and language grew increasingly complicated and diverse.

This cultural diversity—the multitude of ways of living and communicating knowledge—gave humans an adaptive edge. Other creatures adjusted to change in their environment through biological adaptation (a process that requires thousands of life spans to generate and reproduce a mutation to the level of the population). Humans developed analytical tools to identify and assess change in their environment, to search out or devise new strategies, and to incorporate new strategies throughout their group. Sometimes these cultural adaptations worked; people transformed their way of life, and their population thrived. Other times, these changes produced further complications.

Intensive agricultural techniques, for example, often resulted in increased salts in the soil, decreased soil fertility, and declining crop yields. Food production declined, and people starved. Survivors often moved to new regions to begin again. Throughout human history, migration became the common strategy when innovations failed. Again, in these times, culture was essential to survival.

For the human species, culture is our primary adaptive mechanism. Cultural diversity presents us with opportunities to draw from and build upon a complicated array of views, ideas, and strategies. The Endangered Peoples of the World series celebrates the rich diversity of cultural groups living on our planet and explores how cultural diversity, like biological diversity, is threatened.

Five hundred years ago, as humans entered the age of colonial expansion, there were an estimated twelve to fourteen thousand cultural groups with distinct languages, values, and ways of life. Today, cultural diversity has been reduced by half (an estimated 6,000 to 7,000 groups). This marked decline is due in part to the fact that, historically, isolated peoples had minimal immunity to introduced diseases and little time to develop immunological defenses. Colonizers brought more than ideas, religion, and new economic ways of living. They brought a host of viruses and bacteria—measles, chicken pox, small pox, the common cold. These diseases swept through "new" worlds at epidemic levels and wiped out entire nations. Imperialist expansion and war further decimated original, or "indigenous," populations.

Today's cultural diversity is further threatened by the biodegenerative conditions of nature. Our biophysical world's deterioration is evidenced by growing deserts; decreasing forests; declining fisheries; poisoned food, water, and air; and climatic extremes and weather events such as floods, hurricanes, and droughts. These degenerative conditions challenge our survival skills, often rendering customary knowledge and traditions ineffective.

Cultural diversity is also threatened by unparalleled transformations in human relations. Isolation is no longer the norm. Small groups continually interact and are subsumed by larger cultural, political, and economic groups of national and global dimensions. The rapid pace of change in population, technology, and political economy leaves little time to develop sustainable responses and adjust to changing conditions.

Across the world cultural groups are struggling to maintain a sense of unique identity while interpreting and assimilating an overwhelming flow of new ideas, ways of living, economies, values, and languages. As suggested in some chapters in this series, cultural groups confront, embrace, adapt, and transform these external forces in ways that allow them to survive and thrive. However, in far too many cases, cultural groups lack the time and means to adjust and change. Rather, they struggle to retain the right to simply exist as other, more powerful peoples seize their land and resources and "cleanse" the countryside of their presence.

Efforts to gain control of land, labor, and resources of politically and/or geographically peripheral peoples are justified and legitimized by ethnocentric notions: the beliefs that the values, traditions, and behavior of your own cultural group are superior and that other groups are biologically, culturally, and socially inferior. These notions are produced and reproduced in conversation, curriculum, public speeches, articles, television coverage, and other communication forums. Ethnocentrism is reflected in a language of debasement that serves to dehumanize (the marginal peoples are considered sub-human: primitive, backward, ignorant people that "live like animals"). The pervasiveness of this discourse in the everyday language can eventually destroy the self-esteem and sense of worth of marginal groups and reduce their motivation to control their destiny.

Thus, vulnerability to threats from the biophysical and social realms is a factor of social relations. Human action and a history of social inequity leave some people more vulnerable than others. This vulnerability results in ethnocide (loss of a way of life), ecocide (destruction of the environment), and genocide (death of an entire group of people).

The Endangered Peoples of the World series samples diversity in different regions of the world, examines the varied threats to cultural survival, and explores some of the ways people are adjusting and responding to threats of ethnocide, ecocide, and genocide. Each volume in the series covers the peoples, problems, and responses characteristic of a major region of the world: the Arctic, Europe, North America and the Caribbean, Latin America, Africa and the Middle East, Central and South Asia, Southeast and East Asia, and Oceania. Each volume includes an introductory essay authored by the volume editor and fifteen or so chapters, each featuring a different cultural group whose customs, problems, and responses represent a sampling of conditions typical of the region. Chapter content is organized into five sections: Cultural Overview (people, setting, traditional subsistence strategies, social and political organization, religion and world view), Threats to Survival (demographic trends, current events and conditions, environmental crisis, sociocultural crisis), Response: Struggles to Survive Culturally (indicating the variety of efforts to respond to threats), Food for Thought (a brief summary of the issues raised by the case and some provocative questions that can be used to structured class discussion or organize a research paper), and a Resource Guide (major accessible published sources, films and videos, Internet and WWW sites, and organizations). Many chapters are authored or coauthored by members of the featured group, and all chapters include liberal use of a "local voice" to present the group's own views on its history, current problems, strategies, and thoughts of the future.

Collectively, the series contains some 120 case-specific examples of cultural groups struggling to survive and thrive in a culturally diverse world. Many of the chapters in this global sampling depict the experiences of indigenous peoples and ethnic minorities who, until recently, sustained their customary way of life in the isolated regions of the world. Threats to survival are often linked to external efforts to develop the natural resources of the previously isolated region. The development context is often one of co-optation of traditionally held lands and resources with little or no recognition of resident peoples' rights and little or no compensation for their subsequent environmental health problems. New ideas, values, technologies, economies, and languages accompany the development process and, over time, may even replace traditional ways of being.

Cultural survival, however, is not solely a concern of indigenous peoples. Indeed, in many parts of the world the term "indigenous" has little relevance, as all peoples are native to the region. Thus, in this series, we define cultural groups in the broadest of terms. We examine threats to survival and the variety of responses of ethnic minorities, as well as national cultures, whose traditions are challenged and undermined by global transformations.

The dominant theme that emerges from this sampling is that humans struggle with serious and life-threatening problems tied to larger global forces, and yet, despite huge differences in power levels between local communities and global institutions and structures, people are crafting and developing new ways of being. This series demonstrates that culture is not a static set of meanings, values, and behaviors; it is a flexible, resilient tool that has historically provided humans with the means to adapt, adjust, survive, and, at times, thrive. Thus, we see "endangered" peoples confronting and responding to threats in ways that reshape and transform their values, relationships, and behavior.

Emerging from this transformative process are new forms of cultural identity, new strategies for living, and new means and opportunities to communicate. These changes represent new threats to cultural identity and autonomy but also new challenges to the forces that dominate and endanger lives.

Introduction: Challenges to Cultural Survival in the Arctic

Milton M. R. Freeman

The arctic regions, although varied in their physical and cultural character-istics, share many common features. Perhaps most important—when con-sidering cultural survival—is that virtually all of the inhabitants of these high-latitude lands are cultural minorities within their own countries. It is sometimes the small numbers of arctic peoples that causes them to experi-ence a number of problems in common, many of which will be discussed in the chapters in this volume.

DIFFERENT VIEWS ON LIVING IN THE ARCTIC

In the past, and even today in popular writing and documentary films and on television, the survival problems of the arctic peoples have been represented by the struggles of "traditional" hunters and pastoralists as they eke out a marginal existence under very extreme climatic conditions. Indeed, such heroic representations can be found in the earliest writings by European and American explorers, missionaries, and adventurers who could describe the Arctic only in relation to their own familiar existence in temperate—and, to them, far more hospitable—regions of the world.

Certainly, in one principal respect, the Arctic is "marginal" to its inhabi-tants: it is marginal to agriculture. Rather than practice settled agriculture, arctic people have made their living as hunters, fishers, and pastoralists, an adaptation far better suited to the Arctic where the growing season for crops is too short and the soils mostly too poor. However, to the arctic peoples, life in the Arctic is anything but marginal—indeed, the Arctic is heartland and home. Seen through its inhabitants' eyes it is both familiar and secure, and it holds personal meaning that can scarcely be understood by an outsider. Photographs of the Arctic, with their vistas of treeless tundra, rocky outcrops seemingly devoid of vegetation, ice, snow, and overall barrenness, do not show how this region could offer anyone a secure way of life. However, all arctic peoples enjoy the benefit of centuries of ancestral knowledge and appreciation of how to make a living, how to raise families successfully, and how to come to terms with an environment that at times could indeed be very demanding—even life threatening.

Without minimizing the very real hardships that people might sometimes encounter in this region of the world, an understanding of why and how some groups of people consider it a preferred place to live requires that we consider the notion of "culture." Culture is a term that means quite different things to different people.

CULTURE: WHAT IS IT?

To some, culture is something people can enjoy in their spare time—listening to music, reading a good book, watching a play, or visiting an art gallery or museum. Anthropologists, who spend their professional lives studying cultures around the world, understand culture quite differently. To the anthropologists who have contributed to this volume, culture is what people do, the rules they live by, and the values they hold in common with others in their own society. So even within a single country, there will very likely be a variety of different cultures. We often hear social commentators speak of "middle America," which is a way of trying to capture the values of a "typical" or "average" American. However, it should be obvious that despite many aspects of everyday life that all Americans share, the livelihoods and many of the personal and community values that an urban resident of Detroit or Los Angeles possesses will assuredly be quite different from those held by a resident of a small fishing or farming community in Maine or Montana.

CULTURAL DIVERSITY IN THE ARCTIC

In the chapters that follow, it is important to note that cultural diversity exists even within the groups of people presented. This can be illustrated with reference to the Inuit (or "Eskimos" as they were more generally referred to in earlier times). As a cultural group, there are only about 100,000 Inuit living in four different countries: Russia, the United States, Canada, and Greenland (which is part of Denmark). This small population is spread across a huge area extending from eastern Asia, across North America, almost to the western fringe of Europe. The 30,000 Inuit in Canada occupy a homeland larger than the subcontinent of India, which is home to almost one billion people!

Despite the few numbers of Inuit and despite certain common cultural characteristics, the different Inuit groups, as illustrated in several chapters in this book, have made a range of cultural adaptations. Because the Inuit occupy a variety of different landscapes and because each of these landscapes offers different possibilities for making a living, it is to be expected that different adaptations would result over the centuries. What creates these differences is that cultures, by their very nature, never remain static; they change continually to accommodate peoples' ongoing attempts to improve their lives and in response to pressures from the outside world.

These different ways of adapting to different environments are well illustrated by chapters that describe various Inuit groups living in four different countries. The Iñupiat of northern Alaska live in an area where, each year almost without fail, large numbers of whales migrate. Over the centuries, a remarkable whaling culture has developed, shared in the past by their Siberian cousins who hunted these same species of whales. A similar seasonal abundance of whales is seen in west Greenland, where the dependence on hunting large-bodied whales is equally ancient, but the manner in which the whaling adaptation manifests itself today is quite different from that seen in Alaska or Siberia. Indeed, in technological terms (as technology is an important cultural means of coping with our daily needs), west Greenlandic Inuit coastal whaling more closely resembles Norwegian coastal whaling than it does north Alaskan whaling.

THE ISSUE OF LANGUAGE

There are other cultural distinctions between the Inuit of northern Alaska and those of southwestern Alaska. Indeed, they call themselves by quite different names—Iñupiat in the north and Yupiit in the southwest—and speak quite different forms of the Inuit language. The Yupiit of Alaska, however, speak a similar language to the Yupiit of Siberia.

It is well understood that language affects the way people think and the way people understand the world they live in. Language is important in maintaining a distinct cultural identity. Relentless globalizing influences, occurring in the most remote northern communities by means of television and other electronic technologies place a great pressure on native languages and the values that constitute an integral part of these distinct cultures.

Language retention is an issue that affects many indigenous arctic people because colonizing governments have often regarded the languages spoken by so few people as an inconvenience in their dealing with them. It is easier for colonizers to try to replace these indigenous languages. The formal school system is used to weaken the influence of the home where language is acquired naturally. This has happened in Russia with the Evenki, for example. The chapter on the Kaska of the Yukon describes the history of this assault on a people's language and the efforts being made—and the problems being encountered—in attempting to counteract this loss. For the

Greenlanders and the Canadian Inuit of Nunavut, language loss is less pronounced—the children still speak their own language—but even these Inuit are well aware that determined efforts will have to be made to ensure that their language remains alive and part of their system of government.

VARIED THREATS FROM OUTSIDE THE ARCTIC

The global influences that threaten the cultural integrity of arctic peoples are similar to those experienced by most minority peoples worldwide. Examples of these threats from the world outside the Arctic extend even to military activities in the case of the Innu of Labrador. Fortunately the impacts are not from an actual war, but rather from the efforts made by the Western nations to ensure a high degree of military readiness for war. Its vastness and remoteness—its great distance from large centers of population—make it a choice testing ground for weapons of the Western military establishment. These damaging intrusions on ancestral lands of the Innu extend beyond the troubling presence of the military. Damage also results from extensive flooding caused by the production of hydroelectricity for distant markets, road building, mining, and forestry—all practices that interfere with the Innu ways of maintaining an important, respectful relationship with wildlife. Their ways of hunting and gathering provide food and maintain the profound spiritual beliefs that sustain their culture and society.

Elsewhere in Canada, the Cree of northern Quebec face similar industrial intrusions, and in the northern reaches of Norway, Sweden, Finland, and the Kola Peninsula of Russia, another people—the Saami—are facing similar developments that threaten their own cultural survival. All arctic peoples it seems, who once lived in relative isolation, are experiencing a growing encroachment on their lands and resources from industrial societies to their south.

In that regard, people living on islands might prolong the isolation better than those who live on the mainland where roads or railways can more easily push north. It might be thought that the relative isolation of the Aleuts of the Pribilof Island and the East Greenlanders, isolated by the Greenland ice cap to their west and an ice-infested sea to their east, could have constituted a protective barrier to globalizing influences. Regrettably that has not been the case. Although no land-altering physical developments have occurred close to their homes, the ideas developed in distant industrial centers have damaged their lives just as effectively.

ALIEN IDEAS AS THREATS TO ARCTIC PEOPLES

New ways of thinking about nature that have originated outside of the Arctic have caused much damage to the small arctic societies living in even the most isolated locations. These include new notions promoted by urban-based animal protection organizations, organizations that individually, in some cases, and certainly collectively control annual budgets in the millions of dollars. Budgets such as these are certainly much larger than those available to the small arctic societies who might want to defend themselves from the attacks of animal protection organizations. Such wealth is used to buy influence among politicians in Washington, London, Brussels, and elsewhere who know nothing of the needs or circumstances of arctic peoples. Indeed, to politicians dealing with issues of economic or social importance to millions of their citizens, the needs of small numbers of arctic peoples—who are certainly not voters in their political constituencies—can appear irrelevant. It is not only indigenous peoples who are so discounted by distant others; the small-scale fisher-whalers from the remote Lofoten Islands region of northern Norway are equally affected by wealthy protest groups operating artful and emotional campaigns in far distant capitals.

In some ways, this war waged by groups claiming an "environmental" cause is especially unwarranted because northern peoples are not the ones who create environmental problems that require a serious political response. Such unwarranted attacks can destroy—in a few short years—sustainable relationships that arctic peoples have developed over centuries with the animals they hunt or herd. In fact, as the chapters dealing with the seal hunters of East Greenland, the minke whalers of northern Norway, the Alaskan Iñupiat, and the Aleuts of the Pribilofs make clear, the issue is not one of environmentalism or conservation of resources. The animals being hunted are neither endangered nor depleted by the level of hunting taking place.

The opposition to arctic peoples' hunting ways of life results from an emotional attachment that city dwellers in faraway places have for certain types of animals, which unfortunately for arctic peoples include seals and whales. People who early in life come to relate to animals from humanized fictional characters found in children's books and family-oriented television shows and films, extend a deep sense of pity toward "defenseless" animals facing the barrel of a gun. Such emotions and concerns are understandable in people who themselves have never had to kill any animal for food, and who consequently leave that distasteful task strictly to others. However, killing animals for food is regarded as a lawful and justifiable act by the state in our own society and in all Western societies resembling our own; even if the food animals in our society are domesticated rather than wild animals, they are living animals, just the same.

Northern peoples, in common with many hunting peoples elsewhere, are praiseworthy for the emphasis they place on respect for all of nature. Their cultural beliefs demand this respect from those who hunt or herd arctic animals. This notion of respect for animals is mentioned in nine chapters in this book, including those about the Evenki of central Siberia, the Yupiit of southwestern Alaska, the Innu of Labrador, and the Cree of northern Quebec.

CHANGES IN SUBSISTENCE ACTIVITIES

Subsistence remains central to the cultural survival of arctic peoples. The term "subsistence" is often erroneously taken to mean only the bare minimum of survival or scratching an existence from a difficult environment using simple tools. In fact, this is not what anthropologists understand by the term subsistence, even if the term "subsist" (as used in everyday language) certainly does refer to a very minimal and often precarious standard of living. To anthropologists, subsistence refers to those practices and beliefs that are necessary to support, and in turn derive support from, the way people make their living. Thus subsistence does not simply involve a people's livelihood (that is, the economic means of their existence); it also involves a number of related social arrangements, beliefs, and cultural traditions that enable the society to function and that ensure that economic activities are given appropriate value and meaning by members of society. One anthropologist has defined subsistence simply as "a set of culturally established responsibilities, rights and obligations that affect every man, woman and child each day" or, as we read in Chapter 8, subsistence is "about the proper way of conducting social relations among humans and between humans and animals."[1]

The terms "value" and "meaning" necessarily bring to the understanding of the term "subsistence" various spiritual, moral, esthetic, and emotional considerations. Clearly, any threat to a people's subsistence presents a very real threat to the integrity of their society and the fabric of its culture—and hence to the future survival of that culture.

Several chapters in this volume discuss a variety of threats to subsistence. For example, when government policies resulted in moving nomadic hunters into permanent centralized settlements (as in the case of the Inuit, Cree, and Innu in Canada), the manner in which knowledge of hunting traditions was transmitted to the next generation began to be seriously affected. This loss of knowledge and skill also occurred during the resettlement of the reindeer-herding Evenki, Chukchi, and Saami in Russia and the Saami in Finland and the northern regions of Scandinavian countries. The James Bay Cree have recognized the cultural damage such residential changes can cause. They have introduced a hunter-support program to assist those who wish to continue living a hunting and trapping life. Similar efforts to support hunting as a viable occupation have been put into effect in both western and eastern Greenland and by the Innu of Labrador.

The movement of formerly nomadic or isolated groups of northern peoples into permanent settlements or towns presents other challenges; such moves facilitate the introduction of formal programs of state schooling. The impact of school programs on language retention has already been mentioned; schooling has also diminished the social status of the elders who no longer serve as the principal source of useful information. The elders have been marginalized by the government centers' requirement for an influx of outsiders possessing the technical skills needed to run schools, power plants, and medical and administrative services. This influx of skilled outsiders has relegated many local people to low-paying low-status jobs that negatively affected their ability to control their own lives. Formerly independent hunters or herders now increasingly depend on others and on the state, with a corresponding loss of self-esteem and, consequently, a reduced ability to adapt. In many northern communities these abrupt social changes have resulted in a variety of antisocial behaviors, including substance abuse, increased family violence, and suicide.

DIET, WELL-BEING, AND IDENTITY

One of the serious impacts of settlement living involves the increased difficulty of accessing traditional wildlife and fish resources, which may best be found at some distance from the place of now permanent residence. Residents in many arctic communities have experienced a change in their customary diet. Diet is obviously important for health, with the healthiest food being the fresh local foods that a people adapted to eating over many generations. Any change in diet, especially if the new foods are of less nutritional quality or held in less esteem by the people who eat them, will produce negative effects upon peoples' health and sense of well-being. People in the temperate zone who do not harvest local food themselves nevertheless have available a wide variety of foods as a result of efficient and low-cost transportation systems which benefit from the presence of mass markets. This is not the case in the Arctic, where the great distances from centers of agricultural production, correspondingly high transportation costs, and the small size of consumer markets, ensure that imported food is expensive to purchase and often of poor nutritional quality.

Food, however, is not just a source of nutrition; it fulfills many other human needs. We are all familiar with the term "comfort food" and with the craving to eat certain foods because various foods have considerable cultural and emotional value attached to them. The intense longing for familiar foods, which is common to all people, manifests itself in the large number and variety of "ethnic food" restaurants and food products increasingly part of our communities and supermarket inventory.

The saying found in many cultures "You are what you eat" captures the contribution of people's dietary habits, or food culture, to their sense of identity. This is illustrated in the importance the people in northern Norway and northern Alaska attach to maintaining their traditional food cultures by eating whale meat, the Innu of Labrador place upon caribou, the Cree of Quebec place upon geese or fish, and the Greenlanders place on eating whales and seals. The capture of these important foods requires skill and traditional knowledge passed down from ancestors, and eating these foods reinforces a people's sense of who they are and where they have come from in cultural terms.

Of course, because all cultures change, food cultures also change. Over the years, trade items brought into the Arctic have introduced its inhabitants to an ever increasing range of new foods and beverages. The sheep farming culture that has developed in the twentieth century in southern Greenland has succeeded in part because of the growing acceptance of this totally new source of food to the Inuit living in Greenland.

The industrial frontier is encroaching upon the traditional territories of many northern peoples, making it harder to continue taking the food they need from their own immediate surroundings. Flooding caused by hydroelectricity projects, road building undertaken to enable the construction of dams, mines, forestry, and tourism all represent a threat to hunting, herding, and fishing. Furthermore, contamination of the arctic food chain by chemicals used in industries or agriculture great distances removed from the Arctic add to the concern that arctic peoples have for the ecological security and the safety of the food produced in their homelands.

COMMON RESPONSES TO THREATS TO CULTURAL SURVIVAL

Despite the great distance between the small and often isolated arctic peoples, the barriers created by speaking different languages, the different political and national jurisdictions, and the high cost of long-distance air travel, diverse arctic peoples have found ways to learn from each other. In these cases, the successes that some groups have experienced in organizing themselves to fight against oppression and injustice have come to the notice of others who use this knowledge to improve their own lives.

The chapters that follow document growth in the arctic peoples' own organizations—of herders, whalers, hunters, fishers, and trappers—throughout the circumpolar world. In some cases these groups are at the community level (such as the Hunters and Trappers Organizations in Nunavut) or the regional or national level (the Marine Mammal Hunters Union of Chukotka and the Greenland Hunters and Fishers Association). Beyond these local or national organizations, there are now international Saami and Inuit organizations linking all Saami (from four different countries) and all Inuit (also from four countries) into increasingly effective international aboriginal organizations that have achieved official standing.

After having gained a voice, arctic peoples have been able to improve their effectiveness by undertaking research and becoming involved in national and international workshops and conferences, using the courts to seek redress, and joining with aboriginal and nonaboriginal groups in other countries facing similar difficulties. These measures have shown results in protecting languages and subsistence practices, obtaining greater recognition and use of traditional knowledge in environmental management initiatives, and changing some oppressive laws. Obviously, not all measures have been equally successful. Unfortunately, it appears that no country has a blameless human rights record at home—no matter how loudly that particular country may criticize the abuse of human rights in other countries.

It is to be hoped that the future improves for all the societies described in this volume—and for the many other peoples both in the Arctic and elsewhere who are facing similar threats to their cultural survival. Now that the different peoples of the Arctic have begun to communicate effectively with each other, it is likely that improvements in their circumstances will begin to accelerate. Increasingly the victories of some will help others gain improvements in their own circumstances. For this to occur sooner rather than later will require the understanding and support of non-arctic peoples. With this in mind, this volume is dedicated to the hope that a wider level of understanding of the arctic peoples will be gained by the many people living far distant from the peoples described in this volume.

NOTE

1. G. Wenzel, *Animal Rights, Human Rights: Ecology, Economy and Ideology in the Canadian Arctic* (Toronto: University of Toronto Press, 1991), 60.

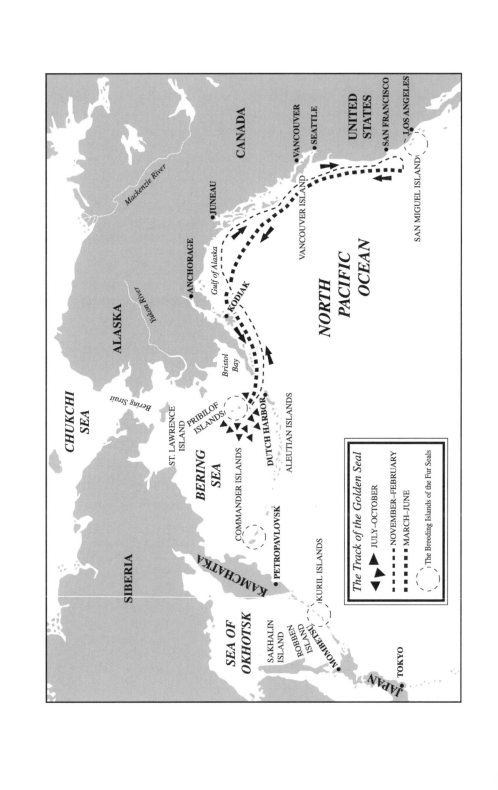

1

The Aleuts of the Pribilof Islands, Alaska

Helen D. Corbett and Susanne M. Swibold

CULTURAL OVERVIEW

The cultural survival of the Aleuts of the Pribilof Islands, Alaska, is one of the most unusual case studies in the Arctic. Taken from their homes on the Aleutian chain to two uninhabited and isolated islands in the central Bering Sea, the Pribilof Aleuts were forced into service to kill sea mammals for two colonial regimes, first Russia and later the United States. The Aleuts were one cog in a wheel of a massive fur industry that lasted 199 years, from which a complex history and unique culture developed.

The People

The seal hunters of the Pribilofs are descendants of the great maritime race of Aleuts who settled along the Aleutian archipelago, a 1,300-km chain of islands extending southwest of the Alaskan mainland. Russians called them Aleut (al'-ee-oot), but their own name is Unangan, meaning "the coast" or "seashore." They are believed to have migrated across the Bering land bridge from Asia between 12,000 and 15,000 years ago. An early Eskimo-Aleut culture began to develop about 8,000 years ago in the Bering Sea and North Pacific region, later branching into the distinctive maritime culture and language of the Unangan along the Aleutian Islands. Living in semisubterranean houses, the Aleuts developed a sophisticated marine technology to cope with the limitations imposed by their environment and rigorous climate. They possessed special skills for hunting marine mammals from skin-covered kayaks, skills that were later exploited by the Russian fur traders who came to the islands after 1750 in search of sea otters and fur seals. In the first fifty years of Russian control, Aleuts died from introduced diseases, wars resisting colonizers, malnutrition, and privation caused by the transport of able-bodied hunters away from their families and villages to hunt sea mammals for the Russians. At the time of contact, the Aleut population is estimated to have been between 12,000 and 15,000.[1] Today, there are about 2,000 Aleuts, of whom only 340 people still speak the Aleut language.[2]

In 1786 Russian navigator Gavriil Pribilof discovered the first of two islands that came to bear his name after a three-year search by some sixty Siberian trading companies for the breeding site of the valuable fur seals. St. Paul and St. George Islands, collectively known as the Pribilof Islands, are the summer hauling grounds for the greatest concentration of Northern Pacific fur seals in the world. Since the animals breed on land, it is relatively simple to round up and harvest them in a convenient location. The islands were uninhabited at the time of their discovery by Pribilof, although Aleut oral history knew them as Aamix, a rich hunting ground once visited by an Aleut chief lost in a storm. At the time of the discovery, Russian traders had nearly eliminated sea otters and were seeking the next most valuable source of furs—the fur seals. The discovery of the Pribilofs extended the Russian fur trade in America for almost another century.

Aleut hunters were taken to the islands, often without choice, on a seasonal basis, and by the 1820s permanent settlements had been established on both islands. Seals were killed ruthlessly until then, when the Russian American Company established a licensed fur-seal monopoly and adopted conservation methods in harvesting seals, taking only three- to five-year-old nonbreeding males and prohibiting the killing of female seals. By the time of the sale of the Russian-American territories to the United States in 1867, the Pribilof Aleuts had attained an enviable status, enjoying full rights as citizens of Russia, literate in two languages, paid fairly for their labor, and retaining their traditional systems of governance.

The second great shock to the Aleut culture came with the American purchase of Alaska in 1867. The Pribilofs were the unpublicized "jewel in the crown" of the Alaska Purchase, and the seal industry generated large revenues for the U.S. Treasury. At first, the Aleuts were paid competitive wages by a series of private monopolies, at a rate comparable to other industrial workers in America. After forty years of private control, however, the fur seal populations had been severely depleted, and the Aleuts experienced privation and malnutrition. The U.S. government took over the industry in 1910, and the Aleuts discovered that the government's agenda for the Pribilofs was seals, profits, and people—in that order. The Aleuts lost the rights they had held as Russian subjects and were now treated as wards of the U.S. government. Every aspect of their lives was interfered with: language, political structures, wages, religion, freedom of movement, and even their choice of marriage partners. This state of servitude to the U.S. government reached its apex in 1942 when the Pribilof Aleuts were evacuated and interned in dilapidated fish canneries in southeastern Alaska until the end of World War II. Many Aleuts died in the substandard conditions, lacking adequate food, water, sanitation, medical treatment, and shelter.

The Americans were also remiss in the first forty years of managing the seal harvest. By the late 1800s, sealskin coats had become so popular that sealers from several countries had launched a spree of uncontrolled high-seas, or pelagic, killing. By 1910 the combination of pelagic sealing, corrupt government agents, who were supposed to oversee the harvest but did not, and greedy monopolies had reduced the northern fur seal from its population of over 1 million animals to only 300,000 animals. In 1911 the North Pacific Sealing Convention was signed by Russia, Japan, Great Britain (for Canada), and the United States in return for a ban on high-seas killing. To compensate Canada and Japan for the loss of pelagic furs, Russia and the United States agreed to share a portion of their controlled, land-based harvests of nonbreeding, three- to five-year-old seals. Scientists from the signatory countries would determine how many seals could be harvested each year and thus maintain a maximum sustainable yield. The commercial harvest was tightly controlled and the killing technique (stunning and bleeding) was assessed as more humane than any other alternative methods. The international treaty, unique in the history of wildlife conservation, brought the seal back to a sustainable population while providing the Aleuts with employment and subsistence food.

The Pribilof Aleuts gained full rights as American citizens, as well as government-level wages and benefits, in the mid-1960s, but their new-found freedom came at a cost. News about this secret federal reserve was beginning to reach the public, and the environmental movement of the 1970s was questioning the wisdom of hunting animals for their skins.

The Setting

The Aleutian climate is so notorious that early Russian missionaries called the area "the place that God forgot."[3] High winds, rain that blows sideways, and thick fog are commonplace. The islands are volcanic, treeless, and covered with thick grasses, sedges, and beautiful wildflowers. Environmental conditions were even harsher on the Pribilofs where there were no natural harbors for protection, no freshwater streams or salmon populations, and fewer varieties of berries. The Aleuts developed respiratory problems associated with the climate, malnutrition, and living in government houses that let in the wind.

3

Traditional Subsistence Strategies

The Aleuts lost their maritime navigation and sea-hunting skills on the Pribilofs when they were forced into a land-based industry that interfered with many traditional subsistence activities. In particular, the men did not have the freedom to fish or hunt during the sealing months. They worked intensively through the summer harvest season, sometimes killing over 100,000 seals in a precise, methodical assembly line of designated tasks. Women and children helped on the killing grounds, gathering seal meat to salt for winter use. During the winter months, the sealing crews were idle, waiting for the next killing season. During this time, the men hunted Steller sea lions from shore, an activity that required a strict code of hunting ethics, respect for elders, and apportionment of meat along extended family lines. Women picked and preserved berries in the summer months and, in early times, gathered crustaceans in the intertidal zone. The rest of the subsistence diet was supplemented by ducks, reindeer (an introduced species), cod, halibut, and seabird eggs. An extensive trade network developed between the Pribilof Aleuts and their relatives on the Aleutian chain, with whom they exchanged fur seal meat for dried salmon and berries.

Social and Political Organization

Unangan villages were traditionally ruled by a chief (*toyuq*), a second chief (*sukaskiq*), and after the coming of the Russians, a chief who was lay reader in the local Orthodox church (*staristaq*). The Russians honored this political system, but the American government interfered with the Aleuts' selection of chief and the distribution of harvest monies. The Pribilof Aleuts formed a tribal council after World War II, but their political structures were consistently undermined by the U.S. Treasury agents who managed the islands. The Aleuts gained more political and economic control over their islands with the passage of the Alaska Native Claims Settlement Act (ANCSA) in 1971. The local land and financial resources now came under the control of native corporations. By the 1980s, a proliferation of modern institutions vied for power in the villages of St. Paul and St. George: tribal council, city council, corporation, and school. This became a source of constant conflict.

The primary social unit on the Pribilofs is the Aleut extended family. Entire families were involved in the fur-seal harvest, and to this day, elders will not eat seal meat that has not been butchered, preserved, and prepared by a family member. Family units are now engaging in the successor to the fur-seal industry, namely, the new day-boat fishery.

Religion and World View

Little is known about Aleut beliefs prior to their contact with Europeans, although early Russian priests reported that Aleuts followed the instructions of local shamans (indigenous priests or ritual specialist) regarding hunting taboos, weather, and predictions for the future. The dimensions of "east" and "above" were associated with the sacred and a universal creator. Sunlight and seawater were regarded as sacred sources of life. This world view meshed with Russian Orthodox Christianity, and the conversion of the Aleuts to this faith was bolstered by the respect shown by missionary priests for local customs and language. Indeed the priests often interceded on behalf of the Aleuts with the Russian imperial government, protecting the Aleut culture from the worst practices of the fur companies. This respectful alliance between the missionaries and the native population and the overlap of world views account for the importance of the Orthodox church in Alaska today. It is regarded as a native institution, the major symbol of Aleut identity, and the guardian of social mores in Aleut villages. On the Pribilofs, the Orthodox churches provided a continuum of ritual and tradition during periods of upheaval. Old melodies are sung in the churches in Aleut, Slavonic, and English. Seasonal subsistence activities of hunting, sealing, fishing, and berry picking receive the priest's blessing, and all the houses in the village are ritually blessed at least once a year.

THREATS TO SURVIVAL

One thing that kept us together was we had a common goal, and that was to survive.
—Maxim Malvansky, mayor of St. George, 1988[4]

Challenges—Then and Now

Today, the villages of St. Paul and St. George are the largest Aleut communities left in the world, with a population of 768 people in St. Paul and 184 in St. George. The Pribilof Aleut culture has survived and adapted to many challenges over the last two centuries: forcible relocation, the influence and culture of two colonial nations, substitution of their traditional economy with a wage-based economy, and suppression of their language, religion, political structures, and human rights. From 1975 to 1985, the Aleuts faced a new, more insidious challenge: the wrath of a Western, urban culture living thousands of miles away. The environmental movement had spawned a new generation of animal rights' activists, who, bolstered by the success of the harp-seal pup campaigns in the Canadian Atlantic, began to pressure the U.S. government to withdraw from the fur-seal industry on the Pribilofs. Despite the differences between the harp-seal hunt and the fur-seal harvest, animal protection groups launched intense, emotional campaigns that treated all seal killing as one. The Aleuts were subjected to hate mail, threats and harassment, legal challenges by humane societies, and negative media coverage.

"The seal harvest is presently a key element of our survival," wrote Aleut leader Larry Merculieff in a 1984 letter. "Thus any attempts to stop it through misdirected emotionalism of people who do not live with nature as closely as we do can only be viewed as violence against us—and the seals."[5] International campaigns devalued seal pelts, making the U.S. government's stake in the harvest increasingly unprofitable. The Reagan administration, seeking ways to cut the budget, decided that abandoning the commercial seal harvest could assuage negative public opinion and save tax dollars. In 1983 the U.S. government announced its withdrawal of its $6.2 million annual allocation to the Pribilofs, the sole economic mainstay of the islands. At the same time, the United States withdrew from the international fur-seal treaty, leaving the northern fur seal without international migratory protection, open to pelagic killing, and without international scientific monitoring and research.

There was little time to prepare a comprehensive community and economic mobilization plan. The government offered no compensation in the announcement of its withdrawal from the seal industry. An intensive lobbying effort by Pribilof Aleuts in Washington, D.C., resulted in a $20 million trust fund to the islanders to assist them to diversify their economy. Both St. Paul and St. George began to prepare to move into fisheries, which by the mid-1980s were booming in the Bering Sea as the result of a change from being a foreign-owned to being an American-owned fishery. Harbors were constructed on both islands to provide safe moorage to the U.S. small-boat catcher fleet. By 1990 St. Paul's harbor was deepened and expanded to accommodate large floating processors and factory trawlers. The Aleuts quickly adapted to a day-boat fishery, and today over 100 local fishers operate thirty locally owned vessels in a million-dollar halibut fishery. The Pribilofs offer the only sheltered harbors in 50,000 square kilometers of rough ocean waters. The crab industry sustains St. Paul today. During crab season, the harbor serves over 230 transient vessels, two floating processor plants permanently moored in the harbor, and over forty floating processors, freighters, and crab vessels within five kilometers of the islands.

Environmental Crisis

This new economy may do more to destroy our habitat and disrupt the wildlife than anything in the island's history, and it has the capacity to accomplish this destruction within a single generation.

—Larry Merculieff, 1997[6]

Once protected by its physical isolation and the secret nature of the federal fur-seal industry, today's Pribilof environment is more vulnerable to catastrophe because of the community's recent entry into the global market place. The Pribilofs are located in the middle of the richest bottom fishery in the world, and during the winter crab season the marine horizon is filled with as many as 300 trawlers, tramp steamers, supply ships, freighters, and fish processors, their lights illuminating the night skies. Fuel barges filled with from three to six million gallons of marine diesel fuel weave their way through the flotilla of vessels, en route to the harbor. Scientists fear that this concentration of vessels around the largest, most sensitive wildlife area in the southern Bering Sea may have catastrophic consequences for marine birds and animals. The introduction of rats through a ship berthed in harbor or a grounded freighter could quickly destroy the Northern Hemisphere's greatest concentration of seabirds and introduce disease to the seal rookeries.

Ten vessels have run aground in as many years on the Pribilofs. The worst was the wreck of a floating processor in March 1989, spilling more than 10,000 gallons of diesel fuel. If the spill had occurred two months later, thousands of nesting seabirds would have been affected. In 1996 a vessel dumped contaminated fuel within five kilometers of the Pribilofs, resulting in the death of about 1,000 King Eider ducks, part of the winter subsistence diet of Aleuts. When the oiled ducks began to wash up on St. Paul's shores, the community was divided between publicizing the negative effects of the fishery and keeping quiet about it to protect their economic interests. "It took a spill to wake people up to focus on preventive action" said Larry Merculieff, who for a decade was the lone Aleut voice addressing the deteriorating health of the Bering Sea ecosystem. "The deterioration is the result of wanton waste of millions of pounds of fish thrown overboard by fishing vessels, discharge of huge levels of contaminants by land and by sea over decades, and the use of the Bering Sea as a convenient dumping ground for non-biodegradable garbage" (personal communication, February 21, 1996).

In 1992 northern fur-seal pups began to die mysteriously in two breeding rookeries on St. Paul. Researchers found the cause of the 20 percent mortality increase to be "white muscle disease," perhaps the result of a toxic substance reaching the pups through mother's milk or their flippers. This was the first documented case of the disease appearing in a marine mammal, having been found only in domestic cattle before. Scientists suspected that contaminant discharges from an offshore fishing vessel caused the seal deaths.

Decades of intensive fishing in the Bering Sea, combined with climatic changes, have led to population declines in over seventeen species of marine mammals, fish, and seabirds. Scientists believe that food stress is responsible for most of the declines. Prospects of a broad ecosystem failure, similar to the crash of the northwestern Atlantic cod fishery, have mobilized a host of committees, working groups, and government panels to focus on the plight of the Bering Sea. They are still grappling to understand the problem, much less knowing how to reverse it. Pribilof organizations have now joined this process. The city council of St. Paul has raised environmental issues to the top of its agenda and it has added an environmental department to its operations. The tribal government decided to sue the vessel responsible for the death of oiled King Eider ducks, resulting in an out-of-court settlement.

Sociocultural Crisis

Aren't we still serving someone else's existence? It's basically taking the same tool that was used before, only it's chiseling a living from the Bering Sea.
—Aquilina Bourdukofsky, 1995[7]

The loss of the commercial harvest was socially and economically catastrophic to the community of St. Paul, the focus of fourteen years of research. Without government subsidies, the cost of home heating, marine transportation, and maintenance of the airport, roads, and buildings skyrocketed. Eighty percent of the wage base in the community disappeared. The insecure future, increasing loss of cultural identity associated with the seal, and lack of respect from urban populations evidenced by attacks on the traditional Aleut sealing practices all led to rapid social disintegration. In the first years after the government pullout, there were unprecedented numbers of suicides and murders, and an increase in drug and alcohol abuse and violent behavior. Politically, three local institutions (municipal government, tribal council, and native corporation) filled the void left by the government, but they all fought with each other. Divisions were intensified by a heritage of oppression and the fact that two institutions were patterned after the dominant society (a municipal government and a for-profit corporation) and the third represented tribal functions. Factionalism, corruption, competition, and constant legal challenges thrived in this environment. The Orthodox church began to lose its position of authority in the community. Changing values influenced by television, materialism, travel, and the disintegration of community sharing contributed to the erosion of social institutions and cultural beliefs and practices formerly of great importance.

The last commercial seal harvest took place in 1985. Since the U.S. Congress failed to ratify the international fur-seal treaty in 1985, sealing on the Pribilofs occurs now only on a subsistence basis. The harvest of as many as 1,600 animals, which is conducted on a voluntary basis by the tribal council, is monitored and supervised by federal officials and a voluntary humane observer. In the first years of the subsistence harvest, the Aleuts countered constant legal challenges by animal protection groups claiming

The late Martha Krukoff and her son, Lawrence, cut seal meat to freeze, St. Paul, Alaska. Courtesy of Susanne Swibold.

that the seal meat was being wasted. Representatives of these groups would appear on the harvest field each summer, watching while the Aleuts butchered the seals and had their meat weighed by a federal official. After years of legal skirmishes, the Aleuts have won the right to take seal meat without harassment. They also fought for and won the right to take seal pelts for a handicraft program, the first time in two centuries that they have had control over the destination of the seal pelts.

Fifteen years after the government withdrawal, the Pribilofs have entered a new era of economic and social stability. In St. Paul, there is a blossoming of self-governance as the more moderate elements of the community take political leadership roles. The community no longer relies on outside expertise to run the village. The political bickering has subsided, and the local institutions concentrate on doing their jobs. Alcoholism and drug use decreased when the island's employers began to enforce sobriety policies and random drug testing. Employees with substance addictions are sent off the island for treatment, and they participate in a mentorship program when they return. Violence, felonies, suicides, and murders, have all decreased. There is a new pride in the halibut day-boat fishery, and people have adapted successfully to a fishing livelihood. Fishing, like the commercial seal harvest before it, absorbs the entire community, involving entire families in its operation. There is a new affluence in St. Paul, where the median household income is $42,000, among the highest in rural Alaska, and there is no shortage of jobs for those who wish to work.

The boom has, however, brought a new set of problems previously unimaginable on these isolated, pristine islands. Each crab season brings 2,000 transients to work in the processing plants or waiting for a ship. "We've become the gas station of the Bering Sea," says the Aleut priest, George Pletnikoff.[8] The close-knit small-town atmosphere has been strained by daily jet service, strange faces in the village stores, and an invasion of urban values into an island setting. Streets are filled with taxis, forklifts, and semi-trucks conveying crab pots. Boat crews buy groceries, find spare parts, hire drivers, drop off the injured, or pick up fishermen flying into town.

Island leaders realize their economy is riding the peak of a Bering Sea fisheries boom. Their economy, like the seal fishery before it, is too dependent on a single resource, and it is completely vulnerable to collapse in global markets, resource fluctuations, overefficient fishing technology, and the rapacious appetites of the corporations that drive this market. Crab quotas have been declining, and St. Paul's $14 million budget immediately registers the effects in reduced taxes, fuel sales, services, and storage fees. "Have we moved from one endangered species to another?" asks city clerk Phyllis Swetzof. "If the fishery went away, we would definitely go into a slump" (personal communication, July 24, 1998). The day-boat fishery is also vulnerable to quotas set by regional fishery councils far from the islands. The 1998 halibut quota was increased, with a corresponding rise in the amount of time devoted by the community to fishing. This resulted in an oversupply of halibut in the processing plant, causing the price to drop by half. Caught in a falling price market, Aleut fisherman continued to bring in more halibut in the hope of making enough money to pay the loans on their boats.

The extended halibut season has interfered with the subsistence seal harvest that normally follows the fishing season. In 1999, 980 seals were taken, compared to 1,345 in 1998. This follows a trend of higher community value being placed on the commercial fishery than the subsistence seal harvest. The Aleuts are asking the federal government to extend the harvest period from one to three months, thereby enabling people to eat smaller amounts of fresh meat rather than freezing large quantities of seal in a short time frame. Frozen seal is now distributed to Aleuts in Seattle, Anchorage, and the Aleutian Chain. Seal meat is no longer the dietary staple on the Pribilofs. In 1881, the average annual consumption of seal meat on the Pribilofs was 600 pounds per person.[9] By 1981 this amount had dropped to approximately 284 pounds per Aleut. Today the figure has fallen to about 40 pounds per person.[10] The decline can be traced to the greater variety of choices in the store and the availability of other subsistence foods (halibut and reindeer), changes in nutritional awareness (less salted meat is consumed), the influence of Western, urban values via television and travel, contaminants in the meat from pollution in the food chain, affluence, and less time to prepare the meat. If the woman in a household dislikes seal meat, her avoidance is generally passed through subsequent generations.

The new fishing economy has reinforced assimilation into global economic markets by merging local fishing councils with multinational fishing corporations. The Pribilofs, like other Alaskan Bering Sea communities, participate in a Community Development Quota (CDQ) program, which attempts to balance inequities between local fishing communities and corporate fish processors. The St. Paul CDQ association receives a 4 percent allocation of the Bering Sea pollock quota and sells this quota to processing companies for about $2 million in annual revenues to be reinvested in fishery development programs. The community receives development funds (reducing pressure on government budgets), and large-scale processors have a competitive advantage to fish in a region. One outcome of this new alliance is a reluctance by the directors of the local fishing council to offend their industrial partners by discussing the environment or the future. By becoming partners in large-scale resource extraction in the Pribilof region, local people are effectively removed from direct, meaningful control and involvement in decisions affecting their region's resources. Indigenous systems of knowledge and prudent use of natural resources are increasingly forgotten in the pressure to increase fishery quotas for multinational fishing corporations.

RESPONSE: STRUGGLES TO SURVIVE CULTURALLY

Taking Control

Two broad patterns can be traced in the fifteen years since the federal government announced its withdrawal from the commercial seal harvest. The first was the work by a generation of Aleut leaders to respond to the crisis and to consolidate and administer the land, equipment, and financial structures under municipal, tribal, and corporate structures. These leaders had the difficult task of balancing traditional Aleut values with elements of Western culture they needed in order to move from being passive wards of the federal government to managing and planning their own destiny. That they have largely succeeded in this task in a short period of time is nothing short of miraculous.

The second trend emerged over the past five years: a cultural revival movement seeking to celebrate the traditional Aleut strengths and the sealing, hunting, and fishing skills that enabled them to survive many difficult challenges over the centuries. This work was begun by one Aleut woman, Aquilina Bourdukofsky, in a quiet, unassuming way. Today, her work, which is flowering in all sorts of offshoots, is manifested primarily in the desire of local people to stop fighting and get to work governing their island and in a renewed sense of their role as stewards of their islands. Bourdukofsky spent a year recording the Aleut language and stories of her father, the Russian Orthodox priest Michael Lestenkof. She thought about the Pribilof history and the sense the Aleuts have of being victims and slaves to an outside authority. "I began to focus on our strengths," she said. "We know our people came here under hard conditions. We took seals in mass amounts for the fur trade. We had to be the ones to do it—we knew when to stop, how many to take. We have to take more ownership, responsibility, and respect for our history instead of dwelling on ourselves as slaves, a skinny evacuated people huddled in corners" (personal communication, August 27, 1998).

The Pribilof Islands Stewardship Program thus began with the goal of reconnecting young Aleuts with their islands and sea. Funded by the island organizations, federal and state governments, volunteers, and environmental organizations, the summer program combines traditional knowledge with Western science, providing young people with the opportunity to work with international scientists researching fur seals, fish, and seabirds. The students gather data, count populations, take tissue samples, and assist in lab work. They participate in the subsistence seal harvest, apprenticing with experienced sealers to learn how to kill, skin, and butcher the seals. They haul meat for the villagers, flesh pelts for a handicraft program, and shear pups for a population census. A skilled "disentanglement team" of young people now roam the fur-seal rookeries, removing the fish nets from the necks of seals that would otherwise die from strangulation. In winter, the young people clean debris from the beaches and seal rookeries. Students have learned traditional Aleut songs, dancing, and drumming, and then how to make their own dance regalia. The program has also spawned a revival of Aleut kayak (*bidarka*) construction in the local school.

Only a decade before, many Pribilovians thought these symbols of Aleut identity had vanished forever. The stewardship camp sparked a resurgence of cultural pride and strengthened ethnic identity in other areas of community life: in the success of the halibut day-boat fishery, in the incipient sobriety movement, in the resurgence of skills among the voluntary subsistence seal harvest crew, and in the blossoming of self-governance. Bourdukofsky is now working on a Marine Messengers Program, in which students from the stewardship program visit other harbor villages and the Alaska mainland to speak about their role in caring for the Bering Sea. "We are now getting outside funding agencies to not just think about investing in the environment, but investing in the indigenous people who grow up in this environment," she says. "That's how we'll make sure we continue to live here" (personal communication, August 27, 1998).

Sadly, the Aleut language is now endangered, and linguists predict it may be extinct by the year 2055. Only the elders still speak it in the Pribilof villages. Attempts to teach it to younger generations through the school have not been successful. The Aleut language is tied to an intimate knowledge of the land and sea, rules of conduct, and a unique way of knowing. The processes of modernization and assimilation into a Western mainstream culture have displaced the language from its context, rendering it a cultural artifact.

FOOD FOR THOUGHT

> I believe we exist generationally. Would we be as strong as we are if we didn't go through the hardships, the slavery? It's powerful to hear the strength of our people—that's what held them together in the past and today.
> —Aquilina Bourdukofsky (personal communication, August 27, 1998)

The story of the Aleuts of the Pribilof Islands, Alaska, is a unique case of cultural survival in the Arctic, a story of resilience and adaptation to an onslaught of assimilative processes over the course of two centuries. The Aleut culture and population flourished on the Aleutian archipelago prior to the arrival of Russian fur hunters in the eighteenth century. Soon thereafter, the Russian American Company enslaved and relocated Aleuts from the Aleutian Islands to the Pribilofs to hunt fur seals. The Aleuts were settled in villages on St. Paul and St. George Islands, where they labored in a land-based seal industry, losing many of their aboriginal subsistence and marine skills. The purchase of Alaska by the United States in 1867 ushered in the second wave of assimilation, and the Aleuts became wards of the American government.

Pressure from the animal rights movement and a declining fur market prompted the U.S. government to abandon the commercial seal harvest in 1983. The government pullout led to catastrophic social and economic effects in the Pribilof communities. The insecure future, increasing loss of identity with the seal, and lack of respect from urban populations led to rapid social disintegration. Local institutions, hobbled by a mentality of dependence and inexperience in self-governance, were divided by factionalism, power struggles, and legal disputes.

The Pribilof communities entered the flourishing Bering Sea bottom fishery, developing harbors, processing facilities, and vessel supply operations. Aleuts achieved a rapid, successful transition to a day-boat halibut fishery, which has brought a new prosperity to the Pribilof communities. However, the marine fishing economy has resulted in several unintended, disruptive socioeconomic consequences: village roads are clogged with harbor traffic, the island water aquifer is strained by the freshwater requirements of the processing plants, and transients have transformed the small village atmosphere in St. Paul. The community's livelihood is now tied to a global market economy and decisions made by fishery councils far from the shores of the Pribilofs.

Efforts by animal rights groups to save fur seals may, in the long term, have led to a reduction in the fur-seal population. An overefficient, mechanized fishery has posed far greater threats to the Bering Sea ecosystem than the seal harvest.

Aleuts have become their own agents of assimilation and modernization through their participation in the fishing industry. This third major wave of acculturation has resulted in the most profound and rapid changes to the Pribilof cultures. A local, cultural, and environmental movement has grown up to counteract the loss of Aleut identity, community cohesiveness, subsistence skills, and connection to the land and sea. In the process of cultural recovery, self-governance, self-reliance, and self-sufficiency are emerging in the community. Finally, the Aleut connection to the fur seal, severed by the collapse of the seal harvest and the disapproval of a Western, urban culture, is now being recovered by a young generation of Pribilof Aleuts.

Questions

1. What are the three major developments in acculturation in the Pribilof culture and who can be identified as the primary agents of change?

2. How did the Pribilof seal harvest differ from other harvests of fur-bearing wild animals? What are the differences between commercial and subsistence seal harvesting?

3. What effects did the animal rights movement have on the Aleut culture? What were its unanticipated effects on the northern fur seal? How has it affected the Aleuts' relationship with the fur seal?

4. How are Aleut attitudes toward their land and subsistence resources changing as new developments alter their culture and lives? What steps are they talking to retain their cultural identity in periods of rapid social change?

5. What does the Pribilof experience suggest about the problems associated with the lack of economic diversification in northern rural economies? Can you find examples of other northern communities that are less reliant on single-resource economies? What are the implications of changes in wildlife-based economies upon northern native cultures and future generations of these societies?

NOTES

1. Margaret Lantis, "Aleut," in *Handbook of North American Indians* (Washington, D.C.: Smithsonian Institution Press, 1984), 163.

2. Valerie Chaussonnet, ed., *Crossroads Alaska: Native Cultures of Alaska and Siberia* (Washington, D.C.: Smithsonian Institution Press, 1995), 109.

3. Michael J. Oleksa, *Alaskan Missionary Spirituality* (New York: Paulist Press, 1987), 3.

4. Quoted in *Tundra Times*, June 27, 1988, vol. xxvi, 1.

5. Letter to Animal Protection Institute of America, April 26, 1984.

6. Ilarion (Larry) Meraulief, "Western Society's Linear Systems and Aboriginal Cultures: The Need for Two-Way Exchanges for the Sake of Survival," in E. S. Burch, Jr., and L. J. Ellanna (eds.), *Key Issues in Hunter-Gatherer Research* (Providence, R.I.: Berg, 1994), 411.

7. Quoted in Doug O'Harra, "A Boom in the Bering," *We Alaskans Magazine; Anchorage Daily News*, March 5, 1995, H-11.

8. Quoted in Miro Cernetig, "The Endangered Hunters of the Pribilofs," *Toronto Globe and Mail*, July 20, 1991.

9. D. W. Veltre and M. J. Veltre, "The Northern Fur Seal: A Subsistence and Commercial Resource for Aleuts of the Aleutian and Pribilof Islands, Alaska," *Inuit Studies* 11 (2): 51–52.

10. Helen Corbett and Susanne Swibold, "Furs, Food and Factions: The Fur Seal and the Pribilof Aleuts," *Wildlife and Local Cultures, Fourth International Whaling Symposium* (Tokyo: Institute of Cetacean Research, 1994), 105.

RESOURCE GUIDE

Published Literature

Bonner, W. N. *Seals and Man: A Study of Interactions.* Seattle: University of Washington Press, 1982.

Jones, Dorothy Knee. *A Century of Servitude: Pribilof Aleuts under U.S. Rule.* Lanham, Md.: University Press of America, 1980.

Laughlin, William S. *Aleuts: Survivors of the Bering Land Bridge.* New York: Holt, Rinehart and Winston, 1980.

MacLeish, Sumner. *Seven Words for Wind: Essays and Field Notes from Alaska's Pribilof Islands.* Fairbanks: Epicenter Press, 1997.

Torrey, Barbara Boyle. *Slaves of the Harvest: The Story of the Pribilof Aleuts.* St. Paul Island, Alaska Tanadgusix Corporation, 1978.

Films and Videos

Amiq: The Aleut People of the Pribilof Islands, a Culture in Transition, 1981– 1983, 1985. 58 minutes. Flying Tomato Productions, 276 Three Sisters Drive, Canmore, Alberta T1W 2M7, Canada.

Laaqux: The Northern Fur Seal of the Pribilof Islands, 1988. 57 minutes. Flying Tomato Productions, 276 Three Sisters Drive, Canmore, Alberta T1W 2M7, Canada.

Peter Picked a Seal Stick: The Fur Seal Harvest of the Pribilof Islands, 1981. 28 minutes. Flying Tomato Productions, 276 Three Sisters Drive, Canmore, Alberta T1W 2M7, Canada.

San: The Birds of the Pribilof Islands, 1990. 58 minutes. Flying Tomato Productions, 276 Three Sisters Drive, Canmore, Alberta T1W, 2M7, Canada.

Internet and WWW Sites

http://www.pmel.noaa.gov/bering

http://www.pmel.noaa.gov/sebscc

http://www.cifar.uaf.edu

http://www.comregaf.state.ak.us/cf_comdb.htm

http://www2.nas.edu/whatsnew

http://www.fas.org/spp/starwars/offdocs/b920617.htm

http://isec.dk/symposia/mm_1st.htm

http://www.nmfs.gov/tmcintyr/mammals

http://www.iato.org

Organizations

Amiq Institute
276 Three Sisters Drive
Canmore, Alberta T1W 2M7
Telephone: (403) 678–5027
Fax: (403) 678–2879
E-mail: amiq@telusplanet.net

Bering Sea Coalition
22541 Deer Park Drive
Chugiak, Alaska 99567
Telephone: (907) 688–2226
Fax: (907) 688–2285
E-mail: Imerculieff@igc.org

2

The Chukchi and Siberian Yupiit of the Russian Far East

Peter P. Schweitzer and Patty A. Gray

CULTURAL OVERVIEW

The People

The Chukotka Autonomous Region of the Russian Federation is inhabited by several groups of native and non-native peoples. The Chukchi and Siberian Yupiit constitute the two most numerous native groups in the region; ethnic Russians and Ukrainians dominate among the non-native population. According to the 1989 Soviet census there were about 15,000 Chukchi and 1,700 Yupiit. More than 90 percent of the Yupiit and most of the Chukchi live within the borders of the Chukotka Autonomous Okrug, but some Chukchi also live in the Sakha Republic to the west and in the Magadan Province to the south.[1]

Neither Chukchi nor Siberian Yupik (the singular form of Yupiit) are self-designations. Chukchi, which has been used by Russians since the seventeenth century, probably comes from the Chukchi term for "reindeer." The term "Siberian Yupik" came into use only recently and partly coincides with the self-designation "Yupigy."

Both the Chukchi and Siberian Yupiit have inhabited Chukotka for several thousand years. The Chukchi language, which belongs to the Chukotko-Kamchatkan language family, shows little dialect differentiation. The Siberian Yupiit speak an Eskimo language (part of the Eskimo-Aleut language family). Until recently, three distinct Yupik languages were spoken in Chukotka; now only two are spoken. Several researchers have concluded that the ancestors of the Yupiit arrived in the coastal areas of

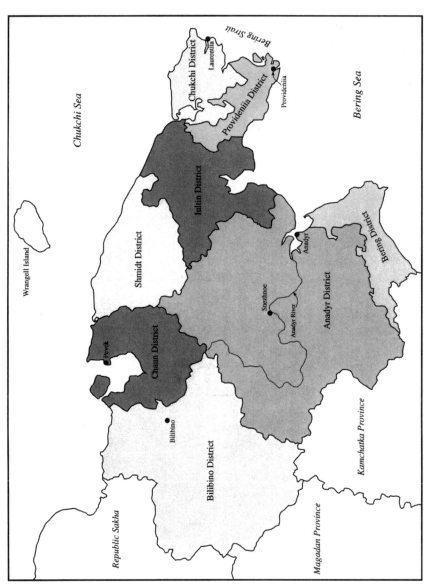

Chukotka Autonomous Region.

Chukotka before the Chukchi, but there is not enough evidence to settle the issue definitively.

The native peoples of Chukotka have had contact with non-native peoples since the seventeenth century, beginning with the first Russian Cossack explorers who moved into Chukotka in search of fresh economic opportunities. These were later followed by American traders with the same goals. The Chukchi gained a fierce reputation during the first half of the eighteenth century, when they successfully withstood Russian military attempts to subdue them. The eastern parts of Chukotka did not come under full government control until early in the twentieth century.

The Setting

Chukotka, located in the far northeast of Russia, is bordered by the East Siberian and Chukchi seas to the north and the Bering Sea to the southeast. It is a huge territory of 737,700 square kilometers, or about two-thirds the size of Alaska. Most of Chukotka, and the entire Chukchi Peninsula, is situated north of the tree line, and the low tundra vegetation is only occasionally interspersed with patches of brush. The fact that the Chukchi Peninsula is surrounded on three sides by the sea results in relatively high humidity and relatively warm winter temperatures. During the short summer, rain and fog are characteristic of the coastal areas. The inland areas of western Chukotka experience lower absolute winter temperatures but without the humidity and strong winds found on the coast.

The Chukchi Peninsula constitutes the northeastern fringe of Russia, and the Bering Strait that separates it from Alaska is only about forty-three miles wide. The Bering Strait is a major transit route for a variety of migrating sea mammals. Locally, the most important sea mammals are several species of whales and seals, as well as walruses and polar bears. Most of the land animals on the Chukchi Peninsula are small, such as lemmings and hares. The most common larger mammals are wolves and foxes. The once abundant wild reindeer, which are no longer found on the Chukchi Peninsula, have been replaced by domesticated reindeer.

The inland tundra region of Chukotka consists of true tundra with numerous lakes, rivers, and low mountain ranges, to mixed forests. Land animals here are the same as those found on the Chukchi Peninsula, with the addition of brown bear, moose, and wild reindeer. Several species of fish are found in inland rivers, the most important of which are salmon, trout, arctic grayling, whitefish, and smelt.

Traditional Subsistence Strategies

The early twentieth century, although far from representing an "untainted past," is characterized largely by self-directed subsistence activities.

The incorporation of Chukotka into the Soviet Union led to far-reaching social, economic, and cultural transformations.

The sea-mammal hunting activities of the coastal Chukchi and Siberian Yupiit shared a number of general characteristics. The most important animals, from an economic point of view, were walrus and several species of seal. During the open-water season, bowhead whales—which were extremely important socially and ritually—were hunted only from a few large villages situated at capes facing the open sea. A few settlements also specialized in hunting gray whales. During the winter sea-ice season, hunting was directed at seals found at their breathing holes in the ice. Boat crews consisting of from six to ten adult male hunters provided the framework for work organization during summer and fall hunting. Sea-mammal hunting was traditionally defined as a male activity, although women could fulfill the social role of male hunters if a particular family or kin group did not have enough eligible males for the task. The gathering of tundra plants (berries and grasses) and the eggs of ducks, geese, and other birds, as well as river fishing, were necessary, but auxiliary, subsistence activities in all coastal villages. Plant gathering, the preparation and distribution of meat, the processing of hides, and the production and maintenance of clothing and gear made from animal skins were among women's primary responsibilities.

In the inland tundra region of Chukotka, the most important economic activity has long been herding the domestic reindeer. Herds were held by families, who worked to accumulate a large number of reindeer and then hired younger men to help tend the herds. The more ambitious among these young men eventually acquired reindeer of their own and settled separately with their own family. The nature of tending domestic reindeer dictated that these family groups were mobile, migrating constantly in search of suitable pasture for their animals. As on the coast, a traditional division of labor existed: men engaged in herding, hunting, and fishing activities; and women cooked, sewed, gathered tundra plants, and took responsibility for setting up and taking down the camp.

Interaction between the Chukchi reindeer herders of the inland tundra and the coastal villagers dates back at least several centuries. Both groups depended upon each other, at least economically, because the reindeer herders were in constant need of sea mammal fat and hides, and the coastal residents sought reindeer meat and hides.

Social and Political Organization

The major difference in the social organization of reindeer herders and coastal residents was that there was a more pronounced differentiation into rich and poor among the herders. However, rich herders could lose their wealth quickly through animal diseases and other misfortune. The coastal residents distributed their harvested resources more equitably. Marked economic differences did not develop until the second half of the nineteenth century, after contact had been established with commercial whalers and traders.

The settled village was the most important social and political unit for the inhabitants of the coastal areas of the Chukchi Peninsula; among reindeer herding peoples, it was the nomadic herding camp. Larger political units consisting of several neighboring villages or camps rarely seem to have formed. Within the coastal villages, the whaling crew, a group made up of relatives and neighbors, was the most important social unit along with the extended family. Among the reindeer herders, the herding camp was the social equivalent of the whaling crew; the herding camp typically consisted of four or five extended families.

In contrast to many other Siberian peoples, neither the Chukchi nor the Siberian Yupiit followed a strict clan organization, although the Siberian Yupiit did have kin groups which resembled the so-called clans of the Yupiit living on Saint Lawrence Island. Both Chukchi and Yupiit had a variety of ways of extending kinship links beyond those used in Euro-American society to create relatives (e.g., the ceremonial exchange of spouses, which results in the members of each family becoming closely related). Marriages did not require any special wedding ceremony or the payment of any brideprice or dowry. However, there was bride service during which the future groom lived and worked with the bride's family for a time, after which both spouses typically moved in with the husband's family. No particular rules governed who an individual could or could not marry, but there was a general tendency to marry within one's own camp or village. Nevertheless, marriages between coastal residents and inland reindeer herders did occur.

Religion and World View

The cosmological views of Chukchi and Yupiit bear many similarities. Among both coastal and inland tundra peoples, the entire nonhuman environment was considered to be alive and endowed with the ability to act and speak. Animals and humans alike were considered to be persons possessing souls, and the boundary between these different categories of persons was easily crossed—animal persons could transform into human persons and vice versa. Species of wild animals and trees, lakes, and rivers were thought to have "owners" or "masters"—spiritual entities controlling resources—with whom humans had to maintain a respectful relationship in order to use the resources appropriately. Male and female shamans had privileged access to the spirit world, which allowed them to cure the sick, prevent misfortune, and predict the weather.

Bowhead whales had the most prominent place in the rituals of the coastal hunters of the Chukchi Peninsula. The ceremonial of boats, which marked the beginning of the hunting season in May, and the ritual greeting of a hunted whale were the major ceremonies. Only the Yupik settlement of Nuvuqaq celebrated a special whaling festival, which took place in winter after the closing of the whaling season and lasted for an entire month. The central theme of the whale rituals among the maritime hunters of Chukotka was the resurrection of the animals, a ritual to guide them back to their "homeland." Seals and walrus, despite their major economic importance, played only a minor role in such ceremonies. However, a respectful attitude toward all game animals was observed, and the captured animals were treated as honored guests to the settlement, not merely as a resource to be harvested.

The western parts of Chukotka first came into contact with Russian Orthodox missionaries during the eighteenth and nineteenth centuries; however, the Chukchi Peninsula was until recently outside the reach of missionary activities. The lack of governmental control of the area prior to the twentieth century prevented the Russian Orthodox Church from establishing a permanent presence. After the Soviet government brought the area under state control, religious activities were outlawed for ideological reasons. Since 1990 a steady influx of missionaries has attempted to reverse this situation. Protestant activists from abroad have clearly outperformed the Russian Orthodox Church in their financial and personnel investment in the region. The native population, especially in the cities, has been the most responsive to these newest Christianizing efforts, particularly among individuals suffering from alcoholism.

THREATS TO SURVIVAL

Soviet Reforms

Despite a long history of interaction with foreigners, the Russian Revolution in 1917 initiated a period of outside influence unprecedented in Chukotka. Following the revolution, the new Bolshevik government began an active campaign to bring "socialist enlightenment" to the "backward" peoples of the far northeast. This was intensified in the 1930s, when Soviet leader Joseph Stalin ordered the forced collectivization of all agricultural activities throughout the Soviet Union. Privately owned reindeer herds were seized and assigned to collective farms, and reindeer owners who resisted were at best simply disenfranchised, at worst killed. The most important social unit now became the collective farm, further divided into work brigades. On the coast, the person formerly the "master of the boat" now became the "brigadier," and his boat crew became a "brigade." Similarly, on the tundra, the herding camp was now called a brigade and was led by a brigadier. All the land in Chukotka was divided up among the newly created collective farms, and rigid boundaries were drawn between them. Thus, while formerly the owner of a herd could make the decision to migrate several hundred miles to find better pasture for his animals, in the collective farm system the herds were forbidden to cross farm boundaries.

The collective farm system in Chukotka evolved from the 1930s up to the present. A large number of collective farms (in which all members ostensibly shared in the farm's management and profits) were eventually converted into a smaller number of consolidated state farms (in which a state-appointed manager made all of the decisions and farm workers merely received a salary for their labor). As a result, hunters, herders, and gatherers were turned into wage laborers who, while technically continuing predominantly to hunt, herd, gather, and fish, no longer had control over the production and distribution of local resources. Reindeer herding, sea-mammal hunting, and fur farming all became branches of the Soviet economy and subject to centralized planning. In the constant quest for greater productivity that characterized this government system, a continual campaign to increase the number of reindeer was pursued until the total number of reindeer peaked at about 500,000 in the late 1980s.[2] Even then, a popular slogan circulated in Chukotka was "Onward to one million!," reflecting an utter disregard for the limited carrying capacity of the tundra pastureland.

Impacts of Heavy Immigration

Throughout this process of the collectivization of traditional economic pursuits in Chukotka, there was a continual influx of Soviet citizens from the European part of the Soviet Union and Siberia, most of whom were Russian and Ukrainian. This massive in-migration significantly changed the social fabric of the villages of Chukotka. At the same time, the more beneficial aspects of state incorporation—schools with native language programs, health care facilities, paid vacations, and libraries—guaranteed a certain level of acceptance of these radical changes. A significant effort was made to transform small numbers of Chukchi and Yupiit into a "native intelligentsia," who would become living examples of the positive power of the socialist social transformation process. These elite natives, who worked as politicians, teachers, doctors, and cultural workers, took up residence primarily in the larger towns and cities of Chukotka. A select few Chukchi individuals held highly visible positions in both local government and the local Communist party organization. Over the years, the second highest post in both the government and the Communist party was almost without exception a Chukchi.

In the name of economic efficiency, a number of prominent (mostly Yupik) coastal settlements were forcibly closed in the Soviet period and their residents relocated. As a result, the following decades witnessed a sharp increase in the number of suicides and other violent deaths, alcoholism, and other social problems. The rate of non-native in-migration increased from the 1950s through the 1980s, coinciding with a campaign of industrial development in Chukotka involving construction, mining, and oil drilling. The total population of Chukotka in 1930 was 14,500, of whom 96.3 percent were natives; by 1970, the population was 100,000, and only 12.8 percent were natives. In-migration to Chukotka continued until 1989, when the population peaked at 164,783.[3] As a result of these drastic demographic shifts, local native residents gradually became a minority in their own settlements and received lower ranking jobs and smaller salaries than the incomers, and the Russian language became the dominant means of public communication.

Current Events and Conditions

As a result of perestroika ("restructuring") in the late 1980s and the collapse of the Soviet Union in 1991, Chukotka has undergone sweeping political, economic, and social changes that have had a significant impact on the social status and living conditions of the Chukchi and Yupiit of Chukotka. Not only did the Russian Federation become an independent country in 1991, but the various territories within Russia began to struggle for autonomy in relation to one another and to the Russian center in Moscow. In 1990 the Chukotka Soviet of People's Deputies declared independence from its parent province, and today Chukotka is an independent territory within the Russian Federation.

While this transformation of the local political structure is meant to signal the arrival of democracy in Russia, it also marks the end of the long Soviet tradition of reserving positions in the government of Chukotka for natives. Although some natives do still hold positions in the administration, the new political power in Chukotka is unabashedly non-native and predominantly Russian-Ukrainian. Building on patterns of the Soviet past, this new government, made up primarily of former communists-turned-democrats, continues to remain under the tight control of a more or less totalitarian governor. Criticism is not tolerated, and opposition is systematically eliminated. This has made it very difficult to develop even a discussion about native rights and interests, much less an active native advocacy movement.

The collapse of the Soviet Union caused a massive out-migration from Chukotka (and many other regions of the Russian Far North). Incomers have left in large numbers to seek the relative economic safety of western Russia. Since this out-migration began, the proportion of Chukchi, Yupiit, and other natives in Chukotka has increased from less than 10 percent to almost 20 percent in 1998, but the overall population of Chukotka had dropped to about 78,000. The increase (from 10 to 20 percent) is an extrapolation based on the reasonable assumption that most of those leaving Chukotka are non-native people.[4] While out-migration continues and the relative percentage of natives to incomers may continue to rise, this does not mean that Chukotka is returning to a social condition in which natives will once again become dominant, or even equal. Non-native incomers continue to exert dominance over a very marginalized native population, for a combination of political, economic, and social reasons. Paternalism, a "benevolent" attitude based on clear-cut hierarchies, continues to be the key characteristic of native–non-native relations in Chukotka.

The Role of the Government

One of the problems in trying to launch a movement for native rights and interests is the persistence of the traditional Soviet understanding of the relationship between social organizations and the government. Thus, the Association of Lesser-Numbered Peoples of Chukotka, which is officially registered as an independent social organization, is entirely dependent upon the Chukotkan administration for financing, making it in some sense a virtual branch of the administration. This compromises the association's ability to raise issues that cast the administration in a critical light.

Moreover, when natives do criticize the administration and ask for attention to specific problems, the administration often responds by denying existence of the problem or by distracting attention away from the problem or toward far less serious problems. For example, instead of attempting to develop a comprehensive program for helping natives attain education that could lead to improved job opportunities, the administration promised to pay a lump-sum monthly compensation to the entire native population, which, when divided among all native inhabitants, came to a one-time payment of about twenty dollars per person.

Another strategy is the staging of elaborate and colorful native holidays, for which no expense is spared. The problem is that natives themselves are rarely if ever involved in the planning of these holidays; they are instead directed to perform their traditional culture for public consumption. Russian holidays are staged as well, with similar intentions. However, natives in particular increasingly express frustration with this ultimately empty attention. As one native activist, who was fired from his job in a village House of Culture because of his open criticism of the local administration, said, "All they do is give us holidays and pretend that everything is fine. They show us off to international audiences and say, 'See how well our traditional cultures are doing!' Dance, sing, they tell us, but they won't help us where we really need help!" (Interview with Patty Gray, Anadyr' District, Chukotka Autonomous Okrug, October 1996).

This young activist recognizes that the greatest irony of these staged holidays is that the daily practice of traditional economic activities, such as sea-mammal hunting and reindeer herding, are the best means to attain cultural survival and revitalization. Yet these pursuits receive the least concrete assistance from the Chukotkan administration.

Environmental Crisis

Official policy regarding the environment during Soviet times was determined largely by attempts to increase the country's productivity and industrial and agricultural output. Consequently, there was little concern about the long-term effects of the Soviet command economy on the natural environment. One of the legacies from this era is the nuclear power station at Bilibino, one of only two such reactors in the Soviet North. For many years, reindeer herders in the region have complained about damage to the pasture inflicted by this industrial project.

Gold and other mining activities are another source of environmental destruction. Currently, the major mining enterprises are concentrated in the northern half of Chukotka. These include the gold mines of Leningradskiy, Polyarniy, Komsomol'skiy, and Bilibino, as well as the tin mines near Pevek. In the late 1990s, commercial bids were constantly being held for the rights to new mining areas in all of Chukotka's eight districts. The low-cost techniques of surface gold mining, which are particularly destructive, make vast stretches of tundra unsuitable for reindeer herding and other subsistence activities. In addition to the purely environmental threat, these mining activities have triggered far-reaching social and cultural changes in as much as most mining towns were inhabited almost entirely by transient incomers. In recent years, several mines and their supporting towns have been closed, creating a patchwork of ghost towns across Chukotka. Typically, little environmental cleanup is attempted at these abandoned sites.

Even the areas little affected by Soviet industrial policies, such as the Chukchi Peninsula, have to bear their share of environmental damage and destruction. For example, the coastal strips of the Chukchi Peninsula are littered with hundreds of thousands of empty oil drums, which were brought in to fuel state farm operations and were never taken out of the region again. Even in the vast, seemingly wild stretches of inland tundra these oil drums can be found. The irresponsible attitude of military personnel toward the natural environment could never be prosecuted, nor could the poaching activities of high-ranking local officials. Everywhere in Chukotka, the fragile tundra is marked with the permanent tracks of all-terrain vehicles (ATVs) known locally as *vezdekhody* ("go-everywhere"), which have become one of the key forms of transportation in rural Chukotka. In 1998 a local law was passed to limit the use of these tracked vehicles by private individuals coming from urban areas (weekenders who used them to take hunting or fishing trips into the tundra); however, these passenger vehicles have become more important in far-flung villages because helicopter travel has been drastically limited by the deteriorating economic situation.

Threats to the Reindeer

One important category of environmental crisis in Chukotka can be classed as a natural one. Chief among this category are the predation of domestic reindeer by wolves, the increase in the size of the wild reindeer herds, tundra fires, and the icing over of tundra pasture in the fall. Wolf predation has always been a problem for reindeer herders; in fact, during the Soviet period, wolves were described as "enemies of the people." Predation became an especially serious problem in the early 1990s, when political and economic changes in Chukotka led to the breakdown of reindeer management practices. While central managers often claim that it is the natives' fault for being drunk and irresponsible and not watching the herds, in fact the increasing wolf predation has occurred when rifles, bullets, and working snowmobiles were in short supply to the reindeer herders. One young herder in the village of Snezhnoe describes his frustration: "Without bullets, there is nothing we can do. We run and scream at the wolves, but they don't pay any attention" (personal communication with Patty Gray, Anadyr' District, Chukotka Autonomous Okrug, June 1997).

Today's "enemy of the people" is not only the wolf, but also the wild reindeer herd, which migrates in several separate groups primarily throughout central and western Chukotka. Besides exhausting the pasture that is needed by the domestic reindeer herds, wild male reindeer regularly drive females off from the domestic herds. The size of this wild herd regularly fluctuates in long-term cycles. Wild reindeer have always interacted with the domestic reindeer population; however, in the late 1990s, the wild herd had grown to an unprecedented size. Estimates in 1998 ranged from 50,000 to 150,000; the official count (in January 1998) for all domestic reindeer in Chukotka was about 150,000.[5]

Tundra fires are another environmental threat to reindeer herding. Chukotka does have a department for battling summer tundra fires, but in the early 1990s, when there was a breakdown in the efficiency of such departments, a large fire that broke out in the Anadyr district destroyed hundreds of square hectares of reindeer pasture. During the winter, a serious threat to pasture occurs when a periodic icing over of the tundra takes place, primarily on the Chukchi Peninsula. Icing over occurs when a late fall warm spell melts the snow cover and is then followed by freezing temperatures. Such icings are said to occur about every seven years. The icings that occurred in 1996 and 1998 caused the loss of a large number of badly needed breeding stock.

Negative Non-Native Attitudes

Chukotkan landscapes show a rather varied picture of environmental degradation; it seems that wherever human activities (other than traditional subsistence pursuits) have occurred in Chukotka, they have left their—mostly damaging—marks. Their roots are found in the Western and Soviet attitude that treats the environment as a resource to be exploited for short-term profit. Since Chukchi and Yupik subsistence activities were incorporated into an economic model based on such an attitude they too became, necessarily, environmentally damaged. Generally, land-based resources (such as reindeer pastures and riverine fishing) have been more seriously impacted than sea-based resources (such as sea-mammal hunting). This also means that Yupik subsistence activities are less threatened by environmental factors than are those of the Chukchi. Maritime subsistence has been much more negatively impacted by national and international regulations imposed by the Soviet state and the International Whaling Commission (see chapters 8 and 12).

Sociocultural Crisis

The severe cultural alienation that afflicted the Chukchi and Yupiit during the Soviet period can still be felt. For example, native language competence, which decreased severely between 1960 and 1990, has not returned to previous levels, despite the fact that the tragic loss of native language and culture is a continuing refrain in Chukotka and a major concern among the Chukchi and Yupiit (primarily the urban intelligentsia) and a few concerned non-natives. Nevertheless, the early 1990s brought signs of hope to the Chukchi and Yupiit, who began to feel again that their cultural heritage was precious after decades of indoctrination to abandon the old ways for the sake of Soviet modernity. The appearance of foreign scholars and tourists, none of whom was interested in the Soviet or Russian cultures clearly reinforced the feeling that traditional knowledge was a resource worthy of being transmitted and documented. Contacts with indigenous peoples from other parts of the circumpolar North and elsewhere opened the eyes of many Chukotkan native leaders to the achievements of those other groups, whom Soviet propaganda had always tried to portray as suffering and disadvantaged under the corrupted rule of capitalism. The large out-migration of incomers also contributed to the general optimism of native leaders. Nearly everybody was convinced that things could only get better. Among the different visions circulated, the most noticeable was the belief that a return to tradition was possible and desirable.

Institutionalized Inequalities

When late-Soviet reforms, such as perestroika and glasnost ("openness"), made it possible to publicly voice criticism about existing conditions, native concerns initially appeared as the most urgent ones. In all of the Chukchi and Yupik villages for many years there had been a pronounced social stratification, which clearly favored the incomers over the native people. Wherever one looked—salaries, housing standards, job and educational opportunities, and health services—the local people were the most disadvantaged. It was thus quite obvious that changes needed to be made to realize a more equitable distribution of social and economic resources.

However, far from improving the conditions of the native population, the post-Soviet trend seems to be a redoubled effort to secure a position of dominance for the incomer population, pushing natives ever farther to the margins of productive society in Chukotka. This trend is linked closely to the arrival of capitalism and democracy in Chukotka. For example, while the socialist system deliberately and openly claimed to provide special programs to facilitate the advancement of natives socially, culturally, and economically (however much these programs may have failed in practice), in the democratic system, everyone—incomer or native—supposedly has an equal opportunity to make his or her own advancement. This is related to the perceived philosophy of capitalism: everyone has a chance to establish himself or herself in business or obtain an education to later secure lucrative employment, and those who fail economically have only themselves to blame. When natives complain about their persistent disadvantages in employment, education, or housing, they are often answered with a recitation of this new philosophy of the new Chukotka. However, since incomers had always occupied the top tier in the Communist party, in government positions, in industry, on collective farms, and in all important cultural institutions, they were already in the best position to take advantage of the changing political and economic circumstances. Natives, on the other hand, lacked the training, experience, connections, and financial resources to take advantage of the new capitalist rules. In the face of persistent criticism, the Chukotka administration has recently adopted a new rhetoric of concern and assistance for the native population; however, beneath the surface of this positive veneer, very little seems to be changing in terms of the structural inequality that exists between natives and incomers.

The New Capitalism

Probably the most serious threat to the cultural survival of the Chukchi and Yupiit in Chukotka is the sweeping program of privatization mandated in Russia beginning in 1992. In Chukotka, the botched implementation of this program has had a disastrous effect on the traditional native pursuits of reindeer herding and sea-mammal hunting. Formerly, collective farms had been entirely subsidized by the state, and their workers had become completely dependent on deliveries of food, clothing, supplies, and fuel. The collective farm was not merely an economic enterprise; it provided the entire social support system for the village by managing schools, stores, utilities, housing, and other essential services. State support was abruptly withdrawn after 1992, the social network of the collective farm was dismantled, and all that was left were the immediate commercial assets (for example, reindeer herds and whale boats).

Reindeer herding and sea-mammal hunting, which had always been primarily subsistence activities for the Chukchi and Yupiit, suddenly had to become commercially viable businesses, paying salaries to their workers out of their own profits. In this, the privatized collective farms failed utterly and miserably. In 1998 most collective farm workers (the majority of whom are natives) had gone a full five years without a single paycheck. The supplies they relied on stopped being delivered, and families began to survive primarily on bread, tea, locally gathered plants, and meat that they obtained for themselves. This has triggered a movement of people seeking work that begins in the collective farm itself: farm workers seek jobs in other segments of the village economy, which have been vacated by villagers seeking better opportunities in the district centers and cities, opportunities which have opened up as a result of out-migration by the urban incomer population to other, more temperate, regions of Russia.

Thus, the economic crisis has severe implications for the cultural survival of the Chukchi and Yupiit. While urban intellectuals frantically seek programs and preserve and promote the Chukchi and Yupik language and culture, the simple fact remains that language and culture are most "naturally" preserved wherever Chukchis and Yupiks are allowed to practice freely their traditional economic pursuits. Native language survives most successfully in reindeer brigades and on whale boats, where it is a working language, not in classrooms, where young people—cut off from their cultural traditions—do not see the relevance of speaking the Chukchi or Yupik language.

RESPONSE: STRUGGLES TO SURVIVE CULTURALLY

Developing Legal Frameworks

A serious obstacle to developing new precedents with regard to native rights and interests in Chukotka (and in Russia generally) is the weak development of the post-Soviet legal system. While many new laws are being passed both at the federal level and within Chukotka, it is widely understood that the laws themselves are usually vague and difficult to implement, and that the enforcement mechanisms are poorly developed. A further

Chukchi family at a fishing camp on the tundra, Provideniia District, 1993.

problem is the lack of agreement between the federal center and regions like Chukotka about who has authority over what; in many cases, laws clearly contradict the Russian constitution, but there is little that can be done to bring about compliance. Yet the establishment of a strong legislative framework for defining the status of native peoples is considered a crucial step before any significant progress can be made.

A national community of advocates (including both natives and non-natives) is working in Russia to develop legal norms, with regard to indigenous peoples, that are consistent in the federal center and in the regions where indigenous peoples live. These advocates face many obstacles that extend beyond the general weakness of the legal system. One problem is that, as a result of a wave of Russian nationalism that appeared in the 1990s, there is a great deal of resistance on the part of many non-natives to pass laws that carry specific benefits for indigenous peoples. Another problem is achieving consistency between federal laws and regional laws. In some cases, rather progressive legislation supporting indigenous peoples has been passed in other parts of Russia, but getting the federal legislature to pass a version of such laws proves more difficult.

In the 1990s, several draft laws have been proposed to the regional legislature in Chukotka that are considered fundamental to the progress of guaranteeing some basic rights for the Chukchi and Yupiit in regard to sea-mammal hunting, reindeer herding, local self-government for native communities, and traditional resource management. The local legislature is very resistant to hearing these laws and, in some cases, has demanded drastic revisions in a law before giving it serious consideration. The one law that seems most likely to be passed is a draft law that encompasses a multitude of issues, which includes the role of government in providing support for reindeer-herding activities. Federal versions of these laws (except for the sea-mammal hunting law), as well as a general law on the status of indigenous peoples, have also been proposed, but the federal legislative body has so far refused to hear them.

Native Activism

To better understand recent local responses to threats to cultural survival in this region of the Arctic, it is necessary to differentiate between at least three distinct phases in the field of native political mobilization. These periods could be called Soviet stagnation, perestroika optimism, and post-Soviet stagnation. The decades prior to the fundamental changes brought about by perestroika saw a period of major social and cultural upheaval for the native peoples of Chukotka. At the same time, because the political system was centrally governed, there were very few channels for expressing discontent or alternative solutions. In theory, joining the Communist party of the Soviet Union was one of the few options available for participating in local and regional decision making. However, most people were aware that real change could never be initiated through such activities, and thus these jobs were often left to opportunistic careerists who cared little about the specific problems faced by their constituents.

Nevertheless, some individuals at different levels of Chukotkan state institutions (from party organizations to schools and state farms), who honestly tried to make a difference, were able to initiate some minor reforms. The new native and non-native "dissidents" of Chukotka (mostly urban intellectuals), on the other hand, were so marginalized that their voices were little heard by the general populace. The most successful strategy used during those days was probably to refrain from any kind of activism. Living one's life by conforming superficially to Soviet demands while ignoring their ideological implications—a kind of "internal emigration"—proved to be a viable cultural survival strategy.

The winds of perestroika quickly changed the level of political activism throughout Chukotka. It became apparent that the existing state or state-controlled organizations—despite their often mind-blurring attempts to reinvent themselves during the late 1980s and early 1990s—were insufficient to addressing most of the pressing needs and demands of the times. In Chukotka, it was especially the native population, primarily the Chukchi and Siberian Yupiit, which felt that it was the right time to publicize their plight (the majority of incomers were busy packing their suitcases and felt little need to initiate local changes). At the height of the period of glasnost, during a period of optimism and excitement in a newly independent Russia, a new movement of indigenous peoples mirrored similar movements taking place in other parts of the circumpolar North (see chapters 5, 6, and 13). At the national level, this was reflected in the creation of an Association of Lesser-Numbered Peoples of the North in Moscow. At the same time, local native associations were formed all across the Russian North, including Chukotka.

In 1989 a U.S.–Soviet agreement made possible visa-free travel for indigenous residents on both sides of the Bering Strait after forty years of Cold War separation. On the Russian side, Siberian Yupik residents actively used this opportunity to visit their friends and relatives on Saint Lawrence Island and on the Seward Peninsula of Alaska; the Chukchi were involved in less travel. The new affiliation of Siberian Yupiit with the larger Inuit world outside Russia (in Alaska, Canada, and Greenland) influenced the formation of the Yupik Society of Chukotka in Chukotka in August 1990. Meanwhile, an Association of Lesser-Numbered Peoples of Chukotka was created to represent all of Chukotka's native peoples; the two organizations continue to exist side by side. Within a few years, both a Reindeer Herders' Union and a Sea Mammal Hunters' Union were created to represent these two predominantly native professional groups in Chukotka.

Despite the high level of superficial activism, the organizational activities of those transitional years reflected the profound influence of Soviet political culture. For example, the general tenor of many organizational activities was to compile problem lists containing complaints ranging from insufficient housing to native language loss. Most of the time, these complaints were passed on to higher authorities with the demand these others take care of the problems. Very few attempts were made to approach the problems through concerted community activism. Because of the decades of life experience within the Soviet political system, where everything— good or bad—came from "above," the thought of trying to change negative circumstances through personal effort was rarely entertained. Even today, this passive approach continues to hamper local initiatives.

Looking Beyond Borders

One of the most positive achievements of recent years are international contacts. The agreement on visa-free travel between Chukotka and Alaska has enabled many Chukotkan residents to cross the Bering Strait to visit friends and relatives, to attend conferences, and to participate in professional exchanges. These travels are happening despite many remaining bureaucratic obstacles. The belated arrival of electronic mail—which became available to the general population of Chukotka in 1998 although it had been available to the administration since 1995—is a hopeful sign. Contact with those beyond Chukotka, who can share ideas and possible solutions to common problems, has long been the most powerful instigator of change in Chukotka. In 1998 the administration began to install a telephone system capable of direct international dialing. Hopefully, these changes will make phone and fax communication with Chukotka more reliable.

An especially interesting project of international collaboration is a whale-monitoring project funded by the North Slope Borough in Alaska and the U.S. National Park Service. Instead of relying on guesses made by biologists, this project documents the movements and numbers of bowhead whales and other sea mammals through direct observation by experienced native hunters. Over several years, this project has provided coastal villages on the Chukchi Peninsula with much-needed cash income and has provided the Iñupiat of northern Alaska with information about little-known whale stocks, which are important in allocation battles with the International Whaling Commission. In 1998 U.S. funding for this project expired, and, although the Chukotkan administration has pledged to finance it for three more years, it remains to be seen whether this will occur.

Finally, some of the above-mentioned native organizations provide important links to global or circumpolar indigenous networks. For example, one of the founders of the Chukotkan Reindeer Herders' Union was also the founder of the National Reindeer Herders' Association, which operates in close cooperation with the World Reindeer Herders' Union. The Siberian Yupiit joined the Inuit Circumpolar Conference, which is one of the most influential indigenous organizations on an international level.

FOOD FOR THOUGHT

The predicament of the Chukchi and Yupiit in Chukotka differs from that of other indigenous peoples around the world primarily because of the socialist history of the Soviet Union. At least in material terms, that period of history is viewed nostalgically by many, including natives, in Chukotka. In comparison with the current situation, the Soviet period was a time when even the Chukchi and Yupiit were comparatively well fed, comfortably housed, and afforded a token measure of prestige in society. In that sense, the advent of so-called democracy and capitalism in Chukotka, however ironic it may seem, has meant a dramatic drop in the quality of life and a serious threat not only to cultural survival, but to physical survival. But the roots of the problems of today can be found in the structured inequalities between natives and incomers that were established during the Soviet period. While in the past these inequalities were deliberately masked by the supposedly benevolent paternalism of the incomer population toward the Chukchi and Yupiit, in the post-Soviet period an attitude of intolerance has developed as the native Chukotkans appear to fall farther behind in these new economic times.

The Chukchi and Yupiit in Chukotka are not a homogenous population. Besides the cultural differences between the two groups, there are significant differences between the urban native intellectuals and those who labor in the villages and in the traditional occupations of reindeer herding and sea-mammal hunting. Today, rural natives are struggling to stay alive. They are aware of the advocacy efforts of their supposed leaders in the urban centers, but it is difficult for them to find these efforts relevant to their own daily lives. Conversely, it is difficult for urban activists to understand sufficiently the problems of rural natives. Moreover, the 1990s have been a period of crisis and upheaval for all of Russia, and the specific problems of these small populations of endangered peoples of Chukotka will most likely remain a low-priority concern on the government agenda for many years to come.

Questions

1. What effects did the different waves of in-and out-migration have on the social and cultural fabric of Chukchi and Yupik culture?

2. What are the similarities and differences in the contemporary problems faced by the Chukchi and Yupiit?

3. How would you characterize the policy of the local government in Chukotka toward the Chukchi and Yupiit, and what are the implications of this policy for their cultural survival?

4. How might future developments of reindeer herding and sea-mammal hunting influence the cultural fates of the native peoples of Chukotka?

5. How do the social and political conditions for indigenous peoples in the former Soviet Union differ from those in other parts of the Arctic?

NOTES

1. "Indigenous Peoples of the Soviet North," Document 67. Copenhagen: International Work Group for Indigenous Affairs, 1990, 13.

2. *Magadanskii Olenevod*, vol. 40, 1998, 12–13.

3. A. N. Kotov, et al., eds., *Chukotka: Prirodno-ekonomischeskii ocherk* (Moskva-Anadyr': Izdatel'stvo "Art-Liteks," 1995); V. V. Leont'ev, "The Indigenous Peoples of Chukchi National Okrug: Population and Settlement," *Polar Geography* 1 (1977): 9–12; I. S. Vdovin, *Ocherki istorii etnografii Chukchei* (Moskva-Leningrad: Nauka, 1965).

4. From unpublished population statistics from the Department of Migration and Nationalities, Anadyr, Chukotka Autonous Okrug.

5. From personal communication from Vladimir M. Etylin, National Reindeer Herders Association, November 1998.

RESOURCE GUIDE

Published Literature

Borgoras, Waldemar. *The Chukchee*. The Jesup North Pacific Expedition 7. Leiden: E. J. Brill, 1904–1909.

Gray, Patty A. "Snezhnoe: Where East and West Collide." *Transitions: Changes in Post Communist Societies* 4, no. 6 1997: 96–100.

Kerttulla, Anna M. "Antler on the Sea: Creating and Maintaining Cultural Group Boundaries among the Chukchi, Yupik, and Newcomers of Sireniki." *Arctic Anthropology* 34, no. 1 1997: 212–26.

Krupnik, Igor I. *Arctic Adaptations: Native Whalers and Reindeer Herders of Northern Eurasia*. Hanover, N.H.: University Press of New England, 1993.

Schweitzer, Peter P. 1997. "Travelling Between Continents: Native Contacts Across the Bering Strait, 1898–1948." *Arctic Research of the United States* 11 (1997): 68–72.

Sverdrup, H. U. *Among the Tundra People*. Translated by Molly Sverdrup. La Jolla: Scripps Institution of Oceanography, University of California, San Diego, 1978.

Films and Videos

Beringia, 1992. Directed by Alexander Burimsky. For purchase and rental information, contact the director through Goskino, Valdaisky pr. 16, 125445 Moscow, Russia.

Chukotka Coast of Memories, 1989. Chronicle of contemporary village life, subsistence activities, and native dancing. Directed by Andris Slapinsh. For purchase and rental information, contact Natasha Diushen, Ruses Street 9–46, LV-1029 Riga, Latvia.

Traveling in the Arctic, 1980. Includes footage of Sakari Palsi's 1917–1918 expedition to Chukotka. Directed by Hanu and Sakari Palsi. For purchase and rental information, contact Hanu Palsi, Suomen Elokuvaarkisto, Finnish Film Archive, Box 177, 00151 Helsinki, Finland.

Copies of all three films are housed at the Alaska Native Heritage Film Center, University of Alaska Museum, P.O. Box 756960, Fairbanks, AK 99775–6960, and at the Arctic Studies Center, Smithsonian Institution, NHB 307, MRC 112, Washington, DC 20560.

Internet and WWW Sites

The Chukotka Autonomous Okrug: An Ethnographic Web Site by Patty Gray
http://www.geocities.com/Athens/Atlantis/7097

Chukotka: Russian Reindeer Country
http://www.informns.k121.mn.us/rfe/chukotka

East of Russia—information page on Chukotka (created by the American Business Center)
http://vladivostok.com/usis/CHUKCHI.htm

Paleoenvironments and Glaciation in Beringia
http://www.geo.umass.edu/projects/chukotka/berhome.html

Rusline—Russian Internet Directory information page on Chukotka (created by the Russian Information and Business Center, Inc., USA)
http://www.rusline.com/oblast/CHUKOTKA/CHUKOTKA.html

United Nations Environment Program, GRID-Arendal, information page on NITs "Chukotka"
http://www.grida.no/prog/polar/add/cip/instit15.htm

Organizations

The Association of Lesser-Numbered Peoples of Chukotka
President: Aleksandr Omrypkir
37 Otke Street
Anadyr', Chukotka Autonomous Okrug
Russia 686710

The Ecological Society of Chukotka "Kaira Club"
Chairman: Gennadii Smirnov
5 Mir Street, Apt. 39
Anadyr', Chukotka Autonomous Okrug
Russia 686710
E-mail: kaira@chukotka.ru
Telephone: (42722) 4–05–87

Native Cooperative "Naukan"
Chairman: Mikhail A. Zelenskii
23 Dezhneva Street, Apt. 1
Lavrentiia, Chukotka Autonomous Okrug
Russia 686940
Telephone: 2–26–69
Fax: 2–27–63

Yupik Society of Chukotka
President: Liudmilla I. Ainana
41 Dezhneva Embankment, Apt. 12
Provideniia, Chukotka Autonomous Okrug
Russia 686910
Telephone: 2–36–47
Fax: 2–21–72

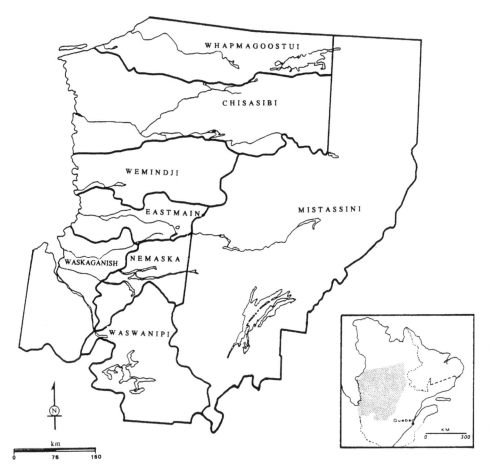

James Bay Cree community hunting areas.

3

The Cree of James Bay, Quebec, Canada

Harvey A. Feit

The James Bay Cree in Northern Quebec, number only 12,000 but they are known around the world for their struggles to survive the massive James Bay hydroelectric projects. Less well known are the threats they face from forestry clear-cutting, pollution of their lands, and the movement to declare the province of Quebec a country separate from Canada.

Three decades of almost continuous resistance to the destruction of their lands and the forced transformation of their culture and society have led them to the forefront of both the international indigenous rights movement and the environmental movement. Their story of successes and failures would hardly lead one to expect that nine communities of hunters, ranging in size from 550 to 3,000 people in a relatively remote area, could have such far-reaching global impacts.

CULTURAL OVERVIEW

The People

The James Bay Cree are a Native American people, or First Nation as they are called in Canada. The term "First Nation" indicates that their presence preceded those of the "Founding Nations" of Canada, namely the English and French. As subarctic hunters, the James Bay Cree have cultural affinities with other First Nations occupying the band of boreal forests that stretch nearly across the full width of the North American continent.

The James Bay Cree speak dialects of Montagnais-Naskapi-Cree, an Algonquian language group, which stretches from the Montagnais on the Atlantic coast of Labrador to the Plains Cree of the western prairies. It is one of only three indigenous languages of Canada that are spoken by enough people that its survival is not at risk.

James Bay Cree identities are also secure from the encapsulation and dominant cultures of Canadians of European descent. Identities are embedded in everyday lives, shaped profoundly by lifelong, daily, face-to-face interactions with contemporaries in small-scale communities. There is a common awareness that the Cree have survived off the food and resources they have received from the land. The Cree often find that they are most autonomous when they use the land and its resources to supplement goods, services, and knowledge from the economic markets, mass media, and government programs to which they have long been tied. Autonomy and freedom are highly valued along with hard work and constant social caring and responsibility for other community members. As the Cree society diversifies and is increasingly impacted by the dominant society, considerable efforts are being made to keep these practices.

The Setting

The James Bay Cree live east and south of James Bay and the southern portions of Hudson Bay, in northern Canada. They have lived in this region for 9,000 years, since the last glacial ice sheet retreated from the region. This region is dominated by the cold arctic air mass in winter, but the summer weather is temperate. In the north there are open forests with stunted trees spaced fifteen to twenty feet apart and patches of open tundra. In the south there are dense coniferous forests with a high proportion of black spruce trees that reach from sixty to seventy feet in height. As a result of its position between the arctic and temperate zones, the region is characterized by some of the most variable climatic conditions in the world. As a result of the influences of the massive inland sea comprising James and Hudson bays to the west and north, the region is also characterized by exceptionally heavy snowfalls. As a result of these local conditions, there is an abundance of water on the lands to the east of James Bay; lakes and waterways make up 15 percent of the surface.

Traditional Subsistence Strategies

Cree hunters express their responsibilities and also dependencies on the land through a series of territory stewards or "bosses." All of the more than 140,000 square miles of land on which the Cree hunt is divided into territories of from 115 to over a thousand square miles, each under the supervision and stewardship of a hunter. The steward and his spouse know the land intimately from years of use, and they decide whether it will be hunted in the coming year or whether the game need to be allowed to replenish itself. They also decide who and how many families will hunt on the land, which game they will try to catch, and which they will allow to grow and reproduce.

Stewards know the animals of their territories well. They may know the locations of as many as 200 beaver lodges and how many adult and young male and female beaver they caught when the lodge was last trapped. Since each lodge has one mating couple, plus some one-year-old beaver and young of the year, hunters keep a record of those they have caught and have an idea which ones are still left. Usually they do not try to kill all the beaver at a lodge, but leave enough adult or yearling beaver so there will be some beaver ready to breed in the coming year. Hunters say that trapping not only helps the hunters and their families by providing them with food—beaver is a preferred meat—and income from the sale of pelts, but it helps the beaver too. When beaver are not trapped, the population of beaver grows quickly to levels that exceed the amount of quality food or the number of sites where colonies can be located, so that the health of the animals deteriorates or they fight each other for lodge sites. In this way, if hunters carefully respect the communications from beaver, then the hunters benefit from the generosity of the beaver who are willing to be killed; the beaver souls, which are reborn, benefit from having abundant food and habitat in which to lead healthy lives. Here social caring and responsibility extend in practice beyond the confines of human society to encompass humans and animals as coinhabitants of a social universe.

The Cree have organized their uses of the land to respect the needs of animals. They use wildlife selectively, hunting and harvesting different species at each season, so that they can hunt efficiently, but also so that they have different kinds of game to use if some need to be harvested in smaller numbers in any year. In the summer months, many different species of fish are the main resource for the Cree. In the fall the large migrations of waterfowl along the coast of James Bay provide a variety of geese and duck species, while moose can be readily hunted in more inland areas. In the winter, furbearers such as beaver, otter, and lynx are trapped, as well as small game—hare, grouse, and ptarmigan—and some moose are hunted in deep snow; fishing under the ice is also possible. In spring, beaver, muskrat, and fish are harvested, along with the returning waterfowl. The Cree employ a number of traditional techniques to regulate their harvests of beaver, moose, geese, and many fish species.

Even though the Cree population has grown dramatically in recent years, Cree hunters have carefully kept their wildlife harvests to levels that do not adversely affect the game populations; rather, they have increased their use of purchased foods to meet the increased food needs of a growing population. The fish and wildlife resources of James Bay are as productive and healthy today as in earlier times because of the respectful use and management exercised by Cree hunters under complex and changing circumstances.

Social and Political Organization

The James Bay Cree emphasize egalitarianism in social relationships, and many details of everyday life are organized so as to respect the competence and needs of individuals. Even young children's wishes are taken into account when planning to move a bush camp or to organize a feast. Social life is organized around extended family groups, distant kinship ties, and bonds of friendship. Outsiders are readily incorporated into Cree social relations but are expected to engage in the extensive sharing and daily reciprocal help that express and reaffirm ties. Families are generally headed by men, who are also the main hunters, but women control much of domestic life and many community-centered organizations and institutions. In addition, any household or subsistence task can be undertaken by a man or a woman.

Despite the strong egalitarianism, the system of hunting territories recognizes a limited number of Cree as the stewards of each tract of hunting lands. Each steward has considerable authority over the uses of the land and where those who are not stewards may hunt. Stewards are generally the older, more experienced hunters. This system provides a judicious balance of leadership in hunting activities that benefit many people. When individuals abuse their leadership and serve only their own personal needs, they lose the respect of others and their instructions are not obeyed. This set of checks and balances has been incorporated into the developing political leadership patterns.

Religion and World View

When we are out in the bush, paddling along in summer, or walking on the ice, the sensitive side of us makes us realize there is a world staring back at us. And we depend on it.

—Paul Dixon[1]

Cree hunters have learned to live in this complex regional environment. In their world view, humans and their societies are part of a wider social universe. The world is not so much filled with natural objects, or things, as it is made up of social beings, or persons. For them, animals are willful beings, each species with its own type of family, knowledge, habitual behavior, and personality, and each animal is God's creation and has a soul.

This way of thinking about the world not only extends to other living beings but to phenomena and objects such as snow, mountains, lightning and thunder, rocks, and lakes. In the Cree world, each of these can be an active agent and therefore just like a living being or person. A. Irving Hallowell, the anthropologist who first described the logic and beauty of this way of thinking in the 1930s, told of one occasion when he heard thunder

42

and an old Cree man casually asked his wife, "Did you hear what they said?"[2]

In this social world, all the activities, behaviors, and signs of animals and other persons are thought of as communication, not just happenings. Thus if a hunter sees signs of an animal, it tells him or her something about what that animal is thinking or feeling. When a Cree sees a moose across a lake in the summer, too far away to be hunted, the Cree may be being told by the animal that he or she will have a successful hunt for that animal in the fall when it is easier to hunt moose. When fewer fish are caught in a fishnet than usual, it may be a sign that the fish do not want to be caught in such large numbers. One observation does not tell the whole story, but if the same message comes repeatedly, and in various ways, it becomes clearer. It is not that the fishermen cannot catch more fish, they clearly can if they keep setting the net. But the fish themselves are communicating that enough—or perhaps too many—have been caught and that the fishermen should not set the net in this area for a while but leave the fish alone to let their numbers increase before fishing here again.

This way of thinking about the world is closely tied to an environmental ethic of respect and responsibility toward the environment. Cree hunters are very careful observers of their world, and the knowledge they have of the lands on which they spend a lifetime of active hunting is typically very detailed and accurate. Scientific knowledge of the region, by comparison, is fragmentary and lacks historical depth, although it too is useful when used carefully. Indeed, the Cree and scientists agree on many things. Nevertheless, Cree hunters are often surprised that knowledgeable scientists often cannot see the ethical responsibilities that flow from their knowledge of the land. They are also surprised when scientists do not respond to the damage being done by developers and government officials by advising them to stop their actions.

The great majority of Cree adopted Christianity in the early decades of the twentieth century. Most became Anglicans, some Roman Catholics, and, after mid-century, many others adopted Pentecostal denominations; others returned to non-Christian Indian religions. Whichever religion they have followed, most Cree believe in a spiritual and social world, in which animals and spirits communicate with hunters. Each of the religious traditions in James Bay has adapted to Cree belief and knowledge.

THREATS TO SURVIVAL

The Effects of Early Contact with Europeans

The culture and society of the Cree have been changing throughout their long history. Long before Europeans arrived, new ideas and innovations were continually being explored and developed. Moose did not move into the James Bay region until after 1910, and the Cree learned how to hunt and manage moose populations in only a few decades.

Change itself is thus not really a threat to the Cree. The Cree have been changing by adopting those aspects of other cultures that they valued; sometimes they have been forced to change by powerful outsiders. However, they have not become just like other North Americans—they are changing on their own trajectory, re-creating the world view, values, and practices that have shaped their lives in ways that fit new contexts and problems. They still share and value the land in a culturally distinctive manner.

Europeans first approached the Cree in search of trade routes to the Orient and later to obtain furs for trade. In the 1670s, the fur trade began in earnest with the founding of the Hudson's Bay Company. From mostly tiny trading posts established around the bay, a small cadre of traders depended on the Cree to harvest furs from the vast surrounding territories using their traditional knowledge supplemented with steel traps, hatchets, and later bait and guns acquired in trade.

The Cree organized trapping for furs as a complement to subsistence hunting, which was of necessity the primary goal. The Cree came to depend on the traders for steel tools, cloth, guns and powder, and, in the twentieth century, tea, flour, lard, and some of other foodstuffs. The traders depended on the Cree for furs and often for food supplies, companionship, and security. Traders sought ways to control the Cree and get them to bring in more furs. The Cree demanded better goods and gifts from the traders as a sign of recognition that they and the hunters were trading partners. The Cree actively defended their extensive autonomy on the land. Many Cree hunters in the 1960s thought the fur trade had been a mutually beneficial experience. Others, however, recalled relatives who had starved in the bush in the 1930s because traders had refused aid and supplies to their families when fur prices declined and they could not pay for necessities, thereby revealing the inhumanity of a profit motive without social responsibility and sharing.

The fur trade lasted for three centuries until, during the years from the 1950s to the 1970s, the Cree began to settle in the government-sponsored communities that grew up around some of the fur trading posts. Not many Cree intended to reduce significantly the amount of time they spent on the land, but they did want their children to get more education in order to deal better with the Canadians who were increasingly intruding on their lands. They were also forced by a decline in fur prices to seek more government assistance from the social welfare system, and governments used this situation to get people to stay in and near settlements where they could receive their monthly social assistance payments.

Government Programs Introduced to Cree Communities

The governments were convinced that hunting was a dying way of life and that those who were hunters at that time would be the last generation. Development of the north would overwhelm and assimilate the hunters and provide new opportunities for the next generations to become wage laborers in the mining, forestry, and energy resource industries which would develop the north. This vision has failed on both counts. Many Cree have continued to choose a hunter's life, or they have developed other ties to the land-based economy. Northern developments have failed to provide jobs accessible or attractive to the Cree or in sufficient numbers to meet the needs of a rapidly growing population.

The improvements in health care that are available in the settlements resulted in a period of rapid population growth. This created constant stress in settlements that were continually short of funds from governments and often desperately in need of more and better housing, proper sanitation and public health services, locally controlled and designed education, and other social programs. Communities have improved slowly over time, but the Cree experience with government-initiated social and economic development planning was one of failure: failure of the government to provide basic and adequate resources comparable to those available in southern towns, failure to provide for local control, and failure to keep promises.

Large-scale Hydroelectric Development

A crisis developed in 1971 when the province of Quebec announced it would start to build the largest hydroelectric project in North America. The province did not inform or discuss the plans with the Cree. Young Cree, who had learned English in the schools, first read about this massive development in newspapers a few days after decisions to proceed with the project had been made. A group of younger Cree from several villages began to discuss how the Cree should respond to this threat. They organized meetings of Cree leaders and elders. The elders declared that the Cree should have a voice in the project, and if they did not, they should to try to stop the project. The elders were shocked at the destruction of the land and animals that would be caused by the flooding. They also proclaimed that this was part of a longer-term pattern of white men—non-Cree—deciding from elsewhere what would happen to the lands of James Bay, and that this pattern should stop.

The people are against the building of dams. The land is what they live off, and that is why they are against it. I know it's going to be bad for people with grandchildren and those yet to be born. . . . It disagrees with me from what I have seen so far. I feel like I have been punched. . . . I have been hurt inside. . . . I never felt that way before. (Abraham Weapinacappo, Cree elder)[3]

Because the governments of Canada and Quebec would not negotiate with the Cree elders and the new generation of leaders, the Cree reluctantly took the province to court to claim their rights to use and occupy the land that would be irreversibly damaged if the project were built. They embarrassed the federal government into giving them funds that would allow them them to make their case. This was the first of a long series of occasions on which the Cree sought to be heard by asking one government, or branch of government, to help it fight another branch of government. The Cree often have had to turn to the judicial system for partial recognition of their rights or to exploit the differences between the federal and provincial governments.

In one significant court case, with the help of a small group of lawyers, engineers, and social scientists, the Cree explained to the presiding judge how the 3,400 square miles of flooding, the more than 300 hundred miles of roads being built to construct dozens of massive dams and camps for thousands of workers needed for the La Grande hydroelectric complex, and the consequent opening of the territory for mining, forestry, and tourist developments would threaten both the land and the Cree way of life.

Two and a half years after the project was begun, and after six months of court testimony, the judge ruled in favor of the Cree and ordered the project stopped. A week later, the court of appeals took the case under review but lifted the order stopping construction while it considered the case. This was both a significant victory and an important loss. Few had expected the Cree to be able to stop the massive project at all. Having done so, even for a week, was a significant victory. The Cree had demonstrated an ability to disrupt plans in a way that could cost substantial time and money.

Many things had to be built in the brief summer period, so even short disruptions could cause long delays; Hydro-Quebec claimed in court that such delays cost it more than $1 million a day. This was cause for concern to both the builders and the financiers because there were still at least five more court rulings to come. The province declared that it was ready to negotiate with the Cree. The victory was limited by the fact that the construction was continuing. It became increasingly clear to the Cree that if the legal process took five years to reach a final decision in the Supreme Court, the project would be almost completed, and the damages would be irreversible whatever the court decided. The Cree therefore felt they had to negotiate.

Larger Political Threats

Quebec has been intermittently governed by a separatist political party since 1976, and two referendums have been held on the issue of whether the Quebecers wish to separate from Canada and establish a separate nation-state. The second of these referendums was won by those in favor of Canadian federalism, but by the narrowest of margins, and future referendums are promised by the separatist party forming the government in Quebec (1999). During the intensely fought separation campaign in 1995, the Cree said that, as a distinct people, if Quebecers chose independence from Canada then the Cree had a right to chose whether they would join an independent Quebec or stay in Canada. They said their lands would go with them. They asserted that they were not a colonized people who could be moved about politically by the decisions of others and that they had aboriginal rights of self-determination. Concern over the treatment of the Cree and the disposition of the extensive lands they use became an important issue in the campaign, although neither the federal nor the provincial government acknowledged Cree rights. The Cree held their own referendum and voted overwhelmingly to stay in Canada.

The campaigns, however, were highly divisive, and they have left the Cree more distant and isolated from the government and public opinion in Quebec. Their struggles for full recognition thus continue, amidst significant victories and ongoing erosions on their rights and lands. As Matthew Coon Come, the grand chief of the James Bay Cree, wrote in 1998:

The myth persists in Quebec and elsewhere in Canada, that this country consists of two founding nations or peoples, the English and the French. This fiction denies our presence, our rights and status, and our role in the history, economy, and the well-being of this country. Now, as Canada debates once more its own possible renewal or disintegration . . . it is our people and our land that is being threatened, and the Crees must be heard.[4]

Ongoing Challenges

The agreement has helped strengthen both full-time and part-time Cree hunting; it has enhanced Cree control of community life and institution; and it has given the Cree some economic autonomy. The process has also strengthened the Cree politically by building leadership skills and organizations.

The negotiated agreement has also failed in important ways. Both levels of government have failed to provide adequate resources to implement many provisions of the agreement. Many Cree lands have not been fully surveyed and marked, nearly twenty-five years after the agreement was signed. The region is still being treated as an uncontrolled resource frontier by corporations in a global economic system that seeks cheap access to resources without concern for conservation or regional development. The agreement has failed to protect the Cree from resource developments in part because the environmental impact assessment procedures have been repeatedly undermined or not applied by both the federal and provincial governments. For example, the government of Quebec has facilitated rapid and unsustainable cutting of the forests of the region. It has justified this by saying the rapid cutting is needed to clear timber from areas that will be reservoirs if future hydroelectric projects are built, but whether the hydroelectric projects that would require these reservoirs will ever be built is very much in doubt. One result of this unregulated forestry is that up to 90 percent of the forested land on some Cree hunting territories has been clear-cut, rendering the steward's lands effectively unusable.

The economic development aspects of the agreement have not been implemented by the governments either. Few Cree were willing to work on the hydroelectric project; only five Cree worked there in 1998. The Cree have not been allowed access to the tourism opportunities that were promised. They are also denied access to modest commercial fisheries or adequate forestry resources which they could carefully manage to provide jobs for the growing numbers of Cree youth who cannot be supported by full-time hunting or by service jobs within Cree communities.

The Cree therefore entered the 1990s as a society still tied to the land and a distinctive culture, as well as a society with an experienced and strengthened leadership and self-governing organizations and resources. They also found their lands and culture under continuing and expanded threats; they found that development has not benefited their communities; and today they are engaged in struggles that are very much like those they were fighting twenty years ago.

RESPONSE: STRUGGLES TO SURVIVE CULTURALLY

> We feel, as Cree People, that by coming to an Agreement . . . that it is the best way to see that our rights and that our land are protected as much as possible from the white man's intrusion. . . . We have always said that we wanted to maintain our way of life. . . . I hope you can all understand our feelings, that this has been a tough fight, and our people are still very much opposed to the project, but they realize that they must share the resources.
>
> —Billy Diamond, grand chief of the Grand Council of the
> Cree, 1974[5]

> If I had known in 1975 what I know now [1990] about the way solemn commitments become twisted and interpreted, I would have refused to sign the Agreement.
>
> —Billy Diamond, Cree grand chief.[6]

Negotiating a Land Claim Agreement

For two years, the Cree negotiated with the provincial and federal governments and with Hydro-Quebec and the other crown (government) corporations that were developing the territory. During that time, the Cree developed a regional association, the Grand Council of the Cree, which united the older and younger leadership of the nine Cree communities and provided essential services the communities alone were unable to undertake. A new regional society emerged from these collaborations, based on the ties that had formerly been established when Cree from different areas would meet at the fur trading posts to sell their fur, but also based on the more recently created ties among the younger generation of Cree who had gone to school together. New communications, joint decision making, and a new regional leadership recognized by all communities were developed in this process.

In some ways, the new political organization reflects the councils formed in each community when the Cree moved into the settlements in the 1950s and 1960s, and it also reflects patterns of hunting territory stewardship. For example, each community gave to the regional organization the mandates it wished to share, and the group tended to give to the communities most affected by a particular choice the main voice in how that decision should be made.

The negotiations with the governments and their development corporations did not provide the Cree with a just or satisfactory settlement. Nevertheless, the Cree were convinced that they had obtained the most they could through the negotiation process and that with the project being built they might be better served by this partial victory than if they allowed developments to go forward without any effective control. This compromise was a very difficult decision to take, and the leadership and communities debated it at length, but in the end they voted almost unanimously in favor of the agreement that had been negotiated.

The Cree, the governments, and the Inuit people of farther north in Quebec—formerly known as the Eskimo—who were also affected by one part of the project, together signed the James Bay and Northern Quebec Agreement in November 1975. It was the first modern treaty signed in Canada. The agreement prohibited Hydro-Quebec from making future extensions of the hydroelectric project without Cree consent; it required some modest modifications to existing plans; and it provided for some programs to remedy those impacts of the project that could be offset, such as improving access to the reservoirs. While the initial La Grande phase of hydroelectric development went ahead largely as it had been planned, new development projects were made subject to social and environmental assessments and regulations.

The governments recognized the Cree rights to hunt on all their ancestral lands, subject only to joint conservation. The Cree control only the 1.5 percent of the land around their communities, and most of the territory was therefore open for development by outsiders. Cree set up their own education and health boards under the agreement, as well as new local and regional governments. They also received cash compensation for damages caused by the projects, which initially totaled $150 million, but now exceed half a billion dollars owing to supplementary agreements resulting from various project modifications.

Support for Cree Subsistence

Our economy is often criticized by those who do not understand, called primitive and old-fashioned. I want you to know it is the best economy in the world. . . . Well, the Cree have survived for thousands of years on hunting, fishing, and trapping. Tell me about another economic system that provided that kind of stability for thousands of years without interruption. The Cree people do not want to give up hunting, fishing, and trapping for an uncertain future. . . . Can Hydro-Quebec guarantee to feed and shelter the Cree people for another 5,000 years? You can see that it is impossible to pay people to give up their way of life, when they depend on the land.

—Edward Gilpin, Jr.[7]

To support hunters, a special program was created in 1975 to provide income security payments to full-time hunters, giving them and their spouses the equivalent of a wage for each day they spent hunting. This was necessary because the prices of furs were unsteady and the costs of hunting were rising; many who wanted to hunt did not have the cash to outfit themselves with basic equipment and supplies. The program has led to more people being able to hunt than ever before and for longer periods. Today, nearly all Cree hunt, and full-time hunters account for about one-quarter of the booming population, not all of whom could be supported full-time on the land.

About one-third of the Cree have regular jobs, but nearly all Cree say hunting and living on the land are vital parts of their lives, and they spend considerable effort and money to hunt and live in the bush part-time. They often hunt on evenings, during weekends, on holidays, and during fall and spring hunting breaks of several weeks when schools and local governments close and the settlements are virtually empty. Cree villages are therefore clearly still hunting communities, but they are on a course of development distinctive to the Cree. Jobs are organized to provide cash incomes but also to provide extensive opportunities for land-based living and hunting.

While the initial compromises made by the Cree in order to gain some degree of control over these development projects did not solve the conflicts at the root of the threats to their land and their culture, the Cree themselves were strengthened by the process of challenging and negotiating with governments and developers. There was a sense of enhanced power from implementing the self-government provisions they had negotiated and, for example, developing schools and health care facilities under Cree control. Cree communities became more vibrant and self-sufficient as people regained control of essential services and a younger generation has grown up with a renewed confidence that they can expand and achieve yet new forms of self-sufficiency.

Diversifying the Local Economy

The Cree also used some of the compensation funds they received to start or to purchase several businesses, including a regional airline, a construction company that builds houses and community buildings in Cree villages and a food and dry goods distributor to supply the stores and restaurants in the villages. Other new businesses developed in the villages include grocery and hardware stores, restaurants, taxi services, gas stations, and small bakeries and other enterprises located in people's houses. These depend on a strong sense of both individual autonomy and community service, values at the heart of the hunting culture that now serve the Cree well while they live in permanent villages.

Building Alliances at Home and Abroad

In 1989, when Hydro-Quebec announced that it would start seeking environmental and social assessment and approvals to build a new hydroelectric project on the Great Whale River, there were divisions within the Cree communities. Some Cree thought it was a chance to strengthen the agreement and get the additional funds needed to improve social and economic conditions in the villages. Other Cree said the hydroelectric project had to be stopped because it had already flooded too much land, damaged wildlife, and threatened Cree culture. However, when Whapmagoostui, the Cree village at the mouth of the Great Whale River, declared that it did not want the project to go ahead, other communities and leaders united behind them. This time the Cree said their position was not, as it had been for the earlier project, "Don't build without our consent," it was "Don't build the Great Whale project." The immediate goal was to prevent the start of construction: to fight before the land was being destroyed.

Cree leaders realized that Hydro-Quebec had spent over $20 billion on the already-constructed La Grande complex, and that the corporation was dependent on international capital markets to raise the funds needed to continue expanding. A key to Hydro-Quebec's plan to convince potential investors that this was a safe and profitable place for their capital was to have an assured market for the sale of the electricity it produced. It did this partly by negotiating for large export contracts for the sale of electricity with Maine, Vermont, and New York state electric utility companies. The Cree realized that, if they could block these contracts, they would undermine some of the economic justification for the project and make it harder or more expensive for Hydro-Quebec to borrow the capital it needed to go ahead. The challenge was for a relatively small indigenous people to make its voice heard in another country and in the world financial centers.

Fortunately for the Cree, some groups in the United States were beginning to question whether their electric utility companies really needed large additional amounts of electricity and, indeed, whether increased energy consumption was environmentally or economically sound. The Cree met with these groups and told them that while Hydro-Quebec argued its energy was nonpolluting, reliable, and renewable, this was not the whole story. Hydroelectricity, the Cree said, flooded massive land areas; destroyed wildlife and habitats; threatened Cree livelihoods, health, and culture; and ignored Cree rights. The Cree also argued against the U.S. utility companies which stated that their responsibilities ended at the international border. The Cree told them that they were exporting environmental destruction and the social costs of producing electricity to Cree lands when they purchased electricity from Hydro-Quebec.

A relatively rapid victory was achieved in Maine, and the Cree decided to undertake a campaign in the other states in cooperation with local organizations. To publicize their campaign, the two communities located at the mouth of the Great Whale River—one Cree and one Inuit—built a combination canoe and kayak—the odeyak—to travel from James Bay through Vermont to New York City for Earth Day 1990. When they arrived in New York City, Grand Chief Matthew Coon Come addressed the massive audience near the tip of Manhattan Island and near the Wall Street financial district, "Hydro-electric development is flooding the land, destroying the wildlife and killing our people, and eventually we will all be victims"[8] Robbie Dick, the chief of the Cree community at the mouth of the Great Whale River, told the audience that the developers "are telling the Americans this is cheap and clean. But it's not cheap for us. When you turn on your switch, you're killing us."[9]

Environmental organizations helped the Cree at each daily stop along the way during their travels. Not all environmentalists supported the Cree, and not all Cree were comfortable working with environmentalists. In addition, animal rights groups were pushing for a ban on the sale of fur pelts, a vital source of income for the Cree hunters, and critical to many indigenous hunters' ability to still live on and protect the land. It seemed a contradiction to the Cree to form an alliance with groups whose antitrapping campaigns aimed to undermine the Cree's own respectful and moral

Overnight camp near the Ottaway River during the fall, in an area that will be flooded if the third phase of the James Bay hydroelectric project is built.

relationship to game and land in the name of a new animal rights ethic that took no account of other cultures and other ways of life.

Researching Other Options

The Cree knew that if they were to make a convincing case they had to show that there was an alternative. They paid energy experts to do a series of studies that showed that energy conservation could save more energy than the Great Whale project would produce—at less cost. Studies also showed that the contract the New York state utility was entering into to purchase electricity from Quebec was financially disadvantageous to the state, because energy prices had been dropping. The Cree also commissioned public opinion polls that showed declining public support in the United States for megaprojects. These results were not lost on U.S. politicians. The New York contract was subsequently canceled by the state utility.

Quebec still wanted authorization for the project, so it submitted 10,000 pages of impact assessment documents to the review boards established by the James Bay and Northern Quebec Agreement. Because the governments tried to weaken the stringency of the review process, the Cree took three court actions to ensure that these were serious environmental and social impact reviews. The Cree argued that these documents did not answer the basic questions—that their purpose was to reassure the public rather than provide essential information for a decision. The board asked Hydro-Quebec to undertake more thorough reviews. A short time later, the premier of Quebec announced that the Great Whale project was stopped and would be delayed indefinitely. It was an extraordinary victory for the Cree and for the Inuit to their north who had joined with them to stop the Great Whale Project.

Expanding Horizons

The James Bay Cree had become leaders in the struggle to gain national and international recognition for the rights of indigenous peoples. With part of the interest from the compensation funds they had received, the Cree have aided other aboriginal peoples who did not have the resources to defend themselves against the exploitation and destruction of their lands by other development projects. The Grand Council of the Cree was also the first indigenous organization to gain recognition as a nongovernmental organization at the United Nations. The Cree leadership found that publicity at the international level was one of the important ways to embarrass and pressure governments in Canada to fulfill more of the obligations they had taken under the treaty. Regional Cree leaders also played an active role at the United Nations in Geneva preparing the draft of the first global International Covenant on the Rights of Indigenous Peoples. This international accord is now being considered for adoption by UN agencies.

FOOD FOR THOUGHT

The system that right now runs this country is a small group of people . . . managed by multinational corporations who feed into the system. That's why it is corrupt.

I still have faith in the people, I still have—to a certain extent—faith in the courts to stop certain mega-projects. Because the way they are built now is unacceptable. And we think we can change that.

—Grand Chief Matthew Coon Come, Grand Council
of the Cree[10]

While Cree leaders and people struggle for the recognition from governments and corporations that they have a right to control their future, Cree lives, culture, and economies are being rebuilt daily by collective Cree efforts on the land and in the communities. The value of the land to all Cree unites their politicians, the Cree hunters, those Cree with steady jobs—

most of whom who hunt part-time—and the growing number of Cree youth most of whom envisage their futures as being based both in the villages and on the land. While jobs are in short supply, and political struggles periodically unify people, the hunting way of life provides a key point of shared value and experience that underpins unity on a daily basis. The other unifying factor is the desire and the active practice of Cree to look after their own communities. Despite serious problems of an inadequate number of jobs—especially among youth—and social ills, Cree villages are socially vibrant because people increasingly find the means to deal with community problems from within their own values, history, and systems of sharing and caring.

Questions

1. What are some of the ways the James Bay Cree have been able to use the values and principles of their hunting way of life to organize their lives in the settlements and the regional politics among their villages?

2. Do you think that Cree society can continue to create lives for Cree youth that combine living in settlements with a life on the land without becoming assimilated? Why or why not?

3. Why are development projects initiated by governments and by global corporations so threatening to Cree lands and ways of life? In what ways have the Cree succeeded in limiting the impacts on their lands and lives from such projects? In what ways have they not succeeded?

4. What are the ways that the Cree have found to fight government decisions within their own country? What ways have they found to carry their struggles internationally and to global financial centers? What material resources and what kinds of knowledge have been critical to the Cree efforts to pursue these struggles?

5. The Cree and the environmentalists share a profound concern for the environment, but they do not always agree. What could environmentalists learn from the Cree about caring for the land? Would it enhance their ability to work together?

NOTES

1. Paul Dixon, "The Link Between the Land and Water Will Be Forever Destroyed," typescript written at Waswanipi, n.d., 2.

2. A. Irving Hallowell, *Culture and Experience* (Philadelphia: University of Pennsylvania Press, 1955), 109.

3. Statement at Eastmain to Boyce Richardson, in Social Impact on the Crees of James Bay Project. *http://www.gcc.ca/Environment/HydroDevelopment/impact.htm.*

4. Matthew Coon Come, "A Message Regarding the Rights of the Crees and Other Aboriginal Peoples in Canada," *Grand Council of the Crees (Eeyou Astchee),*

Never Without Consent: James Bay Crees' Stand Against Forcible Inclusion into an Independent Quebec (Toronto: ECW Press, 1998), 13.

5. Press statement, "A Time of Great Decision Has Come for the Cree People," 1974.

6. Billy Diamond, "Villages of the Damned," *Arctic Circle* 1, no. 3 (1990): 28.

7. In Laurent Lepage and François Blanchard (eds.), *Analyse de contenu des audiences publiques "Grande Baleine": études exploratoire*, Montreal: Hydro Québec 1992, 102.

8. Quoted in Michael Posluns, *Voices from the Odeyak* (Toronto: NC Press, 1993), 32.

9. Quoted in ibid., 33.

10. Interview. "Matthew Coon Coome's [*sic*] Lonely Fight for Democracy," *Nativebeat* 1, no. 9 (1991): 15.

RESOURCE GUIDE

Published Literature

Feit, Harvey A. "Hunting and the Quest for Power. The James Bay Cree and Whitemen in the Twentieth Century." In R. B. Morrison and C. R. Wilson, eds., *Native Peoples: The Canadian Experience*. 2d ed. Toronto: McClelland and Stewart, 1995, 181–223. Published on the Internet at http://www.lib.uconn. edu/ArcticCircle/History/Culture/Cree/Feit1/feit1.html (plus: . . . feit2.html and . . . feit3.html) (1996).

The Nation. A bimonthly James Bay Cree regional magazine edited by young Cree. Beesum Communications, 5678 Park Ave. P.O. Box 48036, Montreal, Canada H2V 4S8. Tel: 514–272–3077; fax:514–278–9914; Web-site: http://www.beesum-communications.com.

Niezen, Ronald. *Defending the Land: Sovereignty and Forest Life in James Bay Cree Society*. Boston: Allyn and Bacon, 1998.

Richardson, Boyce. *Strangers Devour the Land: The Cree Hunters of the James Bay Area versus Premier Bourassa and the James Bay Development Corporation*. Vancouver: Douglas and McIntyre, 1991.

Salisbury, Richard F. *A Homeland for the Cree. Regional Development in James Bay, 1971–1981*. Montreal: McGill-Queen's University Press, 1986.

Tanner, Adrian. *Bringing Home Animals. Religious Ideology and Mode of Production of Mistassini Cree Hunters*. Study no. 23. St. John's: Memorial University, Institute of Social and Economic Research, 1979.

Films and Videos

Cree Hunters of Mistassini 1974. 58 minutes. National Film Board of Canada.

Flooding Job's Garden, 1991. 57 minutes. National Film Board of Canada (coproduced with Tamarack Productions, in association with TVOntario and with the collaboration of TV5).

Our Land Is Our Life, 1974. 58 minutes. National Film Board of Canada.
Power, 1996, 77 minutes. Cineflix Productions (in association with the National Film Board of Canada [distributor] and TVOntario).
Power of the North, 1994. 53 minutes, Wild Heart Productions (in association with MTV, CityTV, MuchMusic [Canadian distribution by Kaleidoscope Entertainment]).

Internet and WWW Sites

Arctic Circle on the James Bay Cree (school oriented)
http://arcticcircle.uconn.edu/Cultural Viability/Cree

Air Creebec (Cree Airline)
http://aircreebec.ca

Cree-Naskapi Commission (Ottawa)
http://www.atreide.net/cnc/

Grand Council of the Crees (Eeyou Istchee)
http://www.gcc.ca

Hudson Bay Region
http://www.sierraclub.org/ecoregions/hudsonbay.htm

James Bay and Northern Quebec Agreement
http://www.inac.gc.ca/jbnqa/index.htm

Mistassini Cree First Nation
http://nation.mistassini.gc.ca/index.htm

Oujebougamau Cree First Nation
http://www.ouje.ca/welcome/chief.htm

School Net on Aboriginal Peoples
http://www.schoolnet.ca/aboriginal/index2-e.html

Organizations

Cree Nation Youth Council
c/o Grand Council of the Crees (Eeyou Istchee)
2 Lakeshore Road
Nemaska, Quebec, Canada J0Y 3B0

Cree School Board
203 Main Street
Baie du Poste, Quebec, Canada G0W 1C0
Telephone: (416) 923–2764
Fax: (416) 922–2072

Cree Trappers Association
Eastmain, Quebec, Canada J0M 1W0

Grand Council of the Crees (Eeyou Istchee)
Ottawa Embassy
24 Bayswater Avenue
Ottawa, Canada K1Y 2E4
Telephone: (613) 761–1655
Fax: (613) 761–1388
E-mail: cree@igs.net

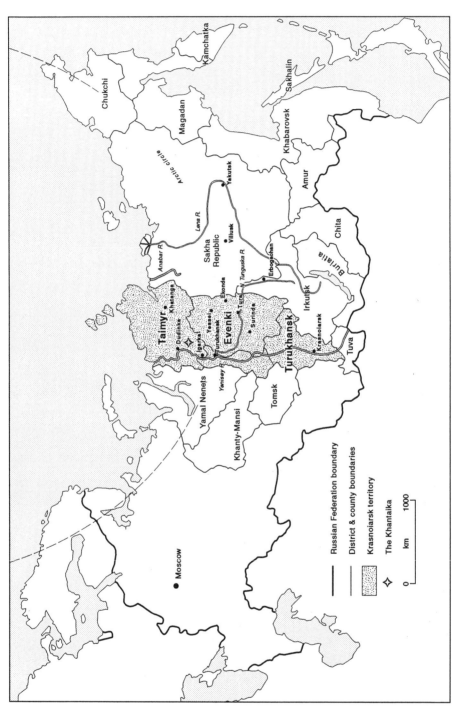

The Evenki Autonomous District and adjacent areas of the Russian Federation.

4

The Evenkis of Central Siberia

David G. Anderson

CULTURAL OVERVIEW

The People and the Setting

The Evenkis are one of the most widely dispersed peoples of the North. Contemporary Evenki settlements are found across the vast territory of Russian Siberia from the divide between the Ob' and Yenisei river basins in Central Siberia, to the mountainous perimeter around Lake Baikal, and extending to the Pacific Coast territories of Khabarovsk and Kamchatka. Evenki settlements can also be found in China and Mongolia. Throughout this large expanse, which represents approximately one half of the Asian continent, the Evenkis, who call themselves by a variety of names, including *bail, khamniganil, orochenil*, are closely related by language and tradition to such neighboring nations as the Evenys, Solons, Negedaletses, and Oroks.

Taking into account all of the places that the Evenkis live, as well as the homelands of their neighbors, this group of indigenous people occupies a territory as immense as those of the circumpolar Inuit or the Canadian Cree Indians. Despite occupying such a large territory, the Evenkis are considered by the Russian Federation to be a "sparse people," a legal designation that entitles them to special privileges. In 1998 more than 30,000 Evenkis were living in the Russian Federation. The major challenge to the survival of this people is their ability to reproduce their language and their culture while being confined to dozens of small communities across Asia in harsh economic and ecologic conditions that have effectively separated the communities from each other.

Traditional Subsistence Strategies

In the past, the Evenkis established their large homeland through extensive travels. They are most famous for being masters of the domestic reindeer. The earliest written records from China mention the Evenkis' use of reindeer transport as early as the sixth century. By riding saddled reindeer, or harnessing them to handmade wooden sleds, the Evenkis were able to hunt or trade over thousands of miles of forest and tundra without any need for money, varied tools, or even forage. Although travel by reindeer is slow by modern standards (seldom exceeding 25 miles a day), reindeer are extremely strong and reliable. Unlike other domestic animals who must have food prepared for them, reindeer are released in open pastures to feed themselves in snow-covered valleys, rugged alpine plateaus, or dense forests. The reindeer simply needed to be rounded up each morning with the use of dogs and lassos to move onward to fresh pastures or a new community.

According to the Evenkis, the secret to holding reindeer is to ensure that each deer recognizes its own herd and the people who master it. Traditionally, reindeer were never kept within fences because the herdsman trusted the instinct of the reindeer to travel together in one group. To gather a herd together, an Evenki herdsman approaches the animals on skiis and sings a loud, slow melody. As the herd approaches the camp, special herding dogs may be used to ensure the herd stays around the camp.

In the autumn, reindeer can be saddled to hunt furbearers such as the Yenisei sable. The Evenki hunter uses a hunting dog to chase the sable into a tree and then fells it with a low-caliber rifle, killing the animal quickly and leaving the skin undamaged. This method of hunting sable is considered to be far more humane than the recent method of using metal traps promoted by the Russian State. In the winter, when snow is deeper, reindeer are often harnessed three or four abreast to pull sleds carrying hunters, families, or freight. At the turn of the century, many trading families assembled caravans (*argishil*) of from five to fifteen sleds to carry fish and fur from the forest to regional markets along the Yenisei River and to bring flour, tea, salt, and other trade goods such as beads, hunting equipment, and cooking utensils back to the taiga, which is the transition zone between the northern forest and the treeless tundra.

The Evenkis rarely slaughtered their own harness reindeer. Instead, they use harnessed reindeer to approach groups of wild reindeer swiftly and silently in order to harvest wild meat. If a domestic reindeer had to be killed because of age, illness, or out of necessity, all parts of the animal would be used. The tough fur from the lower portions of the reindeer's legs was particularly valued for making reindeer fur boots (*bakari*), and the fur from the reindeer's head was used to make round carpets for the tent (*kumalan*). The skin from the body could be used in the autumn to

Reindeer herder and child from the No. 4 Reindeer Brigade preparing to hunt sable, Evenki Autonomous District, November 1992.

make a warm parka, or in other seasons it would be shaved to make durable leather for lassos or summer moccasins. Smoked reindeer hides make warm wall coverings for the cone-shaped Evenki teepees. Almost all the meat of a wild or domestic reindeer can be eaten. The hunter will eat parts of a reindeer frozen raw, such as the liver or brain, thereby obtaining sufficient amounts of necessary vitamins. The stomach and intestine are particularly valued for their nutritious fat. The meat of the reindeer can be boiled in soup or fried over the fire, or, in the spring, the meat of the wild deer can be salted and dried to preserve it for summer.

In addition to reindeer husbandry, the Evenkis set nets for fish and traps for the fur-bearers. The favorite fish of the Evenkis are the taimen and whitefish, both of which can be smoked to prepare *iukalo* (dried fish). The fat collected from the fish can be used as a medicine or to fuel lamps during the dark winters. Hunters construct traps from heavy logs in order to trap arctic fox or wolverine. Although fur trapping and fishing have long been an important part of the Evenki money economy, wild and tame reindeer figure more prominently in myths and shamanistic ceremonies, and today they are considered to be central to the revitalization of the traditional culture.

Social and Political Organization

Evenki social organization has never been strictly regimented as in industrial states. People tend to live and travel together in extended families where a single elderly male is a major decision maker. Men might meet together to decide upon a particular travel route, to choose a time for dividing the reindeer herds, or to organize a yearly plan for trade. Women play a significant role in organizing social life from raising children to governing and adjudicating the day-to-day relationships in the camp while the men hunted or traveled.

With the coming of the Russian conquerers in the sixteenth century, Yenisei Evenki society became more formally male and clan centred. Senior men were obliged by Russian warriors (Cossacks) to pay taxes in fur. Orthodox Christian missionaries baptized individuals and recorded the clan affiliations of senior men in record books as surnames. Taxes were planned and collected at yearly meetings (*suglanil*) located at significant trading centers (such as Turukhansk). The clan structure, as codified by the tsarist Russian state, became even more formal during the Soviet period when Evenki families were organized into clan councils and later collective farms with special production quotas. Despite the complete restructuring of social and political life from 1930 onward, the Evenkis continue to respect those local men and women having special ritual knowledge and elders with life-long experience on the land.

A distinctive quality to Soviet reforms was the establishment of the first autonomous districts for native people. The Evenki Autonomous District was established in the middle of the Yenisei basin in 1930 in order to help Evenki people modernize their economy and culture. The first Soviet institution in Evenkiia was the Tura "culture base" where one of the very first boarding schools was built and where teachers organized themselves into nomadic "red-tent" brigades to travel with Evenki families while teaching their children how to read and write. The language spoken by the Evenkis along the Podkamenaiia Tunguska River, within the Evenki Autonomous District, is considered to be a literary language and is taught in Evenki schools all over Siberia. Since 1989 the Evenki Autonomous District has been the home to the political association Arun which has been one of the leading groups in mobilizing public opinion toward support for the indigenous peoples of Siberia.

Religion and World View

The Evenkis are well known for their ritual specialists who communicate with the spirits of the taiga—the animal masters—who could, during their trances, fly great distances or engage in battles with distant enemies. These specialists were called the *samanil*, a word very close to the Evenki word for knowing (*sama-mi*). When Europeans ventured into Evenki lands in the seventeenth century, they took this word into their own languages as shaman (and shamanism) and then applied these terms to describe similar specialists found in many other cultures across the Arctic and indeed in other parts of the world.

Upon first glance, Evenki shamans use many of the same techniques as other ritual specialists in Mongolia or the North American Arctic. The most visible tool of the shaman is the skin drum, sometimes round, sometimes polygonal in shape. The drumbeat accompanies the shaman during his or her *kamalan*—a performance in which a shaman sings to contact spirit helpers. During the *kamalan*, the shaman may make a request for information about the whereabouts of certain animals or ask for help in healing a patient. The spirit helpers are often embodied in special idols which the shaman hangs on his or her belt. Helpers are associated with a lower, middle, or upper world and can take the form of many animals such as taimen, black bear, or loon. Unlike other ritual traditions, Evenki shamans have great freedom to improvise. Reflecting the extensive travels of their people, shamans often perform their ceremonies in a mix of many languages and use images not only from the taiga forests but also from Buddhism and Christianity. Evenkis never trained to become shamans but were instead chosen by the spirits through prophetic dreams or magical encounters in the taiga. Once chosen by one or more spirits, a shaman could work to improve his or her relationship with the spirit world but could never escape this relationship.

During the height of Soviet power, the influence of shamans was thought to be a threat to the state. In the 1930s, dozens of people identified as shamans were arrested and executed. Because of this repression, or perhaps because of the danger of declaring oneself to be a shaman, most Evenkis say that there are few real shamans today.

Although shamans were directly attacked by the Soviet state, it is important to emphasize that special ritualized knowledge is spread evenly throughout Evenki society. Many Evenkis still watch for omens in their everyday life, from the calls of ravens to significant images in their dreams. Before conducting a hunt for wild reindeer or bear, Evenkis are careful not to boast verbally about their success, and they always show respect for the animal killed. For example, wild reindeer are never slaughtered for sport, and significant portions of the reindeer, such as side fat or bone marrow, is fed to the home fire as a symbol of thanks to the master of the taiga. In addition to powerful or prescient knowledge, Evenkis make use of many elements of the world around them for clinical healing. For example, a shaman may choose a particular domestic reindeer to heal a kinsman of glaucoma or a chronic cough. This reindeer would be dressed in beads and fine clothes, have its legs tied together, and then be carried in to breathe upon the afflicted area.

THREATS TO SURVIVAL

The fourth biannual congress of the Evenki political association (called Arun) held in Tura in September 1998 was dedicated to discovering Evenki survival strategies. According to Evenki participants, the problems posed by new market reforms in Russia are seen to be more deadly than the typhoid and smallpox epidemics of 1914, the political repressions of the 1930s, and the hunger during World War II. The delegates to the conference identified six tendencies threatening their people: the loss of the Evenki language among the younger generation; the weakening of Evenki family structure as a result of enforced migration; a declining birthrate and accelerating death rate; the loss of domestic reindeer herds and, with them, the basis for cultural revival; the appearance of malnutrition in children for the first time in Evenki history; and chronic alcoholism, which contributes to all of the preceding problems.

Villages and the Threat to the Evenki Lifestyles

Most of the contemporary social problems of Evenki communities are connected with the policy of enforced resettlement that was conducted by the Soviet state all across Siberia from 1948 to 1967. Until that time, Soviet teachers and administrators lived beside Evenki families, traveled with them, and taught the children in mobile tent schools. After World War II, Soviet planners thought that it was important to make nomadic hunters and herders more "cultured" by building them stationary settlements, organizing their nomadic households into state farms, and constructing boarding schools. For the first time in their history, Evenkis began to experiment with living within the confines of one valley and one village.

In the early period of these changes, the investment of the state had many positive effects. For the first time Evenki children learned first to read and write in both Russian and Evenki and eventually achieved a full primary education. Many of these children grew up to be leaders in contemporary Evenki society. The early farms specialized in reindeer herding, hunting, and fishing. Because they were heavily subsidized by the state, the Evenkis were guaranteed employment and income. However, in the later phases of this campaign, which more radical, the majority of Evenki people were removed from the forest, and a cycle of dependence was created. In the 1960s, small villages of a few hundred Evenkis were forcibly combined into larger settlements of from 500 to 1,000 residents. The rationale behind these resettlement programs was that resettlement allowed the state to provide cost-effective social services, including health care, electricity, and education.

Life within the villages was not simple. In order to service the expanding array of technical services and facilities, many transient newcomers were invited from the Russian heartland to work as support personnel in these new settlements, for which they were paid good wages. By the mid-1970s, Evenkis found themselves occupying the lowest paid, most labor-intensive jobs while newcomer engineers or teachers received the best housing and highest wages. This discrepancy was most startling when one compared the lifestyle of the Evenki elders, many of whom were forced to live in the crowded apartments of their children and grandchildren, with that of young Russian couples who were given spacious new housing. Although the goal of the village policy was to civilize Evenkis, the result was the creation of a disadvantaged and displaced workforce.

The most noticeable change in Evenki life with the creation of large villages was the loss of the Evenki language among the younger generation. Most Evenki children were forced to remain up to nine months a year in a boarding school while their parents, for the most part, traveled with the reindeer in large orbits around the settlement. As more and more Russian-speaking technical personnel and engineers were invited to work in the villages, the language that the children heard every day was Russian. Within many boarding schools, the Evenki language was taught only as a special subject. Evenki language teachers were obliged to teach with books written in the literary language—a dialect that often did not correspond with the way that families actually spoke at home. The Evenki language has four dialects, and the greatest differences are found along the Pacific Coast where many people find it difficult to understand the language printed in textbooks based on the central Evenki dialect. Many adults today speak of their embarrassment at returning to visit their parents during the summer months only to discover that they no longer understood each other.

A much more devastating effect of resettlement was the stress upon family structure. Not only did children suffer psychologically from being separated from their mothers and fathers, but their intensive education in the villages left them unfamiliar with the skills that they needed to live on the land. In Evenki traditional society, fathers and uncles taught young boys how to catch reindeer with lassos and how to hunt large game in a respectful manner. Women taught their daughters, daughter-in-laws, and nieces how to tend the camp, look after children, prepare food and clothing, and often how to hunt rabbits and set traps. Soviet planners had expected that office jobs and technical labor would soon replace traditional skills. However, a sad irony of the market reforms is that the only sustainable economy in the Evenki District today is hunting, trapping, and reindeer herding—an economy which Evenki youth now find themselves ill-prepared to face.

Although the Soviet policy of civilizing life in the taiga through hastily constructed villages generated inequalities, one could argue that it was a kinder policy than that found in many indigenous villages around the world where policies of genocide are actively practiced. The peculiarity of Soviet development policy was that it was an attack on indigenous lifestyles, not an attack on people. However, the fate of those who did not feel at home in the small, electrically lit apartments of a noisy village was only one short step away from deliberate genocide.

Ecological Challenges

The creation of these small urban spaces across the taiga had peculiar ecological and social impacts. For centuries, Evenkis traveled widely, investing little time in any one place for long. With the creation of villages, those Evenkis who remained tied to the forest found it necessary to travel farther and farther to find fresh pastures and good hunting grounds. Each lengthy trip away isolated them more and more from their children and families, making it progressively more difficult to pass on their skills.

To relieve the problems created by distance, the Ministry of Agriculture provided Evenki villages with subsidized helicopter transport, which shuttled hunters and herders back and forth between their pastures and traplines and the distant settlement where their kinfolk now lived. Initially, this investment invigorated Evenki society by allowing parents to fly into villages every other week to visit with their children. However, these expensive machines proved difficult to support financially in the long term. The introduction of a shift method to reindeer herding had a subtle but devastating effect on the domestic reindeer herds. With a constant interchange of herders, domestic reindeer were born and matured with little constant contact with a single master. The result toward the end of the 1980s was the creation of herds that were undisciplined and difficult to tend. To counter this tendency, Soviet planners constructed long fences, up to 310 miles in length, to ensure that the domestic herds would not run away from their stewards. The parceling of the taiga into fenced areas further weakened the special relationship among individual deer, their herds, and the people who tended them. When the cutbacks in state subsidies made these fences impossible to maintain, the now half-wild animals left their master to roam the tiaga as wild reindeer.

Evenkis in Central Siberia have not suffered as much from intensive industrial resource extraction as their neighbors in the Khanti-Mansi Autonomous District, in the Taimyr Autonomous District, and the Sakha Republic. The impacts of mineral development are nevertheless closing in on the Evenki Autonomous District. To the north, in the city of Noril'sk, one of the largest nickel mines and smelters in the world has polluted the northern boundaries of the district with toxic heavy metal precipitates and acid rain. The effect of this zone of pollution has disrupted the migratory pattern of the Taimyr population of wild reindeer, which had been a stable source of meat for Evenkis living in the northern regions of the district. To power resource development in Taimyr and in the Sakha Republic, large hydroelectric dams have been built upon the Khantaika, Kureijka, and Viluil rivers flooding pastures used by Evenki herdsmen, destroying the migratory patterns of fish stocks, and creating a water system that harbors parasites. In 1998, to counteract the dislocations of the market economy, the administration of the Evenki Autonomous District is actively recruiting foreign investment to develop large oil and gas reserves in the southern part of the district. Preliminary exploration in these gas fields has already disrupted hunting and herding in this region.

The End of Reindeer Herding?

Despite the dislocations caused by enforced resettlement in Soviet times, Evenkis prided themselves on their large, healthy herds of domestic reindeer. An average Evenki settlement supported from twenty to thirty professional reindeer herders who kept as many as 10,000 head of reindeer in herds of 2,000 animals each. The Department of Agriculture demanded that these large herds be culled for meat for the regional centers, but within these industrial herds there were many traditionally trained harness reindeer that were used to supply transport to another twenty or thirty professional hunters. Within three years of turning Evenki state farms into clan councils or private farms in 1992, the number of reindeer in the Evenki Autonomous District alone dropped from 35,000 to 5,000.

There are many reasons for this dramatic decline. One of the major dangers to reindeer husbandry in the Yenisei north region is the threat posed by migratory wild reindeer. These wild cousins of the domestic reindeer move in yearly migrations in herds numbering up to 15,000 animals and can destroy overnight the carefully created relationships between people and domestic herds. During the autumn breeding season, a large population of wild reindeer can sweep a domestic herd away in a single evening leaving the herder and his family with no means of travel. The changing migration routes of the Taimyr population of wild reindeer have already swept away the domestic herds of Evenkis living in Chirinda and are endangering the herds of Evenkis in Ekonda.

Second, due to the lack of support given to professional reindeer herders, many herds of domestic reindeer ceased to be gathered and trained on a daily basis, making them run wild. In the region between the Nizhnaia Tunguska River and the Podkamenaia Tunguska River, the population of wild reindeer exploded between 1993 and 1998 from near zero to 14,000 head, while the number of domestic reindeer still in human hands had declined to a mere 1,000. Those remaining domestic reindeer are under the threat of constant predation from a growing wolf population which, during Soviet times, was culled by professionally hired hunters.

Finally, due to unemployment and the fact that wages were often not paid by state agencies for dozens of months, people slaughtered their reindeer for food or sold them to other hungry relatives.

The flight of the domestic reindeer has had a significant impact upon Evenki society. Practically, with the loss of the local herds, Evenkis are losing access to a resource that enabled them to travel widely without recourse to money or trade goods. In the period in which they can no longer depend upon the welfare state, they are losing their capacity to travel and move freely. Symbolically, the loss of the reindeer implies an end to that part of the Evenki culture that invigorates their folklore and sense of pride as a distinctive people. This loss of self- and collective esteem feeds the cycle of poverty and alcoholism.

Health and Unemployment

The construction of villages also introduced new and unfamiliar health problems. The water around villages gradually became polluted with accumulating human waste, leading to growing problems with gastrointestinal parasites and occasional outbreaks of hepatitis. Other diseases associated with resettlement include tuberculosis, alcoholism, and, more recently, malnutrition, which began claiming the lives of Evenkis toward the end of the Soviet period and which has now accelerated under the effects of market reforms. Until 1992 these ailments were treated by means of free state health care services within villages and emergency medical evacuations to regional hospitals. Since the post-Soviet reforms, doctors have ceased visiting the villages, and health care has become more costly than most Evenkis can afford.

When the Russian state canceled its program of subsidies to these newly built villages in 1991, the wealthy newcomer population abandoned the villages and left their Evenki neighbors to fend for themselves. This outmigration might have been a happy occurrence if it were not for the fact that the centralized nature of these large villages violated the fundamental ecological principles upon which Evenki society was based. In the past, Evenkis were able to hunt and to form and maintain extensive social and economic relationships based on their knowledge of the land and their skilled use of domestic reindeer. The ecological consequences of resettlement inscribed large zones on the landscape devoid of firewood, pasturage, and wildlife making it impossible to travel without a helicopter. Children born and raised in the villages grew dependent on imported sugar, flour, and fruits from the southern parts of the Russian Federation. With the collapse of the redistributive Soviet economy, many young families found that they had neither the money to purchase fuel, ammunition, or machinery to hunt for themselves nor the skills to live on the land with the remaining reindeer.

In most Evenki villages in 1998 over 90 percent of the population was officially unemployed and received unemployment benefits in the form of rations of flour, tea, and salt. This contrasts to a population that enjoyed 90 percent employment as late as 1992 and had a stable wage with which to purchase a wide range of consumer goods. In 1995 the first cases of rickets and thyroiditis were recorded, and epidemic levels of tuberculosis were declared to exist in the villages. These three ailments, associated with a diet of starch and carbohydrates and devoid of protein and vitamins, can be directly linked to the introduction of radical market reforms. Although, at the turn of the century, Evenkis may have starved in the event of an unfortunate hunting season, they had never suffered from malnutrition, resulting from a diet lacking in nutrient-rich fresh meat. Since 1997 conditions in the villages have deteriorated to such an extent that new migratory problems have appeared. If, during the Soviet period, there was an enforced migration from the hundreds of small homes across the taiga, today there is a flight of people from the collapsing villages into the regional centers of Tura, Turukhansk, Igarka, and Dudinka. This migration, necessitated by poverty, leaves the taiga even more barren, and it has created new stresses on the health, sanitation, and social welfare of the residents in these small towns.

RESPONSE: STRUGGLES TO SURVIVE CULTURALLY

Among the sparse peoples of the Russian North, Evenkis have been at the forefront of political struggles to protect their land, language, and lifestyle. During the Soviet period, dozens of Evenki intellectuals received a higher education and achieved important posts within the government structure. Evenki political organizers, such as the past president of Arun, Zinaida Pikunova, have actively brought issues of ecology and assimilation to public attention through articles in the press, establishing contacts with Russian and foreign scholars, and studying the experience of indigenous peoples worldwide.

One of the first struggles that Evenkis fought and won was the cancelation of a massive dam project at Turukhansk which threatened to flood half of the Nizhnaia Tunguska River valley and destroy several Evenki villages. The movement against this project was controversial because local Evenkis had to argue against the opinion of well-placed Evenki politicians, such as Vasilii Nikolaevich Uvachan, who argued for the need for Evenkis to participate in building industrial development. The uniting of Evenkis and Moscow scholars in this campaign in the mid-1980s laid the foundation for Arun. Since then, Arun has participated actively in the formation of the Association of the Sparse Peoples of the Russian North and has sent representatives to Geneva to meet with other indigenous peoples in the International Working Group on Aboriginal Rights. As a result of these experiences, Arun negotiated a path-breaking agreement with the Eastern-Siberian Oil and Gas Company regarding the sharing of profits from the exploitation of natural gas in the Baikit region.

Arun has been careful to argue for a modest expansion of oil and mining developments in the Evenki Autonomous District—but not to argue against all industrial development. In forming their arguments, Arun members point to the positive benefits that Evenkis have received from free state-sponsored education and free medical care. However, Arun has constantly pushed for a controversial distinction between peoples aboriginal to the Evenki Autonomous District and those who are newcomers. Although indigenous Evenkis, Kets, and Yakuts seem to have their rights protected through the fact that they have their own autonomous district, the history of Russian state-building since 1960 has been that state money is invested to help northerners—a category that includes both Evenkis and the majority of the population of the Evenki Autonomous District, which is primarily Russian. Officially, the Russian state does not recognize the idea of indigenous peoples but instead argues that some people are simply more or less numerous than others. Since 1997, while the health of the Evenki population crumbles, Arun has become more radical in claiming that state funds, and funds earned from mineral development, should be sent directly to the people whose ancestors have lived in the north for centuries.

In studying the experience of indigenous peoples worldwide, Evenkis have become interested in the land reservations created in North America for Native Americans. Contemporary Evenkis are attracted to the idea of there being a special place with protected boundaries where indigenous peoples can live on their own lands undisturbed by policies that lead to boarding schools, resettlement, or the disruption of their hunting and herding economy. In 1992, under the influence of Arun, the administration of the Evenki Autonomous District allowed Evenki herders to leave their state farms and establish their own "clan communities." Within a clan community, a group of relatives were given resources such as reindeer and the exclusive right to use specific lands. However, all government funding was removed from these communities. Evenkis living in clan communities continue to struggle for an independent existence; they have discovered that, within a market economy, it is difficult to pay for fuel and transport without government support. By 1997 the approximately 70 percent of the reindeer turned over to the clan communities had been sold or lost, and many Evenki hunters and herders had migrated to the district capital of Tura. In 1998 Evenki politicians began to explore proposals whereby Evenki hunters could share in the monetary wealth from industry and yet retain certain privileges in respect to their lands.

A more radical proposal for supporting Evenki culture comes from those who argue that the entire northern half of the Evenki Autonomous District should be turned into a natural park with strict restrictions on resource development. This proposal has attracted the attention of the United Nations Educational, Scientific, and Cultural Organization (UNESCO) and other international organizations, such as the World Wildlife Fund (WWF). The experience of Evenkis with natural parks has been mixed. In the 1970s, large nature preserves were created in the border region between the Evenki Autonomous District and the Taimyr Autonomous District and in the southern portion of Evenkiia near the Yenisei River. In order to protect these areas and keep the land pure, local Evenki hunters were forcibly resettled by military aircraft away from the lands where they and their forebears had lived for centuries. The present proposal is not nearly as strict, for it gives permission to traditional hunters to continue to travel and hunt in their accustomed areas. However, the question is raised as to whether Evenkis who have lost their reindeer and now hunt with snow-mobiles or with helicopters can be considered traditional. Although natural parks tend to be formed with ideas that are familiar to Evenki hunters, the laws governing parks tend to be made by people who are not themselves indigenous peoples but urban politicians, bureaucrats, or scholars.

Evenkis have also been working with other agencies to try to rebuild their society in a sustainable manner. Since 1995 international organizations, such as the International Red Cross, the Canadian International Development Agency, and the Northern Forum (consisting of state or provincial governments from the circumpolar nations), have shown increasing interest in sending technical assistance to Evenkis, as well as to other indigenous peoples in Siberia. Evenki scholars continue to publish school textbooks in their native language and to push for an extension of Evenki language education into the high schools. Since 1992 a growing number of international scholars have taken an interest in the Evenki language and culture and have written fundamental works on Evenki history in a variety of European languages.

FOOD FOR THOUGHT

Evenkis, like all indigenous peoples in the Arctic, face a contradictory future. They have used the skills earned in harsh boarding schools and competitive work institutions to build their own political organizations and establish contact with international organizations. However, the more closely tied Evenkis become with the international community, the less opportunity they have to practice and maintain their relationship with the spirits of the taiga and the reindeer which once carried them across half of Asia. In the Soviet period, Evenkis suffered from an overcentralized state. In the period of the Russian market economy, Evenkis suffer even more from a lack of interest of the state in their lives.

Questions

1. The resettlement of Evenkis into villages offered many opportunities but also caused great problems. Should Evenki people be forcibly resettled back to the forest?
2. Does the sharp decline in the numbers of domestic reindeer resulting from changing economic and ecological conditions imply that Evenki culture is endangered? Or can Evenkis persist in living their culture within urban conditions?
3. In what ways were Evenki people distanced from their reindeer?
4. Are national parks a good idea for preserving traditional culture?
5. Is there a difference between genocide, and the economic or political actions of an outside agency that threatens to end the traditional life of a people?

RESOURCE GUIDE

Published literature

Anderson, David G. *The Number One Reindeer Brigade: Identity and Ecology of Evenkis and Dolgans in Arctic Siberia.* Oxford: Oxford University Press, 1999.

Bloch, Alexia. "Between Socialism and the Market: Indigenous Siberian Evenkis Grapple with Change." Ph.D. diss., University of Pittsburgh, 1996. Published by University Microfilms International UMI9728658.

Fondahl, Gail. *Gaining Ground? Evenkis and Land Reform in Southeastern Siberia.* Boston: Allyn and Bacon, 1998.

Shirokogoroff, Sergei Mikhailovich. *Social Organisation of the Northern Tungus.* Oosterhoute, Netherlands: Anthropological Publications, 1966 [1933].

Ssorin-Chaikov, Nikolai. "Stateless Society, State Collective: A Social History of the 20th-Century Indigenous Identity among Evenki of Central Siberia." Ph.D. diss., Stanford University, 1998.

Films and Videos

Evenkiiskie geroicheskie skazaniia, 1990. A. N. Myreneva. Novosibirsk: Nauka. (A musicological study of an Evenki heroic ballad with notations and a sound recording.)

Lingren Photographic Collection. Ethel John Lingren. Haddon Museum of Anthropology and Archaeology, University of Cambridge. (A large collection of black and white photographs as well as a 16mm film of Evenkis in Manchuria c. 1930.)

Taiga Nomads: A Documentary Series about the Evenki of Siberia, 1992. 3×50 minutes. Directed by Heimo Lappalainen and Jouko Aaltonon. Illume Ltd., Pasilan Puistotie 4, FIN-00240 Helsinki, Finland. Tel/Fax +358-0148-1489. 16mm and video.

Internet and WWW Sites

http://www.lib.uconn.edu/ArcticCircle/SEEJ/Russia/index.html
"Struggle over Land and Resources in the Russian North"
a site on circumpolar politics and issues with occasional updates on Siberian affairs.

http://www.koeln-online.de/infoe/home.html"
"INFOE—Institute for Ecology and Action Anthropology"
a site with general information about problems facing Siberian peoples.

http://www.spri.cam.ac.uk/people/jeoh2/2evenki.htm"
"Evenki"
an unofficial Web site maintained by a postgraduate student in Cambridge with recent news on Evenk culture and politics and links to other sites.

http://members.tripod.com/~anttikoski/eng_index.html"
"Languages of the National Minorities of Russia on the Net"
a specialized site with information on minority languages.

http://www.eki.ee/books/redbook/evenks.html"
"The Red Book of the Peoples of the Russian Empire"
a reference site of information on all Siberian peoples.

Organization

Political-Cultural Organization "Arun"
Administration of the Evenki Autonomous District
ul. Sovetskaya 2
Tura, Evenki Autonomous District
Krasnoyarsk Territory, Russia 663370
Telephone and Fax: +7-39113-226-55

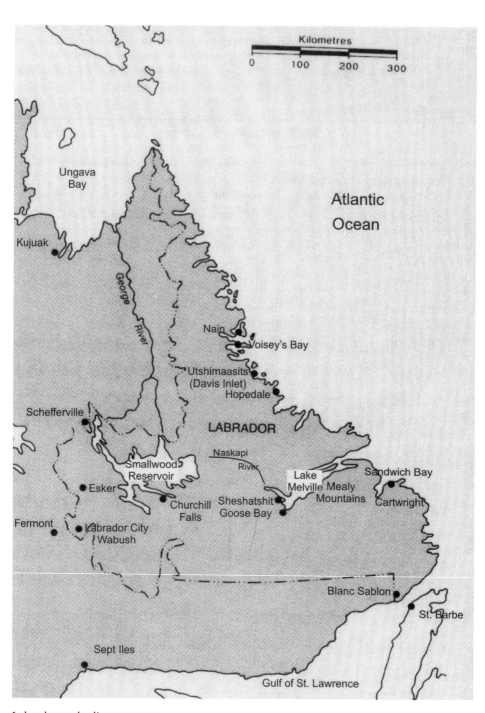

Labrador and adjacent areas.

5

The Innu of Labrador, Canada

Adrian Tanner

CULTURAL OVERVIEW

The People

The Innu, the easternmost of the Cree-speaking people, inhabit the boreal forest and northern Canadian Prairies, from Alberta to the Atlantic Ocean. The word "Innu," in their own language, means "the people," but they are sometimes referred to as "Montagnais Naskapi," which was the term earlier applied to the Innu by anthropologists. Now they prefer their own name for themselves. One of the first North American aboriginal people with whom Europeans made contact, they are also one of the last to be settled into permanent communities. Until the Labrador interior was opened to industrial development in the 1950s, the Innu remained nomadic hunters. As a result of many subsequent developments, as well as new projects in the planning stage, the Innu are now a threatened people.

Indians entered the Quebec-Labrador Peninsula at the end of the last Ice Age, approximately 8,000 years ago. They brought with them and continued to develop a highly portable culture, well adapted to the Labrador environment. The first European traders arrived among them in the late 1700s, although metal goods had previously been obtained through trade with neighboring Indians. In the 1850s, people of mixed Inuit-European descent (known as "Settlers") penetrated the Innu hunting lands and began trapping furbearing animals along some of the interior rivers.

As a result of the decline of the fur trade, the Innu experienced closer contacts with coastal settlements, and many became infected by European diseases. In 1942 a military base was established at Goose Bay, where the

Settlers, but not the Innu, moved in search of employment. In the 1950s iron-ore mines were opened at Wabush, Labrador City, and Schefferville, all connected by rail to a port on the Saint Lawrence River. The Churchill Falls hydroelectric project, which was begun in the late 1960s, flooded important parts of Innu land. Around this time, the Newfoundland government settled the Innu into villages at Sheshatshit, near Goose Bay, and at Utshimaasits (also known as Davis Inlet).

The Setting

Labrador covers the portion of the Quebec-Labrador Peninsula whose rivers flow eastward to the Atlantic, except for small areas along the southern border. The region includes mountains and a wide elevated plain, known as the "Lake Plateau" region, which contains many lakes, drained by a few rivers that have cut deep valleys. The largest is the Churchill River, which flows into Lake Melville, a wide inlet reaching about 200 miles into the interior. On the south side of Lake Melville rise the Mealy Mountains, whose southern face slope toward the Gulf of Saint Lawrence.

The climate of the region is continental. During cold winters the temperature drops to at least 30 degrees below zero, and storms with snowfall are common. Lakes and rivers generally freeze over by October, and breakup of the winter ice usually occurs in June. Summer, although relatively short, can be hot. Forest fires, usually ignited by lightning, occur regularly during the summer months.

The dominant forest species are spruce and balsam fir, with smaller stands of birch, larch, and some other species. In the north and along exposed parts of the coast, tundra predominates, with stunted trees restricted to protected hollows. A variety of small plants, including many kinds of berries, are found throughout the region. The major mammal, and the one of particular importance to the Innu, is the caribou. Other species include the wolf, black bear, beaver, porcupine, otter, lynx, snowshoe hare, squirrel, mink, and marten. Moose, now found in southern Labrador, are new arrivals in the region. Some birds remain through the winter, including ravens, blue jays, snowy owls, ptarmigan, and spruce grouse; others migrate, including Canada geese, many species of duck, osprey, eagles, and numerous songbirds. The region's lakes and rivers contain lake trout, whitefish, pike, burbot, sucker, char, salmon, and ounaniche (a landlocked variety of salmon).

Traditional Subsistence Strategies

To the Innu, this land is not a wilderness, but a familiar homeland. Every lake, river, and mountain is named and filled with historic associations—important events, burials, regular camping places—the stories of which are still told by the elders. The Innu lived most of the year in the interior, hunting both large and small game and fishing, while some spent summers near the coast, fishing and hunting birds. The northern Innu, in particular, depended on the caribou. When the herd was migrating each fall across the George River, many Innu gathered to spear them in the water. The abundance of meat, much of which was dried for later use, allowed them to stay there for many weeks. Gatherings also occurred at other favorable places, such as where geese and ducks arrived in the spring, or where fish spawned in large numbers. The Innu of the southern forests had a variety of animals to hunt, including beaver which provided a fur to be traded to Europeans but also was always an important source of meat.

As nomads, the Innu were well adapted to their environment. They traveled widely in winter, using snowshoes for walking and toboggans for transporting their equipment and supplies. In summer they used birch-bark canoes to travel a vast network of navigable rivers and lakes. Their animal-skin clothing was well suited to the climate. Their comfortable dwellings were constructed with forest materials and covered with easily transported caribou hides.

European arrivals quickly adopted the Innu means of transportation, dress, and habitation, some forms of which are still in use today. Contact with these newcomers little changed the traditional Innu way of life; guns, axes, pots, blankets, tea, sugar, flour, and later chain saws and even snow-mobiles were incorporated into the existing nomadic Innu culture.

Social and Political Organization

The Innu lived in groups of several families, usually related, who co-operated in the hunt and shared the results. Kinship is recognized equally on the mother's and the father's side, so any Innu individual has a wide range of groups with whom to reside. The composition of a hunting group changed over time, and an elder will probably have belonged to many different groups and lived in many parts of Innu territory. At social gatherings, marriages are planned, local groups renew connections, trade was conducted, and through such indirect means, links made with other North American aboriginal peoples. At the *mokoshan*, or feast, sacred foods—like caribou fat and bone marrow—were served, followed by dancing. Other ceremonies marked a child's first steps or the first kill of a major game animal. Major group decisions were arrived at through discussion; the leader voiced the consensus. Leaders were senior men who had gained a reputation as skilled hunters with spiritual power. Innu life was generally peaceful. Elders would seek a resolution to disputes, but individuals could simply separate by joining different hunting groups to avoid social dishar-mony.

Religion and World View

The spiritual aspect of Innu culture was an extension of their relationship with the animals. By dreams, offerings, and songs, each person communicated with the spirits of the animals and other forces of nature. Spirit "masters" directed the movements of particular species. In the hunt, animals were believed to offer themselves to worthy hunters if they were confident their carcasses would be treated with respect. This means never killing for fun or taking more than was needed, butchering the carcass properly, sharing the meat with others, and preserving the bones so they were not gnawed by dogs. Hunters used divination to discover where they would find their next prey. They used the steam tent (elsewhere known as a sweat lodge) for purification in preparation for the hunt. They had shamans, religious specialists who conducted rituals like the "Shaking Tent." The shaman sat inside the tent, which shook violently, and the voices of the various spirits were heard. The audience shouted out questions to the spirits and received answers from them. After the Innu were converted by Catholic missionaries they were told to stop such practices; however, while living in the bush, the Innu maintain much of their traditional shamanistic religion.

THREATS TO SURVIVAL

Western Labrador Mining

Several deposits of iron ore are found in western Labrador. Development in the 1950s required the construction of a rail line, and mines and company towns were eventually opened at Labrador City and Wabush, in Western Labrador, and the Quebec towns of Schefferville and Fermont close to the Quebec-Labrador border. While these mines are all within traditional Innu hunting lands, only Schefferville provided them with any jobs, and this mine has now closed.

These mines have destroyed large areas and polluted the natural environment significantly. The mines also brought thousands of newcomers for the first time into the heart of Innu land. The few Innu who gained employment at the Schefferville mine occupied the lower-paying jobs. With the closing of this mine in 1992 they were left in virtual sole occupation of a ghost town, surrounded by a landscape of abandoned open-pit mine craters, tailings heaps, garbage dumps, and polluted lakes and rivers. There are similar environmental conditions around the other mining towns, and dust pollution has become a major problem. Cottages have sprung up along the roads and the railroad around these towns, from where recreational hunting and fishing are conducted by non-Innu. The Innu must therefore now avoid these regions when they are hunting.

Upper Churchill Hydroelectric Project

To achieve the large storage capacity needed for the Churchill Falls hydroelectric project, engineers had to build a series of long, low dams, which raised the levels of several large lakes to create the huge (2,600 square miles) Smallwood Reservoir, completed in 1974. Ecologically the project was highly destructive and could have been considered an economic venture only by assuming that the land destroyed by the flooding was virtually worthless. In fact, however, the land destroyed was one of the most prized parts of Innu territory, at the hub of a complex web of travel routes where many had gathered each year since time immemorial.

A scientific assessment of the full environmental impact of this project has never been attempted. Large areas of forest were flooded, and wildlife was drowned. Since none of the wood was harvested, standing and floating trees remain a hazard to boating in the reservoir. It has been estimated that 10 percent of the nesting areas for ducks and geese in the Lake Plateau region was lost and at least one of the George River caribou calving grounds was destroyed. When snow and ice melt in the spring, dam gates are sometimes opened, flooding important shoreline habitat downstream. As a result of the project, innumerable Innu graves were submerged, many important prehistoric Innu sites were flooded without record, and numerous Innu hunting camps, to which the occupants planned to return the following winter, were inundated. Consequently, many canoes, traps, stoves, guns, and other possessions, which their owners had left in the bush for use the following winter, were lost. It was no more than good fortune that no Innu happened to be camped in the area when the flooding actually took place. Nobody ever bothered to warn them of plans for the flooding, nor have they ever been compensated for their losses.

The release of nutrients into the water which followed the flooding caused an increase of fish stocks in the newly created reservoir. However, the flooding also caused release of mercury, which became concentrated in the flesh of certain fish and made them unfit for human consumption. Since the Innu ate the fish, 37 percent of those surveyed in 1977 were found to have elevated mercury levels.

Forestry Operations

The upper Lake Melville region has seen several forestry operations. In the 1970s, the Labrador Linerboard project harvested large quantities of pulpwood for shipment to a mill on the island of Newfoundland. The operation clear-cut large sections but then went bankrupt, leaving behind large stacks of wood to rot. Currently there are several competing proposals for wood cutting, including one to harvest 457,450 cubic feet annually and to harvest timber in the area around Cartwright. Regrowth in this environment is slow, and these forests cannot withstand modern commercial harvesting practices. Experts have concluded that, in its haste to lure investors, the provincial government has established unsustainable levels of annual allowable cut. Field observations indicate that, under current forestry cutting practices, little protection is given to streams and water bodies.

Highway Development

The Churchill Falls hydroelectric project resulted in the building of temporary roads between the project and Goose Bay to the east and to the rail line to the west. Soon Goose Bay people began to pressure the government to complete the so-called Freedom Road which would connect them with Labrador City, thus providing road access to the rest of North America. This road, constructed in 1986–1988, now cuts through the center of Innu lands. While it is made use of by some Innu, it has also opened the area for cottages, recreational hunting, and other uses by non-Innu people, particularly in areas adjacent to existing towns. It opens up a large area for which the Newfoundland and Labrador government does not have the resources to control illegal hunting or other environmental damage. The Innu find they must now compete for what are becoming increasingly scarce wildlife resources. For example, a license was recently issued to a Goose Bay butcher to market commercially caribou meat from animals he planned to harvest along the highway.

The growth of Goose Bay has made it the service center for Labrador. In 1996 a proposal was made for the construction of the Ptarmigan Trail, a snowmobile track to provide access in winter between the communities on the southern coast and Goose Bay. This route would pass through the center of the Mealy Mountains, where an endangered caribou herd is located. The Innu saw the proposal as a potential threat, since it would funnel traffic through an environmentally sensitive area of historic importance to them. On the surface, the proposed route seemed unsuitable for its claimed purpose. It would have made more sense for snowmobilers to avoid the mountain area and use their regular route to Goose Bay along the shore of Lake Melville. There was, therefore, a suspicion among the Innu that the real purpose behind the proposal was to open a scenic area—already designated as the site of a national park—for commercial tourism. Once the snowmobile trail was constructed, it was feared that travel facilities such as lodges would become established, and the trail would be upgraded to an all-year road.

Recreational Hunting and Fishing

The Innu, who not long ago were the sole occupants of the Labrador interior, now find they must compete with many commercial and private camps for the region's fish and game. Following the growth of Goose Bay as a regional center, many commercial guiding camps were opened, catering to both resident and visiting sports fishermen and hunters. These camps have placed great pressure on the fish and game in their regions. The Innu report that some of the camps are polluting lakes with oil or garbage. The Innu also find that their own canoes and other property, which they habitually leave from year to year in the bush, are being used, and frequently damaged, by itinerant sports hunters and fishermen.

Military Low-level Flying

Goose Bay was established as a military base during World War II. By the early 1980s the base was being used by British, German, and later Dutch air forces for high-speed low-level flight training over the interior of Labrador and adjacent parts of Quebec. These operations began without any prior clearance under environmental assessment regulations. Military pilots fly as low as 100 feet above the ground in order to learn how to avoid enemy radar. This low-level flight training was initially conducted over Britain and Germany, but public complaints led these countries to seek other localities, especially since the training can involve periodic aircraft crashes. It so happens that the flight paths tend to follow waterways, but it is along these same waterways that the Innu have their camps, since these are their travel routes and the places where most game animals and fish are to be found.

As with the flooding, of the Innu were not informed or asked for their input about the plans for using these hunting lands for military training. When the flights started in 1980, the Innu had only recently acquired the funds to run an outpost program, designed to help some of them get away from the problems of the settlement and spend more time in the healthy environment of the bush. Suddenly, and without any warning, Innu hunters in the bush were disrupted by the explosive noise of jet aircraft screaming past at tree-top level. The Innu who experienced these overflights have complained about what is now known as the "startle effect": disorientation, ringing in the ears, and other symptoms of the sudden shock of aircraft noise. They have told about people who were thrown from their canoes by low-flying aircraft, of children in the camps who became constantly fearful of aircraft, and of the disruptive effects of the flights on game animals. Lakes have been polluted by fuel dumped by the jets. The Innu have documented and reported cases in which their camps were apparently being targeted by aircraft, which overflew them repeatedly. Some aircraft have crashed during training, occasionally starting forest fires. It is apparent that the nesting areas of birds and the calving areas of caribou have been negatively affected. The Innu have brought in neutral observers who have verified their claims, but to no avail; the flights continue and steadily increase in number.

Proposed Voisey's Bay Mining Development

In 1994 a major nickel deposit was discovered at Voisey's Bay, on the Labrador coast between Nain and Utshimaasits. The deposit is close to tidewater; a major portion is close enough to the surface to be mined by the open-pit method; and at least some is of very high quality. The combination of these factors means that the cost of production of at least some of the ore will be relatively low. The region of the deposit has traditionally been used by both the Innu and the Labrador Inuit.

Although the environmental impact assessment of the proposed mine and mill is not yet complete, many serious issues of possible negative environmental impacts have been raised, both at public meetings and in scientific studies. The mine will produce highly toxic tailings, resulting in the danger of pollution. The ore will be transported throughout most of the winter by ship, necessitating ice-breaker assistance. People who hunt on the sea ice in winter, or who travel between the coastal communities by snowmobile on the sea ice, may be placed in danger from leads opened up by the ice-breakers. There will also be a danger of ocean pollution—including underwater noise pollution affecting marine mammals—from these ships.

Some effects of this rich mineral discovery have already been felt. The discovery has started an exploration rush throughout much of northern Labrador. The Innu have noticed that many of the exploration camps have not followed correct procedures for environmental protection, and that provincial authorities have not adequately monitored these operations. Many of the exploration parties left oil and garbage behind when they left an area. In some cases, prehistoric sites have been disturbed. In other cases, bear and other wildlife have been killed or disturbed.

The proposed mine is also having an impact on the negotiation of a settlement of aboriginal land rights in Labrador. Both the Innu and the Inuit have stated that they will not agree to the mine's proceeding until their land claims have been settled. The Inuit have signed an agreement-in-principle, and the Innu were engaged in intensive negotiations starting in 1998. While this situation will probably result in the settlement of these claims more quickly than would otherwise have been the case, hurried negotiations conducted under pressure could lead to mistakes. Both aboriginal groups are also negotiating impact benefit agreement with the mining company, agreements which are intended to ensure that as many aboriginal people as possible obtain jobs at the mine under conditions suitable to them, as well as receiving other kinds of benefits. However, few Innu now have the required qualifications, or the cultural background, for such industrial employment, and there is some doubt about whether suitable training programs can be developed in time to transform them into suitably qualified workers.

Proposed Lower Churchill Hydroelectricity Project

In December 1997, the Newfoundland and Quebec governments jointly announced a plan to generate further large quantities of electric power along the Churchill River. The scheme includes adding to the existing generating capacity of the Churchill Falls project by diverting two additional rivers into this system, as well as building new dams and electricity-generating facilities downstream. In addition to the flooding of Innu land that would be entailed by the project, new electrical transmission lines would be built across Innu lands. The diversion of two other rivers into the Upper Churchill system is sure to entail some of the same negative consequences as did the original Churchill Falls project.

State Administration

When Newfoundland joined Canada in 1949, the new province retained control of the administration of the Labrador Innu, although the Innu in Quebec came under federal authority, as do Indians elsewhere in Canada. The resulting divided administration has created artificial barriers among the Innu. For instance, under federal programs, the Quebec Innu were settled into villages, where they have access to a range of special programs provided by the federal government. Those Innu living in Labrador, in contrast, were at first ignored, and later provided by the province with much inferior housing, schooling, municipal services, and other programs. This division among the Innu was made worse in 1973, when the federal government funded separate aboriginal political organizations for each province. As a result, collective action by the Innu has at times been made difficult.

The settlement of the Labrador Innu into permanent communities by the provincial government was badly mismanaged, and the effects of this are still being felt. The Innu were not invited to participate in the planning of such communities, nor was consideration given to the fact that, as nomads, they were unprepared for the unfamiliar challenges of urban living. Since no school residences were built and children were required to attend school in winter, their parents had to give up hunting virtually overnight but were offered no viable employment opportunities. The first houses provided were little more than shacks, and the promised running water and sewage services did not materialize. In Utshimaasits, these services are still lacking today. The location of Sheshatshit, with its proximity to the growing town of Goose Bay, meant that the Innu experienced forced idleness while they had unlimited access to alcohol. The site for Utshimaasits was selected without consultation with the Innu, on an island that was not a traditional Innu camping place. This site is unsuitable for building owing to shifting soil and has no adequate supplies of water. For several weeks annually, at freeze up and breakup, the residents are unable to reach their hunting lands. Cut off from the activities most valued by their culture, many Innu turned to self-destructive, antisocial activities.

Under provincial jurisdiction, the schools established for the Innu follow the regular Newfoundland curriculum, much of which is irrelevant to them. Most teachers come from elsewhere and have little experience or preparation for dealing with pupils of a different cultural background, particularly since they start school only knowing their own language, Innu Eimun. Schooling has failed to prepare most Innu for employment, but, since children spend more time in school than in the hunting camps, where most traditional Innu knowledge is passed on, it has also contributed to the undermining of the hunting culture. Elsewhere in Canada many northern aboriginal people have acquired local control of schools and have consequently modified the curriculum, altering the school schedules so that children can go with their parents to the bush and introducing aboriginal knowledge and language into the classroom. Such initiatives have hardly yet begun in the chronically underfunded Labrador Innu schools, although a few former Innu teaching assistants have now become qualified teachers.

Another outcome of provincial jurisdiction is that the Labrador Innu now find themselves to be a minority, both socially and politically. While living in the interior, the Innu were in control of most aspects of their lives. Today, living in Sheshatshit and Utshimaasits, they are outnumbered by their neighbors. The current Innu population of Sheshatshit (about 1,100) live close to Northwest River and Goose Bay–Happy Valley, which have a combined population many times this number. Utshimaasits, with about 500 residents, is equidistant between the two larger non-Innu towns of Nain, with 1,100 people, and Hopedale with 625. One implication of this population imbalance has been that when hunting licenses issued by lottery, as was sometimes the case in the Goose Bay area, the Sheshatshit Innu could only hope to obtain an insignificant portion of the total. Among the aboriginal peoples of Labrador, the members of the Innu Nation are outnumbered several times by those of the Labrador Inuit Association. As a result of this minority status, the Innu find themselves increasingly marginalized within Labrador society. Socially, the Innu have few close relations with other Labradorians. Although many of the decisions affecting their lives are made by the provincial government, politically the Innu lack the numbers to affect the outcome of an election in a single provincial riding. When they are forced to resort to the courts to protect their rights, or they acquire international support, there is often a hostile backlash with racist overtones from other Labradorians.

Health Issues

As the Innu have come to spend less time hunting and more time in the settlement, there has been a lowering of the quality of their food and a decline in their general health. Medical professionals have reported that after their Innu clients have spent a significant period in the hunting camps they show a noticeable improvement in their physical health. While out hunting, they have access to a high-quality diet of fresh meat, fish, and berries, and engage in physical activity. In the settlement, where most are dependent on welfare payments, they are mainly restricted to purchasing and eating the cheapest store-bought foods. This diet, along with the enforced idleness of settlement life, has resulted in high rates of stress, obesity, and diabetes. The slum housing conditions in the villages have resulted in an epidemic of tuberculosis.

Even more serious has been the psychological effects, which have been given labels like "post-traumatic stress syndrome." It is clear that, deprived of access to the hunting way of life, many Innu develop a state of hopelessness and loss of purpose, known as "anomie." Such a state often leads to alcohol abuse which, in turn, results in family violence, sexual abuse, and accidental death. Under the conditions of settlement living, Innu parents have found themselves unable to manage their children as they had done in the hunting camps. Children and youth, who have high rates of school dropout and teen pregnancy, have experienced their own psychological problems, symptoms of which include an epidemic of gas sniffing and high rates of suicide.

Cumulative Impacts

While individually each of the above threats constitutes a scandalous injustice, seen together they are indicative of a general and pervasive ignorance and lack of consideration for the interests of the Innu. The combined effect of these threats has been to degrade the environment, leaving less and less land and fewer animals for Innu hunters, who are thus effectively being deprived of the right to pursue their own way of life. The Innu need to preserve their land in its natural state to maintain what they value most: their hunting culture and their spiritual relationship with the animals and the land.

RESPONSE: STRUGGLES TO SURVIVE CULTURALLY

As hunters, the Labrador Innu historically had to face times of uncertainty and shortage. However, nothing in their past could have prepared them for the crisis situation they faced by the early 1970s: forced into unfamiliar settlements, with part of their land invaded by mines and a railway, other parts under water, many of their possessions lost, arrested for hunting for their own food, some of them rendered dysfunctional through depression, alcohol, and sickness. The only response they received to the complaints they made to government officials or to their priests was that these changes to their way of life were for their own good.

Self-Government

The main response by the Innu to the situation they are facing has been to take control of their own affairs. To do this they first organized themselves politically, based on their own understanding of their new situation. Young leaders emerged who used oratory, a skill traditionally valued by the Innu, to assert at every opportunity the idea that they had the right to exercise sovereignty over their own lands. Although numbering only a few hundred, they knew that both Canada and the province of Newfoundland and Labrador were at fault for treating them like a colonized peoples without any rights in their own land, a condition they refused to accept.

In 1973 the Innu helped to establish the Native Association of Newfoundland and Labrador (NANL) and created band councils at Sheshatshit and Utshimaasits, each of which its own chief and council to run most local services in these villages. In 1976 they broke from the NANL to form the Naskapi Montagnais Innu Association (NMIA). Later, this organization was renamed the Innu Nation, and their territory became referred to as Nitassinan. The labels Montagnais and Labrador are foreign terms that have been imposed on them. Starting in the early 1980s, they began to organize with the Innu in Quebec to build political unity between their two groups.

Through their organizations, the Innu have conducted political negotiations with governments whenever they could, seeking every opportunity to take control over whatever programs were available, to regain at least some influence over their own lives. Among the first of these programs was one to address their inadequate housing conditions. In the late 1970s, they began to run an outpost program, which subsidized transportation and other expenses to assist Innu to spend time in hunting camps, away from the problems of the villages. They cooperated with the Inuit to run a court worker program, which assists in judicial hearings by interpreting and advising natives who run foul of the law. Later, they organized the Innu Health Council.

In 1992 two Innu men were sent to British Columbia for training as aboriginal peacekeepers; however, when they returned to Utshimaasits to begin their duties, the provincial government adamantly refused to give them legal authorization as police officers, even though such authorization is a well-established arrangement in aboriginal communities elsewhere in

Canada. Despite this refusal, which continued until 1996, the band and the Innu Nation gave these men the authority they needed to work to address some of the chronic social problems in their community.

In 1991, despite some serious misgivings, the Innu Nation began talks with the federal and provincial governments about their land rights, and in 1996 a framework agreement was signed. In the same year, they signed a self-government framework agreement.

Research

Another important activity the Innu have carried out from the beginning has been to conduct research. The first project was to document their historic use and occupation of their territory, in order to satisfy the government's demands that they make formal claims that their land had, indeed, always been occupied by them. Since then the Innu have regularly updated their research into their own use of the land, and they have continued to document their elders' knowledge of historic land use and occupancy.

In 1981 the Innu commissioned a study to calculate the economic rents owing to them as the result of developments on their lands, such as the iron ore mines and the Churchill Falls hydroelectric project. Starting in 1991 they conducted their own research into moving the settlement of Utshimaasits to a better location. They have also conducted extensive research on existing forestry practices in Labrador and have made plans for a sustainable forestry policy. They have spearheaded several archaeology projects: one in 1995 to assess some of the sites damaged by the Churchill Falls reservoir, and another on the prehistoric Innu use of the region of the proposed Voisey's Bay mining development.

Media Campaigns

When the Innu found that speaking to the authorities about their problems was not particularly successful, their leaders began to address their complaints to the wider public, issuing press releases and holding press conferences. In the late 1970s, as more and more of them were arrested and charged with game law violations, they stopped paying the fines. The court hearings in these cases then became the occasions for public demonstrations. Other Innu turned out to support the accused, and Innu leaders gave statements to the press about their rights to their land and to their hunting way of life. The language of these statements became more confident and self-assertive, and the people began to refer to their sovereignty as Innu and to refuse to recognize the authority of Canada, the province, or the courts. It was at one of these court hearings that the Innu national flag was first publicly displayed.

When the low-level flights began in the early 1980s, none of the Innu

Innu demonstration against low-level military flights at Goose Bay Air Base, 1989. Photo by Bob Bartel.

complaints about the serious negative impacts were taken seriously. However, between 1987 and 1990, when they staged organized protests by occupying the Goose Bay runway and the practice bombing ranges, they were able to shut down the flights and gain the attention of the national media. Several Innu women were particularly important leaders in these protests, drawing sympathetic attention when they traveled across Canada and around the world to publicize their cause. The trials of those arrested at the runway demonstrations, many of whom spent many weeks in jail, also became media events, during which defiant Innu asserted that their land was being invaded by NATO forces and refused to accept the authority of the courts.

The Innu have successfully used protest tactics with other issues. In 1988 they discovered that the province intended to permit a limited hunt of the Mealy Mountain caribou herd, using a lottery system under which only a few Innu hunters would have received licenses. Since the Innu needed the food and considered they had a priority right to the herd, they decided to hold their own preemptive hunt. They announced the hunt publicly, in full view of the media, who covered the event each night on national television news, and Innu spokespersons openly challenged the provincial game authorities to arrest them. The province chose to do nothing.

After a disastrous house fire in 1992, in which several children died, the people of Utshimaasits conducted a public inquiry. The immediate cause was alcohol abuse and consequent child neglect by adults. The same kind of neglect had also caused an epidemic of gas sniffing by children. One of the main general conclusions of the inquiry was that these problems were partly a result of the poor location of the village. In early 1993 a video was taken of children high on sniffing gas, saying they wanted to die. This shocking footage, shown on television internationally, resulted in the arrival in Utshimaasits of newspaper and television reporters from around the world. Largely as a result of the public pressure placed on politicians to do something about the situation, the Innu were able to obtain both an agreement to fund the relocation of their village and funds to send a number of children and their parents away for treatment.

After years of unsuccessful attempts to get compensation for flooding, in 1993 several residents of Sheshatshit announced that, in protest, they were refusing to pay for their electricity, which came from Churchill Falls. They did this by removing the electric meters on their houses.

Later in 1993, at a session of the traveling provincial court in Utshimaasits, the judge handed out a sentence which the community considered to be inappropriately harsh. As a result, several women physically escorted the judge and the rest of the court out of the community. For several months there was a highly publicized standoff, during which the community blocked the community runway so that aircraft could not land and the court could not return. The court was finally allowed back in under an agreement for community participation in sentencing.

After the 1993 discovery of the Voisey's Bay nickel deposit, the Innu complained about systematic violations of environmental regulations at several exploration camps. When the province tried to downplay the situation, the Innu released a video tape showing some of the violations being incurred. Subsequently, the province agreed to pay official Innu environmental monitors to check the camps periodically.

Both the Innu and the Inuit took the position that development of the mine and mill at Voisey's Bay (Eimish) must not proceed until land claims and impact benefit agreements are concluded and the environmental assessment is complete. A demonstration by some Innu, who arrived at the site from Utshimaasits by snowmobile, managed to stop work for some weeks in the winter of 1995. The company also tried to proceed with the building of a road and an airstrip, claiming that these were not part of the mine and mill development. A demonstration by Innu and Inuit was held at the site for five days, until a judge ordered the work to stop while the appeal was heard.

The premier of Newfoundland and Labrador and the premier of Quebec planned a major public event, at considerable public expense, to announce plans to develop jointly a major additional hydroelectric generator on the Churchill River. These plans were disrupted by Innu protesters, angry that once again their land was to be made use of without their participation or consent. As a result, the headline story of the event was about the Innu protest; the plan itself was relegated to second place.

Environmental Hearings

While the Innu have generally mistrusted government-run inquires like environmental impact assessments, they have often used the public hearings to criticize plans and present the results of their own research. They made presentations to the 1978 inquiry into the proposed Kitts-Michelin uranium mine and the 1980 assessment of a Lower Churchill hydroelectric and aluminum smelter plan, developments that were both subsequently abandoned. They also intervened in the environmental assessments of low-level flying and the Voisey's Bay mine and mill development project.

International Campaigns

Since the Innu have asserted that the Canadian state has been violating their rights, it is logical that they should take these complaints outside Canada. Beginning around 1979, they have appeared at a number of international tribunals with the status of an accredited nongovernmental organization to criticize Canadian violations of their aboriginal rights. Starting around 1984, many of these appearances have concerned low-level flying and other military training taking place on their lands. In these campaigns, the Innu have acquired a large number of supporters, many of whom have organized support groups, both within Canada and abroad.

FOOD FOR THOUGHT

Questions

1. Can aboriginal sovereignty, on which the Innu base many of their arguments, be successfully accommodated within a modern state like Canada? Because the Innu are only a small minority in Labrador, granting them sovereign rights over large parts of the territory would seem to be in opposition to the prevailing Canadian ideology that all citizens should have the same basic rights. However, private companies or provincial governments are allowed to control large areas of land. Should Canada want to, what honorable principle could be used to deny the same kind of rights to those who have occupied the land historically and who now have been harmed by being deprived of using these lands?

2. One reality the Innu now face is their economic dependency on the state. While it can be argued that the situation is not of their own making, this dependency to some extent limits their ability to act independently. How can the Innu acquire the money and resources upon which they now depend without being subservient to others?

3. The Innu case also challenges us to examine whether, and how, a subsistence economy, one based not on profit, but on the sharing of only those resources for which there is a known need by the group who consumes them, can continue to exist within a predominantly industrial economy like that of Canada. It would appear that such a subsistence economy is more likely to be environmentally sustainable than industrial ones have proved to be. Would economies related to parks and tourism provide the subsistence basis for a sustainable economy for the Innu? Can groups like the Innu benefit from co-ventures which give them control over some of the more potentially harmful aspects of industrialism?

4. The Innu want their children to maintain the Innu culture and language and its spiritual relationship with the land and animals. They also want their children to be educated in schools to train them to participate in the modern world, if only to fight to protect themselves from the kind of threats discussed in this chapter. Can conventional schools accomplish both these goals? If not, what other means can be used to achieve them?

RESOURCE GUIDE

Published Literature

Armitage, Peter. *The Innu (The Montagnais Naskapi)*. New York: Chelsea House, 1991.

Ashini, Daniel. "The Innu of Ungava. David Confronts Goliath: The Innu versus the NATO Alliance." In Boyce Richardson, ed., *Drum Beat. Anger and Renewal in Indian Country*. Toronto: Summerhill Press, 1989.

Fouillard, Camille, ed. *Gathering Voices: Finding Strength to Help Our Children*. Vancouver: Douglas and McIntyre, 1995.

Henriksen, Georg. *Hunters in the Barrens. The Naskapi on the Edge of the White Man's World*. St. John's, Newfoundland: ISER Books, 1973.

Mailhot, Jose. *The People of Sheshatshit. In the Land of the Innu*. Translated by Axel Harvey. St. John's, Newfoundland: ISER Books, 1997.

Wadden, Marie. *Nitassinan. The Innu Struggle to Reclaim their Homeland*. Vancouver: Douglas and McIntyre, 1991.

Films and Videos

Attiuk, 1963. National Film Board, Canada.
Hunters and Bombers, 1991. National Film Board of Canada and Channel 4.
Place of the Boss, 1996. Canadian Broadcasting Corporation.
Two Worlds of the Innu, 1994. BBC2.

Internet and WWW Sites

Government of Newfoundland and Labrador
http://www.gov.nf.ca/default.htm

Innu Nation
http://www.innu.ca/

Welcome to Labrador
http://www.geocities.com/Yosemite/Rapids/3330/

Organizations

Friends of Nitassinan
21 Church St.
Burlington, VT 05401
Telephone/Fax: 802–425–3820

Innu Nation
P.O. Box 119
Sheshatshiu, Labrador, Canada AOP 1M0
Telephone: (709) 497–8398
Fax: (709) 497–8396
E-mail: innuenv@web.net

Survival International U.K.
11–15 Emerald St.
London WC1N 3QL
England, United Kingdom
Telephone: 0171–242–1441
Fax: 0171–242–1771
E-mail: survival@gn.apc.org
Web site: http://www.survival.org.uk/

6

The Inuit of Nunavut, Canada

Bruce Rigby, John MacDonald, and Leah Otak

Will the Inuit disappear from the face of the earth? Will we become extinct? Will our culture, language and our attachment to nature be remembered only in history books? To realize that our people can be classified as an endangered species is very disturbing. . . . If we are to survive as a race, we must have the understanding and patience of the dominant cultures of this country. . . . We must teach our children their mother tongue. We must teach them the values which have guided our society over thousands of years. . . . It is this spirit we must keep alive so that it will guide us again in a new life in a changed world.

>   —John Amagoalik, past president of the Inuit Tapirisat
> of Canada, Inuit land claims negotiator and chief com-
> missioner of the Nunavut Implementation commission.[1]

CULTURAL OVERVIEW

The People

Long known to others as Eskimos, this indigenous arctic hunting people are now referred to as Inuit (meaning "people"), the name by which they refer to themselves, at least collectively and in an international context. The Inuit who have their homelands in the arctic and subarctic regions of Canada, Greenland, Alaska, and northeastern Siberia, share common cultural and linguistic roots.

Present-day Canadian Inuit are the direct descendants of a people who migrated eastward from northern Alaska to populate the coastal areas of the North American Arctic, Subarctic, and Greenland. The immediate an-

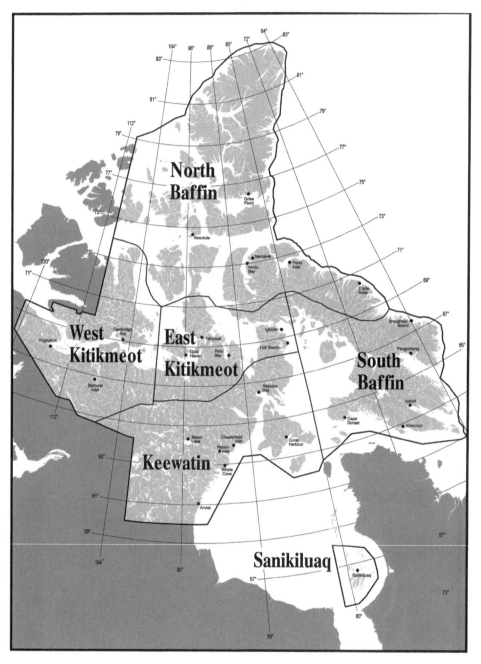

Administrative regions of Nunavut, Arctic Canada.

cestors of the Inuit reached the Nunavut region of the Canadian Eastern Arctic about 1,000 years ago. Here they are thought to have absorbed, or displaced, a previously established hunting people with a similar culture who had occupied the region for at least 1,500 years prior to their arrival.

The population of Nunavut today is found mostly within twenty-six communities spread across the territory's three administrative regions of Kitikmeot, Kivalliq, and Baffin (Qikiqtaaluk). Community size ranges from Bathurst Inlet (with a 1998 population of approximately twenty people) to Iqaluit, the capital of Nunavut, with a rapidly growing cosmopolitan population of nearly 4,500. Also present are the outpost camps in which families follow a more traditional lifestyle for a large part of the year.

A typical Nunavut community has a public infrastructure similar to that found in many small towns across Canada. Government administrative offices, schools, a health center, a Royal Canadian Mounted Police (RCMP) detachment, retail stores, post office, churches, municipal services' buildings, and a community radio station are features found in virtually all Nunavut communities. Other essential items of infrastructure, reflective of the region's remoteness from mainstream Canada, include diesel-powered electricity generators; satellite communications systems for phones, television, and radio; and, of course, airports.

No roads or railways link the communities of Nunavut with each other or with centers in southern Canada. The annual resupply of these communities with essential fuel oil, building materials, vehicles, boats, and other bulky goods takes place by oil tanker and cargo ship during the summer's short, mostly ice-free open-water season. Passengers, mail, and lighter freight items are transported by scheduled or chartered aircraft throughout the year. This reliance on aircraft transport, coupled with relatively low passenger and freight volumes, and the vast distances between the communities, make the cost of living in Nunavut considerably higher than anywhere else in Canada.

The Setting

The newly formed territory of Nunavut, which corresponds roughly to the area north of the current North American tree line, comprises approximately 735,000 square miles. Much of this large area is frequently referred to as a "polar desert." The mean annual precipitation varies from 4 inches in the north to 23 inches in the south of Nunavut, with areas closer to the sea receiving more precipitation than inland areas. The average winter temperatures range from 4°F in the south of Nunavut to −35°F on northern Ellesmere Island, although in the coldest part of the winter, temperatures anywhere in Nunavut may be considerably lower than these average temperatures. Average summer temperatures vary from 50°F in the south to 36°F in the north, although local temperatures vary greatly in relation to proximity to cold ocean waters and the existence of sea ice. Throughout the winter, Nunavut is covered by ice and snow, and the sun disappears altogether for several weeks in those areas located above the Arctic Circle.

The topography is quite varied, with mountainous terrain in the east and flatter areas to the west. The landscape has been greatly influenced by the glaciation that covered Nunavut until approximately 11,000 years ago and today continues to alter the geography of the region. In some areas there are icecaps and glaciers; in other areas, abundant lakes and rivers. Permafrost (permanently frozen ground) occurs widely throught Nunavut. The short growing season, together with low temperatures and lack of precipitation at higher latitudes, restricts the abundance and location of vegetation. Plants generally grow close to the ground, and most vegetation is found in wetter areas, on south-facing slopes, and in valleys.

Wildlife in Nunavut is well adapted to local conditions, with many species migrating into the region in spring and leaving in the fall to return to warmer or more suitable feeding areas outside of the Arctic. Seabirds and several species of ducks and geese often nest in large numbers during the short northern summers, leaving on their southward migration during September. Mammals such as caribou, muskox, foxes, and wolves can be found in many locations across the territory, and the coastal waters have abundant fish (and often shellfish) and marine mammal species such as walrus, polar bear, and several species of seals and whales.

Traditional Subsistence Strategies

The majority of Nunavut Inuit lived in seasonal camps situated in coastal areas and subsisted largely on marine mammals—typically walrus, various species of seal, and, to a lesser degree, whales (beluga and narwhal). This marine-based diet was supplemented by caribou, which supplied—in addition to meat and fat for food—warm skins essential for clothing and bedding, sinew for sewing, and antler for fashioning various tools. Some Inuit who lived inland west of Hudson Bay relied almost entirely on the vast caribou herds migrating through their territory. Arctic hare, muskox, and polar bear were also hunted for food, and the skins were used for a variety of purpose.

Seasonally, the Inuit diet was augmented by fish (Arctic char, whitefish, and lake trout) that were either speared or caught in nets and by hunting geese, ducks, and ptarmigan. The eggs of some species of seabirds, ducks, and geese were collected in the spring, and shellfish and seaweed were also gathered at certain seasons for food. Except for a brief period at the end of summer when berries could be picked and enjoyed, plants were of little significance in Inuit diet, although some were used for medicinal purposes.

Social and Political Organization

Immediately before European contact, the Inuit population of Nunavut lived in numerous, dispersed clusters of small hunting camps, usually situated in coastal areas close to the marine mammals on which they depended. Each of these camp clusters comprised populations whose members viewed themselves, and were viewed by others, as belonging to a distinct, usually long-established, group. The Inuit word ending "-miut," meaning "the people of," was used to denote a specific group, for example the Aivilingmiut of Aivilik (the Repulse Bay region) and the Tununirmiut of North Baffin Island. Each "-miut" group shared a common hunting territory, knowledge base, and often a subdialect of Inuktitut (the Inuit language spoken in the Eastern Canadian Arctic). Subtle, although sometimes pronounced, differences in social organization, hunting techniques, subsistence strategies, technology, clothing, and dwelling structures, as well as intellectual and spiritual life, distinguished each group.

Individual camps within each group tended to be made up of interrelated extended families, living together by common agreement. Sharing of food and other supplies and equipment was widespread in the camps, and in times of need also with people in other camps. Leadership was normally invested in one or two individuals of proven ability whose decisions were followed for the common good. In the event that people seriously disagreed or social conflict arose in the camp, households were free to move away to join camps where other relatives lived. Moving away was the most effective, most common way of resolving social conflict in traditional times.

The organization of camp life, which revolved around the availability of game, entailed a series of more-or-less predictable moves within the local area, by dog team or boat, in response to the seasonal migrations of animals.

Religion and World View

Inuit traditional spiritual beliefs can be characterized as shamanistic, based on the conviction that the universe was peopled with spirits, for everything animate and inanimate possessed an *inua*, a "person," or a soul. In this view, human beings were neither dominant nor superior to other nonhuman beings (e.g., the animals). To survive and flourish, the Inuit had to live in harmony with the other spirits of the world, particularly with those of the animals on which they depended. This balance, which was often difficult to maintain in the face of human frailty because, as one shaman put it, "Human food consists entirely of souls," was achieved through the observance of complex rituals and taboos whose aim was to demonstrate respect for the animals that were hunted, fished, or gathered by the people.

Shamans mediated between their people and the spirit world, making amends for broken taboos, healing the resultant illnesses, and striving to ensure the availability of animals for sustenance. A rich mythology encoded Inuit social values and norms, explained the nature of the universe, and told of other worlds analogous to Earth, accessible only in the afterlife or to shamans in their spirit flights.

THREATS TO SURVIVAL

Explorers and Whalers

Over the past 250 years, periodic encounters with explorers, usually the crews of British naval or mercantile expeditions, had minimal impact on Inuit society and culture. However, in the mid-nineteenth century, British and American commercial whalers began hunting the large bowhead whales off the coast of Baffin Island and in Hudson Bay. This whaling activity, which soon involved the Inuit to an unprecedented degree in European enterprise, exploited their labor, skills, and environmental knowledge in return for wages in the form of trade goods.

Though likely viewed by both parties as materially beneficial, this interaction insidiously foreshadowed the changes that were eventually to strike at the very core of Inuit independence, traditional economy, societal integrity, and health. The Inuit employed in whaling altered their traditional subsistence activities to meet the demands of European commerce. They became more and more dependent on trade goods and began to spend more and more time in camps close to the whaling stations where newly introduced epidemic diseases, against which they had no resistance, took their toll.

Traders

By the end of the nineteenth century, bowhead whale stocks in the Eastern Arctic were seriously depleted, and whale products, chiefly oil and baleen (whalebone), declined in economic value in Europe and North America after the discovery of cheaper substitutes. In the face of these setbacks, outside commercial interest in the Arctic gradually switched from whaling to fur trading, a development that compounded the external pressures on Inuit society already brought about by the whaling industry. The fur trade, vigorously led by the Hudson's Bay Company, gradually resulted in the establishment of trading posts in all regions of Nunavut. Many of these posts, situated close to areas occupied by the Inuit, in time became Nunavut's present-day communities.

The peak of the fur-trading era in Nunavut spanned approximately fifty years, although it continued on a diminishing scale in some areas through the 1960s. Economically, the period was characterized by boom and bust cycles with Inuit economic well-being becoming increasingly dependent on the fluctuation of white fox population numbers and the prices of fox pelts in the distant European and North American fur markets.

The commencement of the fur-trading period coincide with the introduction of Christianity to Nunavut. As the same time, interest in the region was first shown by the Canadian government—initially for administrative and sovereignty reasons—which was signaled by the establishment of RCMP detachments in key areas of the territory.

Missionaries

Shamanism, with its emphasis on spiritual belief, social conformity, ritual, and the afterlife, appears to have made the Inuit amenable to the offerings of Christianity. Of particular appeal, according to some Inuit elders, was the Christians' day of rest—Sunday—seen as a convenient alternative to the frequent, unscheduled abstentions required under their shamanistic taboo system. Christian missionaries first preached the gospel in the Cumberland Sound region in 1894, and, by the late 1920s, Christianity—in the form of Anglicanism and Roman Catholicism—had spread throughout the territory. Missionaries of whatever faith took vigorous action to suppress all shamanistic practices, replacing that religious system with one based on a strict and literal belief in Old and New Testament biblical teachings. More recently, increasing numbers of Inuit have embraced evangelical Christianity. Church attendance in Nunavut ranks among the highest in Canada, and the church plays an active role in community life.

Canadian Government Administration

The involvement of the Canadian government in Nunavut, marginal at best until the middle of the twentieth century, accelerated markedly in the late 1950s and 1960s, triggered largely by public reaction in southern Canada to well-publicized and graphic accounts of starvation among Inuit groups living in the so-called barren grounds to the west of Hudson Bay. With vivid accounts appearing in books and magazines the Inuit suddenly became part of the national agenda. A consequence of this belated awareness was the woefully late introduction of government programs in housing, health, education, and social assistance. These government programs were aimed at alleviating the deteriorating social conditions of the Inuit population that followed the collapse of the fur trade–based economy and the ravages of tuberculosis and other diseases that spread rapidly as Inuit living standards deteriorated.

An immediate result of Canada's wide-ranging administrative move into the Arctic was to draw the Inuit from their scattered hunting camps on the land into government-sponsored permanent communities. Here the Inuit became, in effect, wards of the state living in an unfamiliar and, in many ways, an artificial social environment. Some quantifiable benefits, of course, were brought about by these programs, among them decreasing rates of infant mortality, rising life-expectancy, and greatly increased material security. Socially and culturally, however, the settlement policy was destined to create its own problems. Many Inuit believe that settlement life and the changes it fostered, including the difficulty of moving away from socially disruptive neighbors while living in a government-assigned house or apartment, are the root causes of much of the social malaise and cultural loss experienced in Nunavut communities today. Emil Immaroitok of Igloolik expresses this conviction clearly: "In the old days we were small groups and we hardly had any problems then. But now there's too many people here. . . . There are too many different groups nowadays that live together in one place. There are many problems today. . . . In the past, the elders could deal with the problems . . . but now even the police cannot stop them."[2]

Government Education Programs

The government's school policy, though well intended, was nevertheless culturally invasive. Evie Ikidluak, an Inuk educator from Arctic Quebec, once pointed out that "Inuit are strangers to school but not to education" (personal communication, 1982). The difference is in the approach: in Inuit society children "learned"; in schools they are "taught." Whether in residential or in settlement schools, children now had little opportunity to learn the complex land-based life skills, knowledge, and perspectives of their culture. Inuit adults' roles as educators were weakened, if not entirely usurped, and the education of Inuit children, until now the responsibility of parents and close family members, was largely assumed by schoolteachers who knew little or nothing of Inuit culture or language. In school, Inuit children were taught English, which then became the language of instruction, and led through a curriculum that, at best, reflected little or nothing of their native culture, and, at worst, actively suppressed it.

The schools, however, contributed to a far-reaching and totally unintended outcome. Policy makers and administrators of the late 1950s could not have foreseen that a quarter of a century later their education system would have played a significant role in setting the stage for the development of a vigorous political consciousness among the Inuit that would ultimately lead to the settlement of a land claim involving nearly 20 percent of Canada's landmass.

Threats to Traditional Subsistence

One of the most significant changes experienced by the Inuit during the first half of the twentieth century, during the fur-trading era, impacted Inuit subsistence activities. Because of the need to spend time trapping furs to purchase the now-essential imported trade goods, less time was spent in hunting. In some areas of Nunavut this resulted in hardship when competing demands on the hunters' time reduced the availability of food or of skins needed for winter clothing. In other areas, however, the Inuit adapted well to the changing economy, and participation in the fur trade resulted in many benefits and greater security through the acquisition of rifles, nets, and motorized boats.

During this period, despite a growing dependency on the fur trade and periodic hardships resulting from fluctuating fur prices and game availability, the Inuit social organization remained largely unchanged—with decision-making still firmly in the hands of the camp leaders. Present-day Inuit elders now look back on the fur-trading era—"the old days"—with a certain amount of nostalgia. It was a time when they still had full control over their lives, a time when their culture and language were under no immediate threat. Indeed, for many, life in the fur-trading days defines traditional Inuit culture. Subsequent cultural change and loss among the Inuit are usually measured against the standards of this period.

Contaminants in the Food Chain

A more recent threat to subsistence is caused by the long-range transport of chemical pollutants. Although often thought of as a pristine, untouched wilderness by those living outside the Arctic, Nunavut contains several areas considered under stress from the introduction of chemical contaminants into the food chain. These pollutants result from a number of factors, including the global circulation of the world's weather and ocean currents. Quite apart from the distant sources of some pollutants, there are other, more local sources that include mining, defense, and hydroelectric developments in the north itself (see chapters 3 and 5). Contaminants include heavy metals, such as mercury and cadmium, and organochlorines, such as polychlorinated biphenyls (PCBs), which are all considered potentially hazardous to health if they enter peoples' bodies through the food they eat.

The impact of these chemicals on human health remains uncertain, but monitoring indicates that higher levels of these contaminants are found in the Inuit of Nunavut compared to the levels found in Canadians living outside of the Arctic. This scientific uncertainty itself causes stress among the Inuit as they hear that the seals, whales, caribou, and fish—their traditional foods—now contain chemicals that may affect their health in the future. On the other hand, the stress is not lessened by the sometimes conflicting messages the Inuit receive from the health authorities who urge them to eat their traditional foods because, despite the unknown risk from contaminants, these fresh local foods are more nutritious than imported substitutes.

For those who wish to practice subsistence skills through hunting and fishing and to pass these skills on to their children and grandchildren, the thought that arctic animals may no longer be safe to eat is particularly troubling. Among the Inuit of Nunavut this represents a large proportion of the population, especially in the smaller communities where the consumption of local foods remains high. In the larger communities particularly, some Inuit are consuming more imported store-bought foods which they have been led to believe are safer. The result of this trend is the beginning of a significant dietary change which can lead to health problems and to a reduced opportunity to learn and practice traditional land and hunting skills.

Government Settlement Policy

The fur-trading era effectively ended with the implementation of the Canadian government's settlement policy of the late 1950s and early 1960s, and with it ended the relative independence of the Canadian Inuit. All across Nunavut, the Inuit were brought in from their hunting camps on the land and concentrated in permanent settlements which, for the most part, grew up around the trading posts. One regrettable consequence of this move was that decision making now shifted from the Inuit camp leaders to government-appointed administrators in these new permanent communities.

In these new communities, the Inuit were subjected to a variety of well-intentioned government programs, including compulsory schooling, social assistance, and various economic development initiatives—none of which were of their own making and over which they had little, if any, influence. Many of these programs were in opposition to traditional Inuit social organization and values and tended to alter and confuse established relationships among the Inuit.

Significantly, settlement life also created a barrier between the Inuit and the natural environment, gradually distancing them from their immediate physical and spiritual attachment to the land and its life-giving resources which form the very core and defining features of traditional Inuit culture.

Many Inuit point to their move into the settlements and the subsequent process of modernization as the root causes of the cultural loss they are experiencing today. Formal schooling, in particular, is seen as blocking the proper transmission of Inuit culture, of producing generations of Inuit children who, increasingly, will be unable to pass on to their own children much of the "old" culture. Inuit elders especially, view the weakening of

Inuktitut, the Inuit language, as the most serious threat to the culture as a whole. And they are right, for Inuktitut encodes the entire culture, enshrines values and worldview, and, above all, bestows Inuit identity. As Jane Flaherty points out, "A good grounding in traditional knowledge for today's [Inuit] youth is only possible with a good grounding in the Inuktitut language. Language is culture, culture is language—they cannot be separated."[3]

Aside from the detrimental effects of schooling on Inuktitut, over the past decade Inuktitut has been competing more and more with English for the attention of young bilingual Inuit. Aided powerfully by the English-language media, mainly television, video-taped feature films, and, to a lesser extent, radio and newspapers, the erosion of Inuktitut continues at an alarming pace inviting questions about its viability over the long term. The dilemma faced by Inuit leaders and government policy makers today is how to stem or reverse Inuit culture and language loss while, on the other hand, preparing Inuit youth in Nunavut to adapt and thrive, on their own terms, in the globalizing contemporary world.

Most Nunavut communities, to a greater or lesser degree, experience a disturbing range of social problems indicative of a society undergoing profound and rapid change at the same time as it experiences cultural loss. High rates of unemployment, dependence on government transfer payments, low standards of educational achievement, poor school attendance, a breakdown in the transmission of Inuit cultural values between generations, alcohol and drug abuse, suicide, and increasing crime rates, are just some of the symptoms of an underlying and complex social malaise.

RESPONSE: STRUGGLES TO SURVIVE CULTURALLY

Political Developments

The division of Canada's Northwest Territories into two separate territories, one of which became the new political entity of Nunavut ("our land") on April 1, 1999, is seen as a unique and progressive step in the evolution of aboriginal rights in Canada. Nunavut, which has a public government established through an act of Parliament and safeguarded by the Canadian constitution, will reflect, to a greater degree than any previous administration, the culture, values, and aspirations of the majority of its population, the Inuit. The Inuit population of Nunavut numbers approximately 21,000, which constitutes about 85 percent of the total population of Nunavut. The Nunavut government has an elected legislature of nineteen members, supported by a civil service similar to that found in other Canadian jurisdictions but having a distinctly Nunavut focus and a labor force increasingly representative of the population.

In 1999, the economy of Nunavut was driven, first and foremost, by the public sector. Municipal, territorial, and federal government expenditures and employment in the fields of health care, education, social assistance, housing, municipal services, justice, policing, and transportation constituted the largest input into the economy of Nunavut. At the community level, private sector enterprise was almost wholly dependent on public sector on public sector spending, so that in most communities, almost every dollar spent in retail stores and other privately run businesses was derived directly, or indirectly, from government sources. Even the subsistence activities of local Inuit hunters relied heavily on the proceeds of wage employment, and a major portion of family incomes went to the purchase of expensive hunting equipment such as snowmobiles, outboard motors, boats, and rifles.

Economic activity generating significant amounts of nongovernment income include the Inuit art and handicraft industry, tourism (including sports hunting and fishing), and the fur trade (mainly through sale of seal and polar bear skins). These activities, however, are not equally productive across Nunavut, and they are often subject to changing market conditions in other parts of the world. Most recently, the opening of Nunavut's first diamond mine in the Kitikmeot area, as well as intensified exploration for iron, gold, nickel, and other ore deposits, has increased expectations of the possibility of wages and royalties from the nonrenewable resources sector. Deposits of oil, gas, and coal have been identified in several areas, but the potential environmental impact, market uncertainties or low prices, and the high cost of bringing the resource to market act to restrict exploitation.

Decision making in Nunavut communities frequently focuses on developing consensus on specific issues, which is usually achieved through the wide participation of community members. All communities have elected mayors and town councils. In addition, depending on the size of the community, various committees, societies, and associations oversee specific local affairs and activities. Typically a community has a hunters' and trappers' organization, a health advisory committee, a district education authority, a youth justice committee, an alcohol education committee, and a radio society.

Securing Traditional Knowledge

We need to hold on to the traditional ways of life, but also be educated enough to know about the modern world as well. Traditional knowledge should not take a back seat to anything . . . it is as important to the growth and survival of Nunavut as are computers and school books.
—Jane Flaherty, Grise Fiord, Nunavut, 1998[4]

As pointed out by John Amagoalik, one of the leading statesmen of Nunavut, Inuit culture is vibrant and adaptive and should be very much based on the values and practices of past generations. To achieve this, Inuit in many Nunavut communities are documenting their oral histories and cultural practices and integrating this material into various social and educational programs by a variety of techniques. The recording of this information is viewed as urgent; the elders who have the knowledge are dying, and with them goes the rich contextual information that provides the basis for the facts that need to be collected.

There are many examples of programs aimed at documenting Inuit traditional knowledge. The Canadian Broadcasting Corporation, in providing Inuktitut programming, has in excess of 2,000 oral histories on file. Similar collections have been made by the Inuit Broadcasting Corporation (an organization established to provide Inuktitut language television). Nunavut Arctic College and the Nunavut Research Institute have assisted the Igloolik Elders Society to document systematically a large body of Inuit traditional knowledge. This collection, accessible through computer in both Inuktitut and English, is widely used by schools, researchers, government departments and agencies, and the public at large.

Developing Instruments of Public Government

The creation of the new territory of Nunavut presents the Inuit with a focused opportunity to address some of the long-standing problems that have resulted from the colonial government structures that preceded it. As Canada was once a colony of Britain, the Canadian Arctic has very much been a colony of Canada, with decision making always taking place far away. As such, the existing structures and approaches of government to the administration of justice, health, and social issues have been imported from elsewhere, with control of how such issues are handled remaining in distant cities such as Ottawa and Yellowknife. Many attempts have been made to make the existing systems better reflect local concerns, issues, and needs, but this has met so far with limited success. The establishment of Nunavut, it is widely hoped, will lead to improvements in program content and delivery.

The model for the new government of Nunavut is contained in a document entitled "Footprints in New Snow." The framework presented in this document is based on the premise of a decentralized government working close to the people it serves. While Nunavut will have a capital where many of its executive functions will be located, most government departments will be located in several regional centers at a distance from the capital. This is intended to ensure that the government reflects all parts of Nunavut and ensure that economic benefits are widely available, not concentrated in one main location.

The intent is that the Nunavut government will be based on Inuit values, will be a government that employs the Inuit, and will use Inuktitut as the working language of government. Such intentions will take some time to achieve. However, when implemented, the result will change how Nunavut residents live and will ensure that successes and failures will be "home grown," not imported from elsewhere.

Evolution of a Culturally Sensitive School Curriculum

Although the evolution of Nunavut will play a key role in supporting and preserving Inuit culture, the pre-Nunavut regional boards of education and the government of the Northwest Territories have, for several years, undertaken and promoted programs to present traditional knowledge and culture within the school curriculum. Programs such as "Inuuqatigiit" (the school curriculum from an Inuit perspective) tie modern or Western approaches to learning to traditional knowledge. A good example is provided by the science units which have been developed to explain scientific principles from an Inuit perspective. For example, units have been developed to explain such things as the physics of how a *qamutiik* (sled) is constructed and works and examine the process of fermentation. In southern schools, teaching units on fermentation and organic chemistry focus on bread making or wine or beer making. By contrast, the Innuqatigiit curriculum uses the example of *igunaq* (an Inuit delicacy of "aged" walrus meat) to demonstrate the chemical processes involved in fermentation.

The provision of an overview of Inuit history, from the Inuit perspective, has always been lacking within the overall school curriculum. In particular, although a specific effort has been made to integrate traditional knowledge directly into learning modules, it is only recently that attention has been paid to differences between precontact Inuit history and recent history, and between specific regional interest and those parts of Inuit history that form the basis of important Inuit values. In order to address this need, an overarching history of Inuit, from the Inuit perspective, has been developed. This history consists of in excess of 600 pages of oral stories, legends, and practices from across the Inuit homeland, which illustrate regional similarities and differences. A committee of knowledgeable and respected Inuit has provided direction on all aspects of the project, including comparisons of the older, archaic, Inuktitut with its current form. Ensuring that dialect differences are maintained, while comparing the stories, proved to be very challenging.

The delivery of learning programs in the schools also actively involves the community elders. The programs vary from "elders' story night" (where all the students sleep over in the school gymnasium to listen to the elders' stories), to elders participating in school field trips on the land, to the collection of local place names, or the passing on of general history and practices. In many communities, skilled women participate directly in sewing and clothing-making classes with young girls, and experienced men dem-

Inuit elders and youth join in a celebration of their traditions with drum dancing at an archeological site on Igloolik Island, 1993. Courtesy of Lucy MacDonald.

onstrate and teach the construction of sleds and other traditional equipment and various hunting techniques. Many communities devote significant periods of time to spring camps as part of the normal curriculum. In various ways, community elders participate as facilitators, instructors, and mentors to schoolchildren.

Elders as Part of Society

Apart from their contribution to the learning programs associated with the schools, conscious efforts are being made to ensure that the elders are a significant part of everyday life in Nunavut. Individual elders and elders' groups participate in community justice committees, provide advice and direction to non–school based youth programs, and recognize the achievements of Nunavut residents. As such, elders continue to play a critical role in the transmission of values and knowledge to all Inuit.

Recognizing the Land as a Place for Learning and Healing

Although many communities have some version of a land-skills camp, at which young people are exposed to skills and knowledge obtained from living on the land, the land also anchors other programs of importance to community life. Youth camps are a frequent activity during the summer months, where groups of young people living away from the community participate in various activities that can include science-based learning, a variety of skill-development initiatives, or physical challenges such as learning to travel from a place to place without use of a snowmobile or boat. Sentencing within the justice system also provides opportunities for young offenders, out on the land, to learn about their culture and the importance that traditional values and skills play in life. Conferences and workshops on subjects such as justice, health, and traditional values also often take place in land-based settings.

FOOD FOR THOUGHT

By some definitions, the culture of the Canadian Inuit is, if not seriously endangered at the present time, at least under threat as a result of the rapidity of change caused by global cultural, economic, and environmental pressures. However, while the Inuit generally agree that their culture is being threatened, and that traditional knowledge is being lost, the question remains: What can be done to guard against these events, and how best to address the problems that are the result?

The Inuit have the strength to grow and benefit from the changes that are taking place, but what will it mean to be an Inuk in ten years, in twenty years, or in thirty years' time? Many believe that to be *Inumaariit* (a real *Inuk*), an individual should possess all the skills and knowledge of past generations and, at the same time, be competent in regard to the demands of modern-day living. Is this realistic, and who—and how—should society determine what is best to preserve and pass on to the next generation? Cultures by their very nature are dynamic, adapting, and evolving in the face of the myriad influences they encounter, and Inuit culture is certainly no different in this regard.

In a letter written to the editor of a major Canadian newspaper, Jose Kusugak, the president of Nunavut Tunngavik Incorporated (the land-claim implementing organization) noted:

The statistical data on suicide, alcohol abuse, welfare, etc. may be news to the rest of Canada, but it came as no surprise here in Nunavut.... I write to point out that the Inuit leadership has been hard at work for at least three decades now to rectify the situation, a fact you might have included for your national readership. ... Our land claim and the Government of Nunavut are about control of our land and resources.... We are moving to correct the staggering socio-economic impact on our people of the 1970's fur ban that wrecked the sealing industry in our arctic villages.... We are confident we can build an economy that will restore the dignity and self-respect so many of our people have lost during a well-intentioned, but misguided colonial era.[5]

The evolution of the new Canadian territory of Nunavut will provide Inuit, perhaps to a degree greater than has been possible for other aboriginal groups in Canada before now, with the opportunity to shape their future in accord with the values and cultural norms established by their elders and forefathers. To some, this may not be the definition of a culture that is endangered, but rather a definition of a culture that has been empowered to initiate change to support a commonly held vision. New institutions of government, vehicles for language protection and cultural transmission, will provide the Inuit with a way to protect those aspects of culture that are of value and a way to assist members of their society to become active and contributing participants in the transforming global society. The key question is, How will the evolution take place, and how will the Inuit define what their culture will be? Only time will tell.

Questions

1. Although traditional knowledge is fundamental to Inuit society and cultural identity, how does one validate the information and understandings that are being transmitted to new generations? Is it important to validate such fundamental information and understandings?

2. Given that Inuktitut will be the official language of work in Nunavut, what impact will this decision have on daily life? What are the benefits and disadvantages of promoting protection and widespread use of an aboriginal language for a population of 25,000, compared to promoting the use of Canada's other official languages (English and French) in Nunavut?

3. What are acceptable levels of cultural change for the Inuit? At what point does Inuit culture cease to be distinctive?

4. How can the Inuit organize to preserve the tradition of sharing that was so important to cultural survival while successfully integrating their society into the modern market economy?

5. What advice would you give to ensure that the new structures of public government supported the cultural goals of the Inuit while, at the same time, being fair and equitable to long-term non-Inuit residents of the region?

NOTES

1. Ian Creey, "The Inuit of Canada," *Polar Peoples: Self-Determination and Development* (London: Minority Rights Publications, 1996), p. 146.

2. W. C. E. Rasing, *"Too Many People": Order and Nonconformity in Iglulingmiut Social Process* (Nijmegan Netherlands: Recht and Samenleving, 1994), 1.

3. "Community Profiles on Inuit Traditional Knowledge." Unpublished report. (Igloolik, Nunavut: Nunavut Social Development Council, 1998).

4. Ibid.

5. Jose Kusugak, Draft of a letter to the editor for the *Globe and Mail* (Toronto, Ontario), June 11, 1998.

RESOURCE GUIDE

Published Literature

Alexander, Bryan, and Cherry Alexander. *The Vanishing Arctic*. New York: Facts on File, 1997.

Brody, Hugh. *Living Arctic: Hunters of the Canadian North*. Vancouver: Douglas and McIntyre, 1987.

Creery, Ian. "The Inuit of Canada." In *Polar Peoples: Self-Determination and Development*. London: Minority Rights Publications, 1996.

Damas, David, and William C. Surtevant, eds. *Handbook of North American Indians*. Vol. 5, *Arctic*. Washington, D.C.: Smithsonian Institution, 1984.

Duffy, Quinn R. *The Road to Nunavut: The Progress of the Eastern Arctic Inuit since the Second World War*. Montreal: McGill-Queen's University Press, 1988.

MacDonald, John. *Arctic Sky: Inuit Astronomy, Star Lore and Legend*. Toronto: Royal Ontario Museum and Nunavut Research Institute, 1998.

McGhee, Robert. *Ancient People of the Arctic*. Vancouver: University of British Columbia Press, 1996.

Soubliere, Marion, ed. *The 1998 Nunavut Handbook*. Iqaluit; Baffin Island, Northwest Territories: Nortext Multimedia, 1997.

Wenzel, George. *Animal Rights, Human Rights: Ecology, Economy and Ideology in the Canadian Arctic*. Toronto: University of Toronto Press, 1991.

Films and Videos

Broken Promises: The High Arctic Relocation, 1994. National Film Board of Canada.

Coppermine, 1992. National Film Board of Canada (NFB films are available from public libraries in Canada, or call 212–629–8890 in the United States; website www.nfb.ca)

Everyman: Bishop of the Arctic, 1994, 50-minute color video. A Scorer Associates Production for the British Broadcasting Corporation.

Magic in the Sky, 1981. National Film Board of Canada.

The Baffin Regional Library (867–979–5401) has a reference section that can advise on a wide range of relevant films.

Internet and WWW Sites

Government of the NWT
Education, Culture and Employment
http://www.learnnet.nt.ca/

Indian and Northern Affairs
http://www.inac.gc.ca/index_e.html

News North
http://www.nnsl.com/frames/newspapers/newsnorth/sideindexsetup.html

Nunanet
http://www.nunanet.com/directory.html

Nunatsiaq News
http://www.nunatisiaq.com/nunavut/

Nunavut.com
http://www.nunavut.com/

Nunavut Handbook
http://www.arctic-travel.com/

Nunavut Implementation Commission
http://natsiq.nunanet.com/~nic/

Nunavut Planning Commission
http://www.npc.nunavut.ca/

Nunavut Research Institute
http://apa.nunanet.com/research/

Organizations

Department of Culture, Language, Elders and Youth
Government of Nunavut
Bag 800
Iqaluit, Nunavut Territory
XOA OHO
Fax: 867–979–5220

Inuit Heritage Trust
P.O. Box 2080
Iqaluit, Nunavut Territory
XOA OHO
Fax: 867–979–0269
E-mail: heritage@nunanet.com

Nunavut Arctic College
P.O. Box 160
Iqaluit, Nunavut Territory
XOA OHO
Fax: 867–979–4119

Nunavut Research Institute
P.O.Box 1720
Iqaluit Nunavut Territory
XOA OHO
Fax: 867–979–4681

Nunavut Social Development Council
Box 300
Igloolik, Nunavut Territory

XOA OHO
Fax: 867–934–8073

Nunavut Tunngavik Inc.
P.O. Box 638
Iqaluit, Nunavut Territory
XOA OHO
Fax: 867–979–3240

7

The Sheep-Farming Kujataamiut of South Greenland

Rasmus Ole Rasmussen

CULTURAL OVERVIEW

The People

Although the name "Greenland" is used in this chapter because most people are more familiar with it, what actually is meant is "Kalaallit Nunaat," as this is the name of the country used by its inhabitants who called themselves "Kalaallit." Greenland is generally considered to have been continuously inhabited by native Greenlanders for more than 4,000 years, although this is only partly true. Over that number of years, the changing climatic conditions have, from time to time, attracted and caused the retreat of the distinct groups of people from this, the world's largest island. A general warming of both the land and the sea during the last part of the first millenium A.D. caused the migration northward of important food animals, which in turn encouraged the inhabitants also to move north. It was during this period that Norse settlers from Europe established themselves in the south of the country.

The ancestors of the present-day Greenlanders entered Greenland when the climate started to cool again, settling first in northern Greenland around A.D. 1000 and reaching the southern part of Greenland by the beginning of the fourteenth century. These, the latest immigrants, arrived from the west, about 1,000 years ago, from Canada and Alaska.

The total population of Greenland is about 56,000 (according to the 1997 census). Of this number, approximately 49,000 were born in Greenland. About 80 percent of the population lives in the eighteen municipal centers which, in most cases, are settlements with a population of 1,000 or

Major towns in Greenland (with former Danish names beneath current names).

more inhabitants. Nuuk (formerly Godthåb), the capital of Greenland, has about 13,000 inhabitants. The 20 percent of the population that does not live in the main municipal centers lives in approximately eighty small settlements and fifty scattered homesteads spread along the coast. A few of these are devoted to sheep farming.

Sheep farmers and their families number around 300 people, all of whom live in southwest Greenland. The settlements of Qassiarssuk (sixty-three inhabitants) and Igaliko (thirty-five inhabitants) are the main centers; the others live on the fifty farmsteads and smaller settlements scattered in the three southern municipalities of Narssaq, Qaqortoq, and Nanortalik.

During the 1970s the number of people engaged in sheep farming peaked at more than 500. At that time, Qassiarssuk had 106 inhabitants; 65 lived in Igaliko. Owing to the severe economic and environmental problems experienced during the late 1970s, the number of residents in those settlements decreased drastically. Within a relatively few years, the total number was reduced by one-third but then stabilized around the present level, partly as a result of various initiatives taken by the home rule government. One goal of the Home Rule Government, starting in 1979 after about two hundred years of Danish colonial rule, has been to fully develop Greenlandic resources in order to improve Greenlanders' self-sufficiency. In regard to sheep farming, this has required determining how best to increase the production of sheep on a sustainable and economic basis.

The Setting

The southern tip of Greenland is situated at latitude 59 degrees north, and the northernmost land is at latitude 89 degrees north, nearly 1,900 miles away. The southern tip of Greenland is approximately at the same latitude as Oslo, Norway, or Anchorage, Alaska, where conditions suitable for agriculture exist. However, due to the east Greenland current, which transports vast amounts of ice from the Arctic Ocean and from eastern Greenland glaciers southward along the eastern coast and around the southern tip of Greenland, the climatic conditions in Greenland are markedly different from other areas at the same latitude. The Irminger Current, a northward flowing branch of the Gulf Stream originating in the Caribbean region, creates warmer conditions on the western coast of Greenland, especially on the southern part of the western coast, even though these areas are also affected in the summer months by the presence of ice arriving from the eastern coast.

Except in a few very sheltered places, the climate prevents the growing of trees in Greenland. Southern Greenland, however, provides very good conditions for grass and dwarf scrub vegetation, and the general appearance in many of the fiords in southern Greenland is of abundant vegetation.

It was this abundance that inspired the Norsemen, who visited southern Greenland at the end of the tenth century A.D. in search of new land, to name the country Greenland. Compared to the overgrazed, eroded fields and hillsides in Iceland, where they originated from, this new land looked green and promising.

Traditional Subsistence Strategies

The traditional subsistence activities practiced by the Inuit of Greenland were based on using all available resources, with emphasis placed on the marine mammals. Greenlanders hunted on land, at sea, and on the sea ice; they also fished and gathered mussels and seaweed as well as a few species of plants and berries on land in the summer. Seal hunting especially was a key element in their subsistence, for seals provided necessary food during winter time, oil for the lamps, and skins for clothing, shelter, and boats.

There were no permanent settlements because hunters had to be able to move to where the resources were available. There were particular places where people gathered during the winter season and other places favored during the summer season. These places were where the resources were at their seasonal peak abundance.

With the arrival of the Lutheran missionary Hans Egede in 1721, at a place close to Nuuk, colonial relations became established between Greenland and Denmark, and profound changes were set in motion in Greenland society. The Danes established a number of more or less separate "colonies" (trading stations) along the coast, usually manned by a few dozen people; these colonies maintained close links to the central administration in Copenhagen. A general characteristic of the settlements was the high degree of self-reliance they developed in order to survive. A ship from Denmark arrived once, or maybe even twice, each summer, bringing products needed for the settlement's own survival as well as supplies for trading with the Inuit.

Contact with these European colonists and their culture caused dramatic transformations among the Inuit. Although in the early years of contact, Inuit economic strategies continued to be based on their traditional hunting, fishing, and gathering of local resources, over time expanding reliance on trade goods obtained from the colonies led to a growing dependency and consequent increased vulnerability for the society. Thus, instead of establishing supplies for the winter season and skins for the maintenance of clothing, footwear, and boats, they traded the skins and the blubber for coffee, sugar, and guns.

This increased dependency on trade goods caused such a change to the traditional way of life that even some of the colonists became worried. Around the middle of the nineteenth century, it was recognized that there were already too many Greenland Inuit who no longer had hunting as their main trade. Thus, in formal letters from one of the Danish colonial traders to the authorities in Denmark, there is a report warning of the decline of health standards, the poor maintenance of the kayaks used for hunting, and the growing dependency of the local hunters. This trader warned that there were limits to the benefits of increased trade and the consequent dependency it was producing—and that the limit was being reached. In time, for many, this limit was definitely surpassed. From a self-sufficient, nomadic group of people, the Greenland Inuit had become dependent and sedentary.

Social and Political Organization

Before colonization, the Greenlandic system of sharing and exchange was based on reciprocity, and the extended family groups were, for all practical purposes, self-reliant. When large animals were caught, the catch was shared among community members according to well-established rules and practices.

After the connection between Denmark and Greenland was made in 1721, the Royal Greenland Trade department with its trade monopoly, established in 1776, became the basis of the colonial relationship. The first general regulations from 1782 stressed that the administration should put the best interest of the Greenlanders first, with trading interests as the second priority. Exactly what would constitute the best interest of the Greenlanders was very much debated, but a general impression was that colonial policies were not to interfere too much with the traditional lifestyle—except, of course, in the area of trade.

With the creation of a native advisory council in 1862, in the form of a committee of stewards appointed for each community, a new era was established. This was followed in 1911 by elected local and (two) regional councils, which gave the Greenlanders at least some elements of local government. In 1953 the Danish constitution was amended to give Greenland two seats in the Danish parliament; Greenland was now recognized as a county, equal to other counties in Denmark. This marked the end of the formal colonial relationship, and Greenland was thereby constitutionally incorporated into the Kingdom of Denmark. In reality, however, colonial relations continued until home rule was established on May 1, 1979. Home rule was the result of Greenlanders' persistent work for liberation after more than 250 years of a colonial and quasi-colonial relationship with Denmark.

Religion and World View

Contact with European cultures dramatically transformed many elements of the traditional Inuit society. A key element in this transformation was the introduction of religion, partly through the Danish Lutheran Church and partly through the Moravian Brethren (Herrnhutian Mission) of whom the most well-known missionary, Samuel Kleinschmidt, developed a writing system for the west Greenlandic language, based on the Latin alphabet.

One positive by-product of missionary activity was that most children in Greenland went to school, and as early as in the middle of the nineteenth century it was recognized that almost the whole population of Greenland could read, and the majority could also write in their own Greenlandic language. The first newspaper in Greenlandic, *Atuagagdliutit*, began publication in 1861; this paper is still published today. It was only much later, during the period of rapid and comprehensive modernization in the 1950s and 1960s, that Danish became a language of any importance in Greenland.

THREATS TO SURVIVAL

Changes Resulting from Modernization and Climate Change

Until the beginning of the 1900s, hunting sea mammals was the basis of the economy; fishing was a necessary but neglected and nonprestigious secondary activity. As the twentieth century progressed, the need for blubber and marine-mammal oil products in Europe decreased as mineral oils became available and less expensive and as industrial whaling grew to satisfy the demand that still existed for edible oils. Thus, as the market for blubber was reduced in importance, fishing was introduced as a new commercial activity in Greenland. The development of fisheries in Greenland took place relatively slowly, and in the 1920s the fisheries were directed principally toward Greenland halibut, arctic char, and capelin, together with a developing inshore cod fishery.

After World War II, national as well as an international pressure made it essential to improve the living conditions in this highly dependent, poor country. The development of Greenland was to be based on a modern industrial fishing industry using the now abundant cod resources. As a consequence, modernization programs in the 1950s and 1960s were directed at centralizing all economic activities in a few large settlements, where modern fish-processing plants were built, new concrete multistory apartment buildings were constructed, and living conditions began to resemble those found elsewhere in the industrialized world.

The decision to base the modernization of Greenland to a great extent upon cod fisheries was influenced by changes in the sea temperature, which occurred during the twentieth century, and which resulted in an abundance of cod and a scarcity of the traditionally hunted marine mammals. However, more recently, during the 1970s and 1980s, sea temperatures have cooled, and cod have been replaced by shrimp and Greenland halibut—as well as seals and various whales—all of which are cold-water species.

Shrimp fisheries are now the main economic base of the society; more than 90 percent of the value of Greenland exports are derived from shrimp and shrimp products. Apart from the massive transfer of funds from Denmark, fisheries are the most important economic activity conducted in Greenland today.

Challenges Associated with the Development of Agriculture

Parallel to the development of fisheries—but on a much smaller scale—is the development of sheep farming, which also was initiated at the beginning of the twentieth century. The founder of commercial agriculture in Greenland was Reverend Jens Chemnitz from the settlement of Frederiksdal. During a stay in Copenhagen in 1905–1906, he tried to generate interest in sheep farming in Greenland, which, according to his experiences, had the potential for succeeding in the southern part of Greenland. The Royal Greenland Trade Company (KGH) asked Reverend Chemnitz to go to the Faroe Islands in order to learn about Faroese sheep farming and to take a flock of sheep back to Greenland. In 1906 the first eleven sheep (nine ewes and two rams) were shipped from the Faroe Islands to Julianehåb (today's Qaqortoq) in southern Greenland; later, another eight sheep arrived.

The starting point for this agricultural trial was Frederiksdal, where the sheep seemed to thrive. When these imported animals produced a large number of lambs, it was possible to extend sheep farming to other locations. For example, Amos Egede in Igaliko started his operations in 1914 with just two ewes and one ram. At the same time, a small flock of Scottish sheep was maintained in Julianehåb, and after assessing the local area for sheep rearing, a local entrepreneur named Lindeman Walsøe brought 170 sheep from northern Iceland and established the Sheep Production Station in Julianehåb in 1915. The present Greenlandic stock of sheep seems to have developed from a mixture of these Faroese, Scottish, and Icelandic strains, with clear dominance of Icelandic genes. In order to expand sheep farming in southern Greenland, a system of lending out ewes and rams was started, whereby anyone interested in farming could receive some sheep and repay the loan when their own flock grew in number.

During these early years, sheep farming was only a supplement to the fundamental activities of fishing and hunting. This changed in 1924, when Otto Frederiksen settled in Qassiarssuk and created the first full-time commercial sheep farm in Greenland. He had borrowed 145 sheep from the Sheep Production Station in Julianehåb, with the understanding that every time lambs or sheep products were sold, one-third of the revenue would be used as repayment for the original flock of sheep. In 1926 he bought some calves and in 1927 a horse, and during the next three years he was able to pay off the debt for the original sheep. In 1935 the farmstead was expanded; it now consisted of a large house for the family to live in and a number of barns for his stock, which consisted of 300 sheep, two cows, and six horses. During the same period of time, another fourteen farms were established in Qassiarssuk. Thus the first Greenlandic community based primarily on sheep farming came into existence.

By 1935 eight sheep-farming settlements had been established, of which Qassiarssuk and Igaliko were the largest. Smaller settlements, like Igaliko Qujalleq, developed in other locations where good sheep forage was to be found. During the next ten or fifteen years, sheep farming as an occupation grew steadily, and most of the localities with the potential for sheep rearing were occupied during this period. The slaughtering of some animals was carried out at the farmsteads, but larger numbers were slaughtered at the Sheep Production Station in Julianehåb which, for a long period of time, became the center for the distribution of meat. Most of the meat was sold in the southern part of Greenland where boat transport facilitated local distribution, although the meat from about 700 animals was also sent to Godthåb and other more northerly settlements where Danes—more familiar with the taste of lamb—worked and lived. However, the major part of the meat was exported to Copenhagen where it was sold. These exports accounted for nearly 80 percent of the value of sheep production, but following the outbreak of World War II regular communication between Greenland and Denmark was lost, and Iceland and the United States became the most important export markets. Sales of sheep products also quadrupled in Godthåb and the more northern Greenland settlements.

Besides the distribution of fresh meat, a substantial part of the meat was preserved in different ways. Most was salted, but other meat products were developed, so that the total distribution of sheep products accounted for more than 100 tons, or an average annual consumption of around 22 pounds per capita. This was an important development, even though the consumption in other parts of western Greenland was minor compared to the average consumption in southern Greenland where the annual consumption of sheep products was around 66 pounds per capita.

Other attempts to develop agriculture were made during World War II. The rearing of hogs was attempted but was quite limited as there was no locally produced food for them, and the import of fodder resulted in too expensive a meat product. Although these pig-farming trials provided partial replacement for imported meat during the war, they did not last longer than the war years. Another trial of greater importance involved attempts to grow potatoes. During the war years, potatoes were imported from the United States, but since they were very expensive there seemed good reason to grow them in Greenland. A total production of more than 15 tons per year was the result. Other vegetables were more intensively produced, such as beets and rhubarb.

During the first decades of sheep farming in southern Greenland, most

The sheep-farming community of Igaliko, showing the infield areas used for winter pasture, 1996. The stone wall in the foreground is the remains of a Norse church.

of the slaughtering took place on the farms or at the Sheep Production Station in Julianehåb. Transporting most of the sheep by boat from the farms to Julianehåb substantially reduced the farmers' profits; therefore, plans were developed to establish another slaughtering facility in the center of the sheep-farming district, in Igaliko, where about 60 percent of sheep production occurred. However, building the new slaughter facility was delayed and when a brand-new plant for shrimp production was built in Narssaq in 1949, it was decided to design that facility so that it could be used to process fish and shrimp during most of the year and then operated as a slaughter and meat processing plant during September and October.

A key element in the development of agriculture in Greenland has been the question of access to sheep farming: who could become a sheep farmer? In recent years it has been impossible for any individual to own land privately in Greenland. According to a ruling in 1929, access to land used for sheep farming is given to sheep farmers who enjoy the right to use the land for that purpose. These rights extend to use of the land required in order to construct a farmstead, and land that is referred to as the "infield area." This right is transferable to the farmer's sons and daughters, as long as they want to continue sheep farming and as long as they continue to take care of the area. Taking care of an area means carrying out different types of pasture development, such as removing stones, fencing the pasture, and creating and maintaining the drainage and irrigation systems. The farmer enjoys exclusive use of the land around the farmstead—the infield area—but does not enjoy exclusive access to grazing areas outside the infield area. Although the home rule government introduced a new set of rules in 1979, the fundamental right of access to public land has not been changed in any significant way since the 1929 regulations were established.

Environmental Crisis

Accessing Sufficient Winter Food

Traditional Greenlandic sheep farming, as it was introduced at the beginning of the century, involved extensive grazing during summer when the sheep were unattended in the hills and mountains, going wherever the grazing was good, and being left to care for themselves. There are no predators in southern Greenland, except during the lambing season when ravens, foxes, and eagles may attack newborn lambs.

In those early years of Greenlandic sheep farming, the winter situation did not differ much from the summer situation, except that attempts were made to keep the sheep close to the farm. Traditionally there has been no systematic gathering of fodder for winter feeding because of the special winter climatic conditions in southern Greenland where, approximately every second or third week but with no determinable regularity, a warm Föhn wind sweeps down from the Greenland ice-cap and removes the major part of the snow cover. With the snow cover reduced in thickness, the sheep are able to access food, especially the dense mats of dwarf birch and willow found beneath the snow cover.

Problems arise, however, when the Föhn winds do not arrive. If, for some reason, the Föhn does not arrive for several weeks, the accumulating snow cover prevents the sheep from reaching their food, which occurs from time to time. An even more severe situation arises when a Föhn wind blows for a very short duration or brings limited warmth. At such times, only the top layer of snow melts, after which, with a return to normal cold winter conditions, the melted water on the top of the snow freezes to form a layer of ice which totally prevents the animals from reaching the vegetation beneath the snow. When this happens, numbers of sheep starve to death unless the farmers can supply them with hay, grain, or other suitable feed. This severe situation happened in the twentieth century approximately every fourth year, resulting in great fluctuations in sheep numbers.

Originally this variability in winter weather was considered an unavoidable natural event which could be overcome only by expanding the stock in good years in order to ensure the survival of a sufficient number of animals to rebuild the numbers during the following years. Recently, however, this has been considered a growing problem because commercial sheep farming requires more stability in economic returns. One attempted remedy during the 1960s was to import fodder; however, in the long run, this proposed solution to the problem proved to be far too expensive.

The Threat of Overgrazing

Another serious challenge associated with sheep farming is the necessity of preventing overgrazing, especially in areas close to the settlements. The sheep are very selective in their search for food, and too much grazing on limited areas causes a change in the composition of vegetation that is unfavorable to sheep farming in the long term. In severe cases, the complete removal of vegetation cover can occur, leading to soil erosion. Indeed, during the century preceding the Norse arrival in Greenland in A.D. 982, uncontrolled sheep farming in Iceland had led to deforestration and the loss of substantial amounts of farmland caused by serious soil erosion after the sheep had removed the vegetation. It was such overgrazing in the tenth century that forced Icelanders to search for new land, which led to the establishment of Norse settlements in southern Greenland.

Sociocultural Crisis

If sheep farming is to survive as an occupation and cultural adaptation in Greenland, it is necessary not only to solve the environmental problems, but also to answer questions concerning its social and economic viability. When sheep farming was introduced in the early 1900s, general living standards were low compared to today, and for most Greenlanders the main focus of activity was satisfying subsistence needs. This was also the case for the sheep farmers at that time.

Greenland sheep farmers were involved in fishing and hunting as well, and the farming activity supplied only a part of their incomes. As the modernization process progressed during the 1950s and 1960s, however, the focus changed and farming was regarded more and more as a self-contained activity, and farmers became less dependent on other sources of income. At the same time, the general living conditions in Greenland were improving, and higher standards were expected in housing, education, medical services, and communications. The larger settlements could provide most of the expected services, but the growing population in these settlements resulted in increased pressure on the vegetation in and around the settlements, resulting in less fodder for the animals, smaller animals, and subsequently less income for the farmers. In addition, severe winters could cause a serious loss of sheep and prevent farmers from having adequate incomes the following year.

While the settlement structure worked against the economic interest of the farmers by concentrating the population, it was very supportive of the social and cultural development of the sheep-farming settlements. In the settlements were found the schools and school dormitories that allowed children living in more remote farms to attend school for three or four days each week and return home for the weekends. The settlements also provided medical services—usually in the person of a midwife who had also been trained as a nurse—and church services. The general store, a crucial facility for community residents, provided mail and banking services, as well as supplies of fuel and winter fodder, food items, clothing, hardware, and other needed goods. The store also served an important social function and assisted in the cultural development of the community; here discussions were held and views were exchanged when people met during the day.

The declining number of farms during the 1970s caused a severe threat to the continued viability of the sheep-farming communities. The farmers could see no way out of the squeeze between the environmental problem resulting from their need to increase sheep numbers, and the economic reality of the extremely expensive imported winter fodder. One obvious solution was to give up farming, move to the larger settlements, and start working in fisheries.

RESPONSE: STRUGGLES TO SURVIVE CULTURALLY

Rationalizing Sheep Farming in Greenland

Government Support for Farming

With the establishment of Greenland Home Rule in 1979, a new national policy was formulated which emphasized that the development of Greenland's economy should be based on living resources and should take place with due regard to the traditional settlement pattern—where the small settlements were considered to be the backbone of the settlement structure.

Sheep Farmers Answer the Challenge

For the sheep farmers, headed by the director of the Sheep Farmers' Organization, Kaj Egede, it became important to develop a sustainable farming system. The key question became, Was it possible to solve some of the critical limitations existing in the system—including the production of sufficient fodder—to sustain a self-sufficient farming system?

The first step in answering this challenge was to analyze the potential productivity of the vegetational resources in order to determine the sustainable basis for future sheep farming. This matter raised several questions, for although this study would provide a full assessment of the existing vegetational resources, it was also necessary to determine the practical significance of this potential source of winter fodder. That is to say, it was necessary to locate and assess the pasture areas occurring within a practical distance of the sheep farms.

The second step was to answer a number of sociocultural questions. For example, How should the new settlement structure be organized in order to facilitate social interaction among the farmers, including the sharing of machines and equipment, without causing overgrazing of specific areas? A system of fences placed across the mountains and hills made it possible to keep the sheep in smaller flocks within specific areas and thereby reduce the grazing pressure on the areas close to the settlements. In general, the fields around the settlements were kept strictly for winter fodder production and were therefore inaccessible to the sheep at other times.

Other questions stressing sociocultural issues included rights to ownership of the land, ownership of the sheep, numbers of sheep farmers would be allowed to own, the ability of farmers to sell land or buildings, and the right to inheritance of the children.

The third step involved designing suitable farm buildings; keeping the sheep in barns during the winter months was considered to be the best way to overcome the hazards sheep encountered during winters. At the same time, keeping the sheep in barns would reduce the food needs of the sheep and enable the farmers to look after their health and take care of other problems that might arise.

The fourth step involved clearing fields for winter fodder production and erecting new barns. Many of the farms were built quite close to each other, but in the case of the more isolated farms, it was necessary to build connecting roads between the farms. This had the added benefit of enabling better social interaction to occur.

Private ownership of land in Greenland is not allowed by law; nevertheless, if the Sheep Farmers' Organization recognizes an individual as a sheep farmer, that individual is granted access to specific land areas, as well as undisputed possession of a farmstead. The farm equipment is considered private property, and therefore the farmer needs to pay for it, just as the farmer will have to pay for improvements to his or her farm buildings.

Limits on Sheep Farming in Greenland

When accepted by the Sheep Farmers' Organization as a farmer, the farmer agrees to produce winter fodder on the infield areas around the farmstead. To be accepted as a sheep farmer, however, the individual is required to have been educated as a sheep farmer at the Sheep Farmers' School in Upernaviarssuk, South Greenland, or to have gained similar qualifications, for example, at the sheep farmers' school in Iceland. When a sheep farmer retires, his children have first priority to take over the farm, but they will have to be accepted by the Sheep Farmers' Organization.

Sheep farmers in Greenland are allowed to keep no more than 400 ewes, which allows a reasonable income but can be maintained on a sustainable basis through the winter on locally produced winter fodder. The number of lambs produced determines how many animals the farmer has for slaughter; the expected ratio is around 1:1; that is to say, each ewe on average will produce one lamb each year. By improving health and winter fodder production, it should be possible to increase the number of lambs and therefore also the farmers' incomes. The long-term goal is for each ewe to produce two lambs each year.

Achieving Sustainable Agriculture

As a consequence of this rationalization process started in the early 1980s, it seems that the number of sheep in southern Greenland has been stabilized at the reasonably high level of 20,000 ewes. It has been possible to prevent the yearly fluctuation in numbers experienced in earlier times by keeping the sheep in barns during the winter where their nutritional needs are less than if they were outside finding their own food. Today, most of this winter fodder is produced locally, and imported fodder with high nutritional value is added only in small quantities. This supplementary feed is necessary in order to increase the number of lambs produced. Within the last twenty years, the number of lambs each ewe produces has increased significantly, from a level below 0.7 lamb per ewe per year, to more than 1.0 today, an increase in production that subsequently contributes to the farmers' imcomes. It is expected that this production level will continue to increase.

Approximately two-thirds of the lambs produced each year are sent to Narssaq for slaughter. From there the meat is distributed as frozen products to be sold in shops and supermarkets throughout Greenland. The remaining one-third of the lambs are slaughtered on the farms and sold directly by sheep farmers to consumers as fresh meat. The total production of at least 400 tons of meat makes an important contribution to the total amount of meat available for consumption in Greenland.

Agricultural Development in Greenland

The Sheep Farmers' School in Upernaviarssuk is in continuous operation, and the interest among young Greenlanders, especially from southern Greenland, for the sheep farming vocation is high. At the same time, the Upernaviarssuk facility conducts a number of research and development activities, for example, testing new and improved strains of grass for the hayfields and seeking to improve the local sheep breeds. In addition, the school develops seeds for beets, rhubarb, and other vegetables grown by the farmers for home consumption and maintains more than thirty years of continuous research evaluating the performance of selected varieties of trees that may be suitable to grow in sheltered places in southern Greenland.

As a result of these recent changes in the Greenland sheep-farming system, the situation today shows an overall rise in total lamb production, despite there being a smaller number of ewes today than existed thirty years ago. Economic analysis clearly shows that sheep farming contributes positively to Greenland's economy.

A Successful Farmers' Organization

During the 1930s, the sheep farmers started organizing themselves into in workers' unions, first as local community organizations, but later as one organization: De samvirkende Fåreholder-foreninger (the United Sheep Farmers' Organization) or SAP. In 1948 the first copy of a magazine for the newly organized sheep farmers, designed to distribute information about sheep farming as well as generate general communication among farmers as a basis for social and cultural development, was produced by SAP. SAP arranges an annual gathering for all members, which usually takes place in Qaqortoq. This large festive event involves meals eaten together, games, and other cultural activities.

The board of governors of SAP is elected from among the sheep farmers, who also appoint the director, who is their spokesperson when approaching the home rule government or conducting other official business for the organization.

One of the initiators of modern sheep farming in Greenland, the director of the Sheep Production Station in Julianehåb, Lindeman Walsøe, wrote in 1935,

Sheep farming seems to have been established as a sound vocation for the Greenlandic population already in this generation, and when the next generation grows up those who as children have been living among sheep farmers and sheep—then the full exploitation and understanding will be established. There needs to be at least one generation to create a population of herders out of a population of hunters. The children of the present sheep farmers—they are the ones to further develop the sheep farming system.[1]

This is exactly what has happened. Today, based on the various reforms and ongoing improvements that have occurred, sheep farming is a viable system of food production in Greenland. Besides contributing to the national economy, and creating better living conditions for the people living in southern Greenland, sheep farmers have created the basis for a whole new cultural development. Greenland sheep farming is a good example of sustainable development in the Arctic, as it takes into account not only environmental concerns, but also the economic, social, and cultural dimensions of this concept. What is important to keep in mind is that these activities, including the planning, the structuring, and all the decisions, have been made by the Sheep Farmers' Organization and subsequently by the sheep farmers themselves.

FOOD FOR THOUGHT

It may seem a contradiction in terms to discuss the development of agriculture in Greenland, considering the common understanding of Greenland as a part of the Arctic. Most people picture the Arctic as dominated by snow and ice, polar bears, seal hunting, and very long and harsh winter conditions. It may also seem just as contradictory that Greenlanders, with their long tradition of hunting marine mammals, became settled agriculturists.

Nevertheless, agriculture had been part of the Greenlandic reality since A.D. 982 when the Norse first arrived at Brathalið (the Norse name for the settlement which today is called Qassiarssuk). After the Norse left Greenland some time between 1400 and 1500, there was a period of more than 200 years when no new attempts were made to practice agriculture. However, during the colonial period, and especially at the beginning of the twentieth century, successful attempts at farming were made, leading to today's limited—but seemingly sustainable—livestock production. At the same time, this development has resulted in a very distinct culture, which is a very obvious characteristic of southern Greenland today.

When discussing the development of sheep farming, it is important to understand that this particular development is only a very limited part of the huge transformation that has occurred in Greenland over the last two centuries. Greenlanders have made the change from a self-sustaining hunting society to a highly integrated industrial society; from a society dependent on hunting to a society whose economy is now mainly based on fishing and income transfers; from a traditional to a modern society; and from a Danish colony to a self-governing part of the Danish realm. Although many other profound changes have taken place, this short list mentions some of the more important developments. The successful introduction of sheep farming, which started as a limited experiment, has contributed to this overall national transformation.

In a few generations, a population of hunters and fishers have been able to develop a distinct cultural adaption based upon farming and sheep herding. Within a short span of years, they have successfully adapted to using a variety of entirely new environmental resources and practices in order to become successful sheep farmers. Step by step they learned about specific environmental conditions, how to to interact in new ways with nature, and how to promote their new economic opportunities without compromising the environmental integrity of future generations. They have also been able to contribute significantly to the national economy and to be players in the global economy.

This development has been initiated locally, largely by local people and entirely governed by the people involved in the trade. Some people from outside the local community have been involved but only to the extent required to transfer some technical information to local expert practitioners.

In many ways, this is a development which, although it began early in the twentieth century, exemplifies what since the 1980s has become known as "sustainable development" (as defined in the Brundtland report of the U.N. Commission on Environment and Development). In the case of Greenland, those involved in the development gave careful attention to safeguarding the environment while creating an innovative yet viable economy together with the needed social and cultural arrangements and political institutions.

Questions

1. What characterizes a culture? Use our own culture as an example.

2. In what ways is the Greenland sheep-farming example typical or nontypical of cultural development?

3. Although many cultures appear to incorporate new ideas and technologies easily, others appear to stagnate or even to deteriorate. What are some positive and negative cultural developments that affect your own society?

4. The potential for sheep farming in Greenland existed for many centuries before it was (re)introduced at the beginning of the twentieth century. What triggered interest in this activity, and what were the circumstances that allowed it to become successful? What potentials in your own culture have not yet been realized?

5. The development of sheep farming in Greenland required a degree of government support and local initiative, including a few key individuals who started the process. Do you think this is generally true in the case of important social, cultural, and economic innovations?

NOTE

1. J. Fisker, ed., *Narssak'* (Gylling: Nordiske Landes Bogforlag, 1981), 91 (author's translation).

RESOURCE GUIDE

Published Literature

Friis, Peter, and Rasmus Ole Rasmussen. *Fåreavlen og den Samfundsmæssige rigdom.* Roskilde, Denmark: RUC, 1984. (A history of sheep farming in Greenland; in Danish, with statistics and maps.)

Krogh, Knud J. *Viking Greenland*. Translated by Helen Fogh and Gwyn Jones. Copenhagen: National Museum, 1967.

Statistics Greenland. *Greenland Yearbook*. Nuuk, Greenland: Statistics Greenland (annual publication, in English since 1996).

Trap, J. P. *Danmark*. Vol. 14, *Grønland*. Copenhagen: G. E. C. Gads forlag, 1979 (in Danish).

Videos

For videos on sheep farming in south Greenland, contact:

Kalaallit Nunaata Radioa
P.O. Box 1007
DK-3900 Nuuk,
Greenland
Fax:+299–2–4703

Kujataata Radioa
P.O. Box 158
DK-3920 Qaqortoq
Greenland
Fax:+299–3–7334

Internet and WWW Sites

Greenland Home Rule
http://gh.gl

Greenland Tourism
http://www.greenland.guide.dk/

Organizations

Savaatillit Peqatigiit Suleqatigiissut Siunnersortaat (Sheep Farmers' Organization)
SPS, Augo Lyngesvej B1262
DK-3920 Qaqortoq
Fax:+299–3–7306

South Greenland Tourism
P.O. Box 128
Torvevej B68
DK-3920 Qaqortoq
Fax: +299–3–8495

8

The Iñupiat of Alaska

Barbara Bodenhorn

CULTURAL OVERVIEW

The People

The Iñupiat are an Inuit people living in the coastal regions of the Alaskan Arctic—from the Canadian border to the village of Wales on the Bering Strait. "Iñupiat" means "real people." The Iñupiat, as with Inuit living elsewhere in Alaska, Canada, Greenland, and Russia, have depended on hunting sea mammals to make up the bulk of their diet for at least 2,000 years. Bowhead whale and walrus continue to be of immense importance to the Iñupiat inhabiting the northern and northwestern coast of Alaska.

As is common among the Inuit in general, the Iñupiat are hunters who have developed a masterful technology that enables them to survive in the severe Arctic environment. This technology includes clothing and shelter designed to keep humans warm at −40°F as well as the intricate construction of tools needed to hunt and process food.

The regional Iñupiat population was about 2,900 in 1840 when commercial whalers first crossed the Bering Strait. That population declined to just over, 1,000 following the influenza epidemic of 1918 and then increased steadily through the 1960s and 1970s. The U.S. government built a hospital in Barrow and schools in several villages during the first decade of the twentieth century and began encouraging people to move into these settlements. By 1980 the regional population was registered at 4,209; it had risen to 6,538 in 1993.

Today, the Iñupiat live in permanent villages, yet they still move across the land, the ice, and the oceans to hunt or fish according to the season.

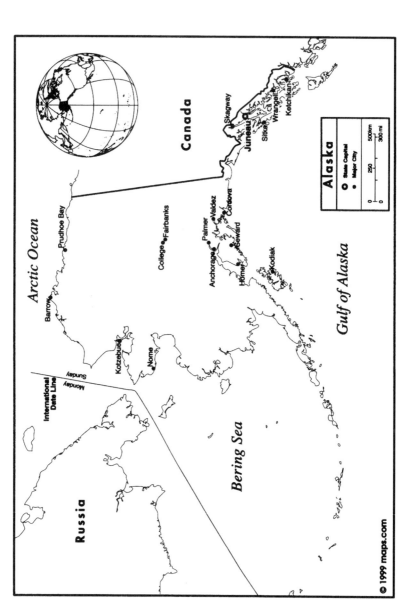

Alaska

State Capital
Major City

0   250   500km
0   300 mi

Arctic Ocean

Barrow

Prudhoe Bay

College Fairbanks

Canada

Skagway
Juneau
Sitka
Wrangell
Ketchikan

Palmer
Valdez
Anchorage Cordova
Seward
Homer
Kodiak

Gulf of Alaska

International Date Line

Monday Sunday

Kotzebue

Nome

Russia

Bering Sea

© 1999 maps.com

Used by permission of MAGELLAN Geographix, Inc.

The communities of Point Hope or Barrow, for example, grew up around existing major communities; others, such as Wales and Wainwright, became important during the height of the commercial whaling era in the late nineteenth century; still others, such as Atqasuk and Nuiqsut, were established after 1970.

As in many hunting societies, the food people eat may have been caught by a member of the household or provided by another hunter. Store-brought goods are often available even in remote villages, but hunted food continues to provide the staple Iñupiaq diet. It is not uncommon to hear, "I'm Iñupiaq; I eat Iñupiaq food." The customary diet of traditional food continues to be central to what it means to be Iñuqiaq.

The Setting

The region occupied by the Iñupiat consists of a low-lying coastal tundra plain. The many streams, rivers, and lakes contain a variety of fish species, many of which are important food species for the Iñupiat. This plain and the foothills found farther inland contain herds of migratory caribou, and the mountains beyond the foothills are home to bears and Dall sheep. During the spring, numerous geese and ducks arrive, leaving the region at the end of summer. Berries and some edible plants occur throughout the region.

The coastal waters contain a number of important marine mammal species. Bowhead whales appear in the spring on an eastern migration to their summering areas in Canadian arctic waters. In the early fall, as it migrates westward again, it enters within hunting range of the three easternmost Iñupiat communities. Beluga whales, and more rarely gray whales, are also found from spring until late summer in these same coastal waters. Walrus and three species of seal also occur in these waters; polar bears are more frequent visitors once the sea ice forms in the fall, but may be found on shore at any season.

Traditional Subsistence Strategies

We eat the animals of the seas. We eat animals of the land. We have two sources for our subsistence, we who live on the shores.
—Patrick Attungana of Point Hope, speaking to the Alaska Eskimo Whaling Commission, 1985[1]

The term "subsistence" in Alaska—as in so many other parts of the North—is not just about getting food on the table; it is also the proper way of conducting social relations among humans and between humans and animals.

In Alaska, the Iñupiat consider whaling their most important activity and indeed generally define themselves as whalers. However, despite the importance of whales, the Iñupiat in Barrow also enjoy eating waterfowl, many kinds of fish, harbor and bearded seals, walrus, beluga, caribou, Dall sheep, polar bear, and even the occasional moose as part of their hunted diet. Greens and berries collected on the tundra customarily have provided important sources of vitamins. Today no special occasion would be complete without *agutaq*, or Eskimo ice cream, which is made from whitefish, caribou fat, and salmon berries. Hunting, which takes place virtually year round, demands a precise knowledge of the environment in order to obtain a variety of different resources on the edge of the ice, the open water, the shoreline, the inland river systems, and the tundra.

Successful hunting depends on environmental conditions, technology, and cooperation with others. Young people continue to learn a great deal by going out with others, watching, trying, making mistakes, and trying again. Technology developed over the centuries continues in use: skin boats for ice-filled waters, knives to cut blocks of snow needed to construct a shelter, the *ulu* (woman's knife) that allows a skilled woman to skin a seal in barely a minute, and clothing that keeps a hunter's body temperature constant regardless of his activity. Today, of course, these items are supplemented with such items as high-powered rifles, snowmobiles, outboard motors, and citizens band (CB) radios.

Social and Political Organization

The people that work together survive and those that try to make it on their own were always the ones who were found dead somewhere along the line due to starvation, because they were not able to work together with their family ties or their relative ties.

—Tom Brower, Barrow[2]

For several centuries before Europeans appeared on the scene, Iñupiat social groups ranged from small, seminomadic bands exploiting river systems to large, permanent communities located where migrating bowhead whales pass close to shore. Over time, people organized to exploit these resources in institutionalized ways, many of which continue to be important today. A single hunter can bring home a seal or a caribou, but whales or walrus are more effectively hunted by a group of hunters. The larger the group, the more formally organized it is likely to be, formed around a core of people related through kinship or marriage. Whaling crews, headed by a whaling captain and his wife, endure over time and constitute an important social unit throughout the year.

As in many hunting societies, virtually all activities involved in procuring, processing, and distributing hunted food have traditionally been divided into men's and women's work. In general, men manufacture tools, hunt and fish, and butcher the largest animal (such as walrus and whales).

Pulling a bowhead whale ashore from a fall hunt, Barrow, Alaska, 1997.

Women fish, skin, and butcher smaller animals, prepare and distribute food, and, above all, sew the clothing that is crucial to survival. Thus men's and women's work complement each other and ensure the survival of both the household and the group as a whole.

Definite leadership positions existed in the established whaling communities; whaling captains and their wives had status and authority, although some families were more influential than others in leadership and economic affairs. Shamans, the religious specialists in a society, were both feared and respected. As long as people could move around on their own, these leaders depended on the goodwill of their followers for the labor needed to carry out their tasks. Leadership was never permanent, but it was important and the whaling captains often met together to decide on important issues for the entire community.

Whaling captains continue to play an important political role in village life today. In the late twentieth century, however, government became much more complex in Alaska, with various local and regional tribal governments having different areas of responsibility. Thus the Iñupiaq Community of the Arctic Slope is a regional tribal organization that includes the eight villages of the North Slope. Each village has its own native village council as well. There are also local and regional corporations formed under the terms of the Alaska Land Claims Settlement Act of 1971. At the same time, Alaska, as one of the fifty states of the United States, has its own governmental structures and areas of responsibility.

The North Slope Borough is a home rule borough that spans about 88,000 square miles. The eight settled communities within its boundaries are incorporated as cities under state charters. Whether people live in a small village or in a regional center with thousands of inhabitants, their life in Arctic Alaska not only demands detailed knowledge of how to survive on the ice and tundra, but also requires a good understanding of overlapping and complex political organizations.

Religion and World View

In the traditional Iñupiaq world, animals as well as humans were thought to possess souls and to act with intent. Hunting in many respects is a sacred activity; customarily it was aided by charms, amulets, or divination, but today it is primarily dependent on the hunter maintaining a correct attitude toward his or her animal counterparts. Although individuals possessed varying degrees of ritual knowledge that enabled them to act effectively in the world, the shamans, who were specialists, were called on to help in times of sickness or animal shortage.

The relationship between animals and humans is considered one of mutual cooperation and respect. Animals give themselves up to deserving hunters but only in conjunction with the proper behavior of both husband and wife. Customarily, amulets and charms were part of a man's tool kit for a successful hunt. His clothing could carry the power to attract animals, which was created during his wife's sewing. For her part, a wife is still expected to maintain a peaceful state of mind and to share her husband's catch generously when he brings it home to her. In part, this is done because husbands and wives are expected to help each other. Just as important, however, proper behavior on both their parts is thought to be important in convincing animals that they have found good hosts to whom they can give themselves. "The animals come to me, they know I share," said Harry Brower, Sr., of Barrow (personal communication to Michael Jeffrey, 1984). It is that relationship that led Elijah Kakinya (an outstanding hunter from Anaktuvak Pass) to say, "I'm not the great hunter; my wife is" (personal communication to Leona Okakok, 1983). He was not referring to her ability to kill animals but, rather, to her ability to attract them to him.

Anyone who helps during the hunting will earn a share of the catch. This sharing is especially important to those who cannot take part for one reason or another. Shared food constantly travels between households often between communities, to parents, siblings, and others who may not be so fortunate. Sharing reflects the way many Iñupiat regard the social relationship between humans and animals: humans share with each other so that animals will share with them. This is most clearly stated during the community feasts that celebrate a successful whaling season. According to Patrick Attungana, the whale "gives itself to all of the community,"[3] and in order for the whale spirit to return, the whale meat must be shared throughout the community. Nalukataq (a traditional festival marking the end of the whaling season), Thanksgiving, and Christmas continue to be events during which all of the whaling communities of northern Alaska give thanks in their own way for the generous gift of the whale and celebrate it with feasting, singing, and traditional dancing. Thus, not only is the opportunity to eat Iñupiaq food important for one's own sense of Iñupiaq identity, the opportunity to share it with others is crucial in creating a sense of Iñupiaq community.

The dominant religion in Alaskan Iñupiaq communities today is Christianity, in various denominations. Whalers today now sing hymns while the whaling feasts of Thanksgiving and Christmas take place in the community churches. Patrick Attungana of Point Hope, a whaling captain and an Episcopalian minister, told the following story in 1985 to illustrate his understanding of the relationship between whales and human beings.

When the whales travel, they know about Saint Lawrence Island, so when they reach there, one of them stops, like they are camping, allowing themselves to be killed. Some of them keep travelling, and when they reach Point Hope, one of them camp at Point Hope, caught by one of the whalers. As they keep on travelling, when they reach Barrow, one of them camp, caught by the whalers.

When the whale is caught, just the body dies; the whole whale gives itself to all the people . . . the whale being or spirit never dies. The whale that was like camping at Point Hope knows when the whales return [as they begin migrating south again]. And the whales that are going back know the whale had stopped to camp. When the whales get to the camp, the dead whale's being or spirit return to the live whales. The returning whales begin to listen to the whale that had been like camping. He tells them that his hosts were good, the married couple were good to it. Some of the whales tell the returning whales that their hosts did not treat them right.

The whale that had good hosts starts wishing and telling others that it will camp again the following year. The other whale who did not have good hosts says that it will not camp again, but will go to a different whaling crew the following year.

When you hunt the animals in harmony, you don't have problems catching the animals. That is what needs to be thought about. If the hunters from Barter to Saint Lawrence Island hunt in harmony, the animals will keep going. They will catch the animal.[4]

THREATS TO SURVIVAL

Loss of Traditional Knowledge

These things we use now don't last forever, they break, get destroyed. If you leave your way of living to your children, it will never go away.

—Ernest Kignak, Sr., Barrow[5]

The institutions controlling daily life underwent massive changes during the twentieth century. An excerpt from William Oquilluk's history of the region speaks of "five disasters." The first three disasters, which occurred in ancient times and killed most of the people, were natural ones. The fourth disaster was the 1918 influenza and tuberculosis epidemics which he experienced as a young man. The fifth disaster, he believes, is occurring "maybe now." For him, this latest disaster is not about global warming (although people certainly talk about that) but rather is about the loss of knowledge: "There are not many old people left. The rules and stories of our ancestors are being forgotten. The people do not know who their relations are."[6]

Although close to half of the Iñupiaq population on the North Slope is still fluent in the Iñupiaq language, that fluency may not now include the very detailed vocabulary that describes the land, the ice, and the animals. Some elders worry that if young people do not learn about their surroundings in their own language, important knowledge will be lost. Many men and women on the North Slope are knowledgeable today about the land and about book learning, but it takes concentration and determination to learn in both modes, for they are two different ways of knowing.

Recently, two changes that have affected this issue have occurred in Barrow. In 1980 school lessons were taught almost entirely in English; Iñupiaq language and culture classes took up about forty-five minutes of the school day. On the other hand, public meetings (e.g., of the city council or the North Slope Borough Assembly) were conducted and broadcast on the local radio entirely in Iñupiaq. The message to everyone was that the language of government was the local language. Since the early 1990s, however, as more non-Iñupiat have been elected to public office, these public meetings have taken place in English. In the schools now, students may enroll in a total immersion program for the first few years of schooling, in which the entire school day is conducted in Iñupiaq. Some parents, however, are afraid that their children will be disadvantaged in the future if they are not learning English from the very beginning. How to balance knowledge in both systems continues to be troubling for many people.

Increased Outsider Interest in the Land

Geographical isolation and extreme Arctic conditions have sheltered Inuit communities to some extent because European and Euro-American settlers have not wanted to turn their hunting territory into farmland. After the end of World War II, however, the location of Alaska near the Soviet Union made it a strategically important area, and distant early warning (DEW-line) radar stations were constructed along the Alaskan coastline, usually within a mile or two of an Iñupiaq village. These construction projects became a regular source of wage labor for the Iñupiat and created a permanent non-Iñupiaq presence close to, but never part of, virtually every Iñupiaq community. At about the same time, it became increasingly clear that the region was a potential source of vast amounts of oil, and indeed, in 1969, a huge oil deposit was discovered at Prudhoe Bay, about ninety miles east of Barrow.

Suddenly the land itself was of tremendous interest to non-Iñupiat. Until this time outsiders had appeared only fleetingly to take away renewable resources (baleen from whales, furs, and so forth), leaving the Iñupiat more or less alone on their land to continue living their own lives. Now, however, the federal government, the state government, and many oil companies concentrated their attention on the land itself as a valuable resource. By the late 1970s, the Prudhoe Bay oil field was the site of a massive development undertaken by a number of multinational oil companies.

Between 1980 and 1993, the total population of the region increased by 55 percent; overall, the Iñupiat still form 74 percent of the regional population. Most non-Iñupiat live in Barrow, where they constitute 39 percent of Barrow's population. In the smaller villages, non-Iñupiat residents rarely make up more than 10 percent of the total population. The Iñupiat are still a clear majority in their homeland.

Economic Inequalities in the Region

As a result of these oil developments, the North Slope is comparatively affluent. In 1993 the average Iñupiaq household income on the North Slope was $44,551; personal incomes averaged $10,765. However, there are major differences between the incomes of non-Iñupiat residents and Iñupiat residents: the average non-Iñupiat household income in Barrow was $74,448, with personal incomes averaging $29,525.[7] These differences are even greater in the surrounding villages.

Outside of Barrow the economic situation is less economically satisfactory, and underemployment is a real problem. In 1993 (the most recent year for which comparative statistics are available), more than a third of the workforce outside of Barrow worked for less than forty weeks each year, and many families fell below federal poverty-level standards.[8] The cost of living is high in Arctic Alaska: it costs $116 a month to heat a home in Barrow (where natural gas is nearby), but it costs more than double that ($295 a month) in Atqasuk where one pays for imported fuel oil.[9] It also costs money to prepare for hunting: guns, ammunition, snowmobiles, sleds, and fuel are requirements for even the most basic trip. "Nowadays, you have to work to go hunting," May Panigeo observed (personal communication, 1984).

People use different strategies to obtain money for hunting, as well as the money needed to access food from others. A relatively small but regular amount of money is earned directly through subsistence activities; for example, dried fish and seal oil are bought and sold, and some hunting equipment continues to be made and sold locally. A *ulu* (woman's knife) can fetch from $50 to $75; a warm parka, many times that—a sturdy sled, more again. Carved ivory, *ulus*, parkas, and mittens are all on sale on consignment at the local store.

In some cases, people work intensively (earning overtime) for a few months, which allows them to accumulate the cash needed to go hunting. In other cases, a family member might work full-time and donate money on the understanding that the entire family benefits from the hunt. Sometimes someone who cannot hunt will give a relative a gun as a Christmas or birthday present and receive, in turn, shares of the meat from the hunter. Tom Brower's statement about the importance of family ties when times are hard continues to be as true in the late 1990s as it was decades ago.

Still, it is clear that life is easier for some and much harder for others. Historically, Barrow has had richer families (usually whaling captain couples) and poorer families, but these differences are becoming more and more evident today. The fact that virtually all of the less well-off families are Iñupiat can create considerable tension between local residents and people coming in from the outside looking for work.

Allotments and the Alaska Native Claims Settlement Act

In our society—you use it—it's yours. There was no need for a title—it's everybody's. [I] have seen change from the both sides. . . . We were caught up in a white society in black and white when we did not even know that we needed that black and white. . . . We did not learn how to keep title—or we would have all of the title up on the North Slope, completely.

—Raymond Neakok, Sr., Barrow[10]

When Alaska became a state in 1959, the territory was more or less categorized as huge empty space that belonged to no one except the federal government which controlled 97 percent of the land. The federal government recognized that the forebears of the Iñupiat had lived on the land well before any European had arrived, and they recognized that something had to be done about the legitimate claims of these indigenous peoples to their homeland.

When it became clear in the 1960s that the coastal region potentially had huge oil deposits, the state of Alaska began making its first land selections as a newly created state of the union. Alaska native protest was immediate, and the federal government imposed an initial land freeze in 1966 which prohibited the state from making further selections until indigenous claims had been settled. Then, in 1968, oil was discovered in Prudhoe Bay.

A second land freeze stopped all further land transactions, and the process of settling native land claims began in earnest. After long and intense negotiations, the final form of the Alaska Native Claims Settlement Act (ANCSA) awarded 44 million acres of land and $962.3 million to Alaska native corporations. On the North Slope, the Arctic Slope Regional Corporation (ASRC) was designated to receive about 4 million acres of land and $52 million from which each of the region's eight village corporations was to receive a portion.[11]

Negotiating the terms of ANCSA caused a great deal of conflict, but there was another issue that had to be decided before ANCSA could be passed. In 1906 the federal government had passed the Native Allotment Act, under which eligible natives throughout the United States were entitled to surface rights to 160 acres of unclaimed land. Since land had never been a scarce resource in Alaska, this act had received little attention—until the discovery of oil. Since ANCSA explicitly extinguished all further claims to land, it was believed that the allotments ought to be applied for before ANSCA was passed.

Allotments have been the source of tension and conflict on the North Slope since the late 1960s when the implementation of the Native Allotment Act began. There have been numerous conflicts with the government over the claims process and between individuals with competing claims. Conflicts have arisen also because of the very notion of land ownership: some people are concerned that the law is changing attitudes about the land and about the people's relationship to it.

The original Native Allotment Act states that eligible applicants must be able to establish "potentially exclusive use and occupancy" of their claim. Exclusive use means that only the person putting forward the claim has used the territory. Raymond Neakok has been quoted about the impossibility of applying this notion to Iñupiaq territory: "You use it—it's yours." When you leave and someone else comes along, they can use it as well. "If you can get out there, you can go hunting,"[12] was the way Ernest Kignak put it. In fact, he chose not to apply for an allotment at all because he could not agree to the conflict the process seemed to create:

I applied for a lot, but my mind didn't like that idea. Since time immemorial it's been this way—when people travel up there on the land, up inland, it doesn't matter if they're from Barrow or from any other place—if they get up there, they can go hunting. This also applies to the oceans. So, thinking about this lot thing, if they are fighting over the land, I don't want to be a part of it. I don't have any lot up there at all.[13]

Conflicting Goals Within Native Corporations

Despite these conflicts, ANCSA was passed (although the Arctic Slope formally dissented), and land selections were made which have, in turn, created real dilemmas for the corporations involved. The ANCSA corporations are supposed to act in the best interests of Alaska native people as a whole and to protect their lands. Simultaneously it is their job, as with any other U.S. corporation, to earn profits for their stockholders. By developing resources and producing profits, Alaska native economic development should help the state's overall economic development. But, of course, that at times conflicts with the need to protect the habitat from the damages that development projects may bring.

There is another potential problem. Initially, the land and the shares were in protected status: they could neither be bought nor sold. However, according to the terms of ANCSA, after twenty years, the land could be sold on the private market if that seemed to be a good idea. In fact, if a corporation were not making any profit—perhaps because it had no opportunities to develop resources that would not endanger the local habitat— the land could be sold off in order to pay taxes owed or meet other financial obligations.

The question of who might be shareholders in the future was also of concern. Under the original terms of the act, 100 shares of stock were issued to eligible Alaska natives who were born on or before December 19, 1971. The only way people born after that date could obtain shares was through inheritance or purchase. Thus, they could be "shareless" until well into adulthood. This could effectively disenfranchise a whole body of young people and divorce them from decisions made regarding the land.

One of the consequences of these acts has been to classify every piece of land the Iñupiat come into contact with during the course of their daily lives. Both in town and out on the tundra, land belongs to individuals, native corporations, the state, or the federal government. Each classification carries with it rules and regulations concerning who can use it and for what purpose.

Restrictions Placed on Whaling

In 1977 the International Whaling Commission (IWC) proposed to ban the hunting of the Alaskan bowhead whale. This proposal was based on two contentious assumptions: (1) the population of the bowhead whale in Alaskan waters had been reduced to fewer than 1,000 whales, and (2) the Iñupiat culture had so dissolved that the subsistence hunts no longer deserved protection. The Iñupiat vigorously set out to prove both assumptions wrong.

Although a whaling ban was not put into effect, very restrictive quotas were imposed on the Iñupiat whaling communities. The immediate result of the quota was to turn whale meat from a staple food into a scarce resource. Arthur Neakok, a Barrow whaler, remembers receiving sleds full of meat and *maktak* (whale skin and blubber) as his personal share as a whaling crew member in the 1960s (interview with author, May 29, 1986). Eben Hobson, Jr., remembers slabs of *maktak* on the kitchen table every night at supper; now it is brought out for visitors and on special occasions (personal communication, 1997). In 1976 it was not uncommon for a household to receive 100 pounds of meat at the Thanksgiving distribution; in 1985, a family received between 10 and 20 pounds (personal communication, 1985).

Restrictions Placed on Other Food Species

Whales may be of central importance to Iñupiaq social life, but they are by no means the only food in the Iñupiaq diet. Nor are they the only food species to be controlled by outside agencies. For example, the Walrus Protection Act (1941), the Fur Seal Convention (1966), the Marine Mammal Protection Act (1972), the Endangered Species Act (1973), and the Alaska National Interest Lands Conservation Act (1980) are all federal statutes that allow the Iñupiat to hunt their marine resources for consumption and use, but limit or forbid their sale. The International Migratory Bird Treaty regulates the harvest of waterfowl, such as ducks and geese, which makes up a significant part of the preferred diet of many Iñupiat.

Thus every element of the Iñupiaq diet is now under external regulation. This situation is made more complex by the fact that the federal government has legally stated that indigenous peoples have a special status because of their history and therefore may hunt species that are prohibited to others; however, the constitution of the state of Alaska specifically forbids discrimination on any basis whatsoever. As a result, Alaska denies Alaska native peoples their aboriginal rights because such rights are not enjoyed by other Alaskans. In addition, although the Marine Mammal Protection Act (a federal law) specifically allows Alaskan whalers to sell meat and *maktak* in Alaska, this is forbidden by federal agencies to appease animal protection interests. The state and the federal governments have been negotiating an acceptable definition of "subsistence" for several years.

RESPONSE: STRUGGLES TO SURVIVE CULTURALLY

Responding to the Pitfalls of ANCSA

By the early 1980s it was clear to many Alaskan native groups that ANCSA held some very nasty potential traps for them. One of the first actions taken by the Alaska Federation of Natives was to invite Justice Thomas Berger from Canada to conduct a review of the act. Berger traveled throughout village Alaska talking to anyone and everyone who had concerns. He also attended a series of discussion meetings in which participants tried to develop some viable strategies to cope with the various problems created by ANCSA. Since then, different corporations have adopted several kinds of strategies for guarding against the loss of their land.

Under the terms of the Alaska National Interest Lands Conservation Act (ANILCA) of 1980, some corporations have moved to separate their land from other assets and protect it under ANILCA so that it remains outside of the commercial market. Barrow's village corporation has designated certain parts of its lands as permanent subsistence areas and has sought to diversify its investments off the North Slope.

Most corporations have instituted a buyback policy so that if individual shareholders decide they want to sell their shares, the shares do not go on the open market but instead go back to the corporation. That way, they will at least remain within the Iñupiaq membership. At both the corporate and the individual levels, the status of the land continues to be fraught with difficulties. At the same time, people remain determined that ANCSA will not become the last great scheme to divest indigenous peoples in the United States of their country.

Protecting Iñupiat Access to Whales

The formation of the Alaska Eskimo Whaling Commission (AEWC) in 1978 by the bowhead whalers provided a body through which the Iñupiat could organize scientific research and simultaneously lobby strenuously in the international arena for recognition of the profound cultural importance of whaling to Iñupiaq communities. As a result of effective opposition from the Iñupiat, the whaling ban was not put into effect. Instead, in 1979, a whaling quota set a limit on the number of "strikes" (a strike occurs when an exploding harpoon grenade hits a whale) and the number of actual whale kills the Iñupiat hunters were allowed on a yearly basis. For the first time, externally imposed restrictions were placed on this most central of Iñupiaq food resources.

Several strategies developed to cope with the changed circumstances, and other strategies were directed to changing the restrictions for the better. At the household level, members often whale with different crews, any of which may receive shares of a whale depending on whether they struck it, killed it, or were one of those helping to tow it to shore. Thus by joining different crews, household members have access to the largest possible number of shares.

At the community level, whaling captains' associations decide on the most useful strategies for each year and ensure that crews have equal chances to hunt whales. In Barrow, if one crew strikes and misses, for instance, it is meant to withdraw for a day to give another crew a chance. The communities of Barrow and Wainwright have chosen to hunt different size whales and to use different technology in response to the quota. Because it is a small community, Wainwright's quota during the 1980s was only two strikes per year. If they lost a struck whale, often they could not try again. They chose to hunt the largest whales—up to sixty feet or more—to obtain more meat. Since these large whales pass Wainwright when slush ice is no longer a problem, they use fast aluminum boats with outboard motors to pursue the whales. They rarely have an unsuccessful year. On the other hand, big whales have tougher *maktak*, and they are harder to land on the ice and butcher. Wainwright crews have lost parts of several whales because the ice broke or because the meat spoiled before they finished butchering the animal. Barrow whalers hunt for the smaller, better-tasting whales. Because these whales pass by earlier than the biggest ones, when loose ice remains a problem, Barrow crews still use skin boats which work better than aluminum ones in these conditions.

The AEWC, which was formed in response to the threats posed by the IWC, consists of whaling captains from all ten bowhead whaling villages in Alaska. Its primary role is to mediate between the IWC and the individual member villages. It was also key in gaining the right for the Iñupiat to monitor their own hunt without outside interference. The AEWC administers the quota—shifting strike or kill quotas from one village to another—to ensure the total allowable catch is effectively utilized.

Since its organization, the AEWC has also undertaken a number of initiatives to protect aboriginal whaling. These include, for example, promoting scientific research to establish the size and the health of the bowhead population, research into improved technology so that the hunting weapons are safer and more effective, outreach to other whaling communities in the United States and abroad, lobbying at the federal level for tax relief for whalers, and lobbying to ensure that sustainable use of bowheads continues to provide benefits to Iñupiat communities.

As of 1989, the IWC recognized the AEWC's claims that the bowhead population was several times larger than the scientists' original estimate. At the same time, they recognized that Iñupiaq whaling could not simply be dismissed as a kind of weekend trophy hunt, and they accepted the view that Iñupiaq whaling and Iñupiaq culture are closely bound together. On the basis of these findings, the quota has been regularly raised over the past several years as the bowhead population continues to increase.

On the other hand, some individuals and crews have stopped whaling, and others stay out on the ice after the quotas have been reached to protest this interference with their aboriginal right to hunt for subsistence. These protesters claim that neither the IWC nor the AEWC has the right to prohibit a subsistence hunt, and so they refuse to comply. For the most part, however, the AEWC is regarded locally as an effective political instrument, and although one never knows what the future will bring, whaling did not seem to be as threatened an activity in the late 1990s as it did in the early 1980s.

Overcoming External Threats to Subsistence

With regard to the large number of regulations imposed by governments to safeguard wildlife species, the Iñupiat fully agree with the need to maintain the health of animal populations. The autonomy of the hunter and the special relationship existing between humans and animals, however, is felt to be threatened by such impositions which, in some cases (as with the bowhead whale in 1977), are not scientifically justified concerns. In addition, the irony of the threat to animal habitats posed by what is perceived as relatively unrestricted industrial development does not go unnoticed: offshore oil exploration, for instance, is thought to be much more threatening to the health of the bowhead population than Iñupiaq whaling. A number of hunters feel vulnerable: "We are the endangered species!" one man remarked after a recent meeting (personal communication, 1981).

People exercise many ways of dealing with restrictions. Some have avoided the conditions by more or less discreetly ignoring the externally imposed regulations and going about their business. Others have said, "We will not whale while this quota business is around" (personal communications, 1983), not wishing to break some rules in order not to break others. People have attacked the imposed conditions by openly defying them, by appearing at hearings repeatedly to testify against both regulations and development schemes, and by going to court. This, in itself, is a cause of added tension. Having to fight for one's rights in an intensely adversarial setting requires breaking Iñupiat cultural rules concerning harmony and cooperation. Some have indicated that balancing both worlds is difficult but can be done (personal communications, 1982). For others, however, the pain runs very deep, and there are many men in Barrow who hunt with joy and find it difficult to stay in town. According to Attungana, "We need to be in harmony today, making it easier concerning our animals."[14]

FOOD FOR THOUGHT

Iñupiat still say, "I am Iñupiaq; I eat Iñupiaq food." And they still say that the best part of living in a village is the way people share. The core of sharing is hunted food, however, and hunting is threatened from many directions. As with many other arctic peoples, the Iñupiat are faced with regulations over every aspect of their lives. It is no longer true that "if you can get out there, you can go hunting," as Ernest Kignak said not very long ago. The land may be off limits, and regulations cover the harvest of all of the animals hunted by the Iñupiat. These regulations not only make it difficult to live, they also create tensions between people.

Local strategies have been highly organized, both within the region and across regional boundaries. The AEWC, which brings all bowhead whaling villages together, has been an effective lobby internationally; local whaling captains' associations have met regularly to respond to changing local conditions. In terms of the problems contained within ANCSA, corporations have come together to try to avert some of the biggest threats to their members' title to land. Corporations continue to find themselves in the contradictory position of being responsible for protecting the land and for finding resources to generate a profit. It is impossible to live without access to significant amounts of money. It costs money to heat houses in town and it costs money to go hunting. Over the past twenty years, many jobs have been increasingly professionalized, so that it is more and more difficult to use work as one of several subsistence strategies.

The harvest of animals is regulated—often by agencies located far away—and people are increasingly concerned about the habitat itself in which animals and people live. There is evidence of changing climatic conditions in Arctic Alaska, and it is not at all clear to what extent the environment the Iñupiat have so skillfully adapted to over thousands of years will continue to support the relationship between human and animals that has been the center of Iñupiaq social life.

Questions

1. The Iñupiat have been in contact with non-Iñupiat for hundreds of years. What is different about the contact they have had with non-Iñupiat in the twentieth century?

2. Are the problems the Alaskan Iñupiat face basically the same as the ones confronting the Inuit in Canada or Siberia? Compare any two Inuit groups in terms of one or two issues they face and the strategies they have developed to address them.

3. Why is whaling so important to the Iñupiat?

4. Should indigenous peoples in Alaska be able to hunt animals that no one else is allowed to hunt?

5. What are some of the ways in which the Inuit have been represented on film? Do you think these images have anything to do with their own lives?

NOTES

1. Patrick Attungana, Address to the Alaska Eskimo Whaling Commission, in *Uiniq: The Open Lead*, trans. James Nageak. April 1(2): 16, 1986.

2. In S. B. Day, *Tuluak and Amaulik: Dialogs on Death and Dying with Inuit Eskimo of Point Barrow and Wainwright, Alaska* (Minneapolis: University of Minnesota, Bell Museum of Pathobiology, 1973), 75.

3. Attungana, Address, 16.

4. Ibid., 17.

5. In Barbara Bodenhorn, *Documenting Inupiat Family Relationships in Changing Times*, vol. 1 of *Family Strengths* (North Slope Borough, Barrow, Alaska: Iñupiaq History, Language and Culture Commission, 1988).

6. In William Oquilluk, *The People of Kauwerak: Legends of the Northern Eskimo* (Anchorage: Alaska Pacific University Press, 1981), 150.

7. North Slope Borough, *1993/1994 Economic Profile and Census Report*, vol. viii, Barrow, Alaska: North Slope Borough Department of Planning and Community Services, 5–15.

8. Ibid.

9. Ibid., 46.

10. In Bodenhorn, *Documenting Iñupiat Family Relationships in Changing Times*, 17.

11. Thomas R. Berger, *Village Journey: The Report of the Alaska Native Review Commission* (New York: Hill and Wang, 1985), 6.

12. Ibid.

13. Ibid.

14. Attungana, Address.

RESOURCE GUIDE

Published Literature

Berger, Thomas R. *Village Journey: The Report of the Alaska Native Review Commission.* New York: Hill and Wang, 1985.

Blackman, Margaret. *Sadie Brower Neakok: An Iñupiaq Woman.* Seattle: University of Washington Press, 1989.

Chance, Norman A. *The Iñupiat and Arctic Alaska: An Ethnography of Development.* Toronto: Holt, Rinehart and Winston, 1990.

Fienup-Riordan, Ann. *Freeze Frame: Alaska Eskimos in the Movies.* Seattle: University of Washington Press, 1995.

Nelson, Richard. *Shadow of the Hunter: Stories of Eskimo Life.* Chicago: University of Chicago Press, 1980.

Tukummiaq, and T. Lowenstein. *The Things That Were Said of Them: Shaman Stories and Oral Histories of the Tikigaq People.* Berkeley: University of California Press, 1993.

Videos

Umiaq: the Making of a Skin Boat. Barrow, Alaska: Alaska Eskimo Whaling Commission.

Internet and WWW Sites

"Gifts from Whales," Bill Hess, 1998
http://www.nativepeoples.com/np_features/. . . s/1998_summer_article/whales_fe

Ilisagvik College
http://ilisagvik.co.north-slope.ak.us/

Iñupiaq History, Language and Culture Commission
http://www.co.north-slope.ak.us/ihlc

North Slope Borough
http://www.co.north-slope.ak.us

Nuiqsut Arctic Resources
http://www.nsbsd.k12.ak.us/nuiweb/kjreso.htm

"Subsistence in Alaska," 1995
http://www.ptialaska.net/~outdoor1/images/subak.html

"Whaling Rights in Alaska," Demarus Tevuk
weber.u.washington.edu/~rural/fieldnotes/detevukpaper.html

Organization

North Slope Borough Planning Department
P.O. Box 69
Barrow, Alaska 99723
Telephone: (907) 852–0320
Fax: (907) 852–0322

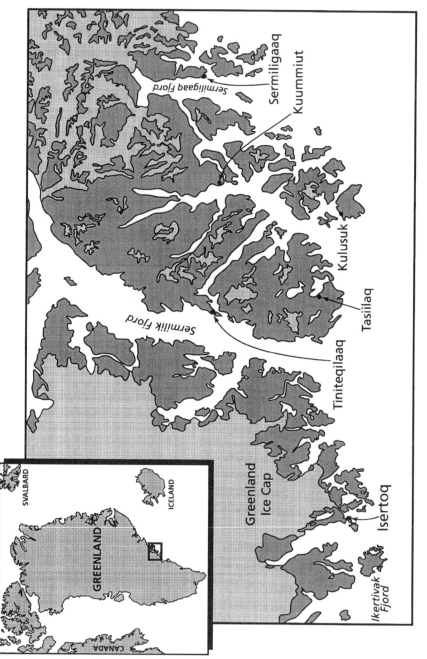

The territory of the Isertormeeq and neighboring communities, East Greenland.

9

The Isertormeeq of East Greenland

Grete K. Hovelsrud-Broda

CULTURAL OVERVIEW

The People

The Isertormeeq are an Inuit people from the village of Isertoq, in the Ammassalik District on the eastern coast of Greenland. There are five other villages in the district: Tiniteligaaq, Sermiligaap, Kulusuk, Kuummiut, and Ikkatteq, and one town, Tasiilaq (previously called Ammassalik). The ancestors of the Isertormeeq most likely arrived in the area during the thirteenth or fourteenth century. The traditional house forms, their small clustered winter settlements, the harpoon types, and other items of material culture of the East Greenlanders are nearly identical to those of the prehistoric Inugsuk people who lived in western and northwestern Greenland.

Although the area surrounding the island of Isertoq has been occupied for centuries, the first officially recorded settlement of Isertoq is 1909, when a family of eleven occupied one stone and turf house during that winter. Isertoq was an attractive place to live because of the local abundance of seals, polar bears, and narwhal, which fulfilled the needs of food, clothing, and materials for shelter. The population increased steadily from 1909 until the 1980s. The local population has fluctuated from year to year until the early 1970s, reflecting the seasonal seminomadic migratory patterns of the residents. Since 1990 the population has stabilized to about 170 inhabitants living in thirty-seven households. There are approximately 3,000 East Greenlanders today, who occupy the coast from Isertoq to Ittoqqortoormiit.

The language spoken by East Greenlanders, Tunumiit, belongs to the Eskimo-Aleut language family and is similar to that spoken in the Canadian

Arctic, among some of the Alaskan native groups, and in parts of the Russian North.

The Setting

The village of Isertoq is approximately 50 miles west-southwest of the town of Tasiilaq. To the north, Isertoq faces the Greenland ice cap which climbs to more than 10,000 feet above sea level, and to the south it is exposed to the North Atlantic Ocean. To the east, the village is sheltered by many islands, inlets, and fiords that freeze over for long periods of time yet are the habitat of ringed seals and some fish species throughout the year. To the west, many islands and the large and virtually impenetrable fiord of Ikertivaq separate the village from the Greenland ice cap. The exposed land where the Isertormeeq live is just a small, narrow strip between the ice cap and the Atlantic Ocean.

Isertoq, at 65 degrees north latitude, is close to the Arctic Circle and thus has sunlight throughout the year; however, the days in the winter are quite short, with only three hours of sunlight on the winter solstice (December 21). Conversely, the days are long in the summer, with twenty hours of sunlight on the summer solstice (June 21). The seasons are marked by very short spring and fall seasons, heavy snowfalls in the winter, and dry summers. The village is frequently exposed to extreme weather conditions. Dry high-velocity winds (called *piteraq* in the East Greenland language), forming on the Greenland ice cap and with speeds of up to 180 miles per hour, can occur year round. Storms from the southeast (*neqqajaq*) bring heavy snow or rain.

Other than occasional foxes, arctic hare, and domesticated sled dogs, the only mammals found on land around Isertoq are polar bears. The sea, however, is rich in marine mammals, with seals the most abundant. The most important seal species for the Isertormeeq is the ringed seal. Other species include the hooded seal, the bearded seal, and the harp seal. Only a few walrus are seen each year, but small schools of beluga occasionally travel through the area. The narwhal is a more frequent, but seasonal, visitor as is the minke whale, which appears only during the summer.

Traditional Subsistence Strategies

We are still seal hunters deep inside. Sealing is one of the foundations for our culture and history. In the past—still not so far in the past—seal hunting was the basis for the very existence for us Kalaallit (Greenlanders). Without seals—no survival. Seals gave us food, clothing, footwear, housing, heat, light, tools and other articles for everyday use, toys and decoration. Seals were crucial in how we see the world, and in our myth of creation.

—Paviâraq Heilman, minister of fisheries, Greenland.[1]

Isertormeeq hunter readies his dog team for seal hunting on the spring sea ice.

The subsistence strategies of the Isertormeeq in the 1990s resembled those of the 1890s. One important aspect of these strategies, both in the past and in the present, is their thorough knowledge of the local environment, the behavior and ecology of the animals, and the preparation of foodstuffs and skins. The Isertormeeq still live close to their natural environment and continue to rely on locally available natural resources for their nutrition.

Seals have always been the main resource taken in their subsistence activities, both for the meat and the pelts. Seal meat consumed on a daily basis represents the main source of protein and essential nutrition for most Isertormeeq. "To eat seal meat is to be a Kalaallit [Greenlander]," the Isertormeeq often say. Also, the diet of more than 350 sled dogs in the village consists mainly of seal meat. In addition to seals, the Isertormeeq hunt various kinds of birds, walrus, narwhal, beluga, and polar bear, and they fish for salmon, arctic char, polar cod, and a number of other marine species.

The women gather berries, plants, shellfish, and birds' eggs. The eggs and shellfish are usually consumed immediately, but the berries and plants are soaked in seal oil and stored for winter consumption. "For us Kalaallit, berries and plants are our vegetables," they say. About forty different plant and animal species are consumed regularly in the village. The country food is supplemented with a wide variety of store-bought foods.

One of the main differences between past and the present subsistence is in the technology currently employed in hunting and gathering. Traditionally, hunters used kayaks covered with sealskin and used dog sleds and harpoons made from drift wood, bone, and ivory. Likewise, women's tools for flensing seals and preparing the skins were made from bone, driftwood, and ivory—all locally available materials. The technology began changing with the arrival of the Danish colonizers, but only up to a point, for not all the traditional technology has been replaced by imports. In the 1990s, a hunter uses a mixture of traditional items, such as harpoons and dog sleds, and imports, such as fiberglass skiffs, outboard engines, high-powered rifles, and seal nets. The women also utilize a combination of locally made traditional and imported tools in processing skins and meat.

Social and Political Organization

Currently, the basic social unit in Isertoq is the nuclear family, and the extended family plays an important role in the social life of the members of each household. Prior to contact, with Europeans, the East Greenland nuclear family lived in stone and turf houses in the winter, shared most often with extended family members (and sometimes with non–family members). "It was so still and warm in those houses. A *piteraq* could be blowing outside, but inside it was quiet," older people recall (personal communication, Biate Gadegaard, 1994).

Food was always shared with everyone living in the same house, and it was shared with anyone who was hungry. "Nobody is hungry when others have food," people say. Generosity is a trait that has often been used to describe the Inuit in general. People continue to share their country food readily with others; sharing of country foods creates and maintains social relationships which remain important to the community today.

Traditionally there was no formal authority or political figure among the Isertormeeq. It was an egalitarian society. In the past and the present alike, a skilled person is respected, as is an elder with great experience. There is no doubt that, in the past, some people may have had a higher status than others—especially a person who was a particularly successful hunter or an *angakok* (shaman). Today this has changed because Greenland follows the Danish democratic system with elected officials and formally constituted council meetings at all levels of government. It is, however, often difficult to arrive at consensus at the village council meetings because people are reluctant to make a decision on behalf of someone else. This reflects a strong belief in individual autonomy that is deeply embedded in the East Greenlandic culture: "You must not ask me what that little child wants to do. How can I know what someone else wants?" a resident once told me (personal communication, Biate Gadegaard, 1994). Nevertheless, Isertormeeq are active participants in the political process because they have, to a great extent, adjusted to the Danish form of government.

Religion and World View

There were both traders and missionaries among the Danish colonizers, and most East Greenlanders had been converted to Christianity by about 1921. However, the original cosmology and belief systems have not vanished entirely. The Isertormeeq continue to consider themselves an integral part of the environment in which they live. The earth is seen as having supernatural elements which give life. As a result, they have great respect for the animals they hunt and that allow themselves to be killed to provide life to humans. Their perspective is one of balance: a hunter must not capture more than is needed to sustain the life of humans. To do otherwise is to offend the animals. One hunter once told a story about his last polar bear: "I came out the morning after I had caught a big polar bear, my thirteenth, and all his paws had been cut off. This was a sign from the spirits that I had now caught my last polar bear. When the spirits cut all paws off a bear during the night it means that a hunter will not survive if he hunts any more bears. I have not hunted a polar bear since" (personal communication, 1995).

The Isertormeeq believe that a person has an independent will because he or she has a personal soul (*tarneq*). When a person dies, the soul becomes a free soul and will travel, after a period of purification, to the land of the dead and settle there. Only the name soul remains on earth after a person dies. The name soul will move into the body of a newborn infant who has been given the same name as the deceased person. With the name, the child inherits some of the special qualities and knowledge of the person whose name he or she has received. Each Isertormeeq is usually given four names, each with a connection to a deceased person. A deceased person cannot be referred to until a newborn has been given that person's name.

Another important aspect of the traditional world view is also related to the importance of the soul, and it centers on the *angakok*. The *angakok* was believed to have control over evil spirits who had the power to harm people and rob a person's soul. Those souls could be recovered only through the countermagic of another *angakok*. The *angakok*'s ability to foretell the future and restore the life balance gave him (or her) a position of authority, influence, and power. The power presumably weakened the moment the shamanistic seance was over, but it was regained as soon as the *angakok* was needed again. Thus, the *angakok* was not regarded as a leader. In fact, the East Greenlandic dialect does not contain a single word for "leader."

THREATS TO SURVIVAL

The Anti-Sealing Controversy

You seem ready to let us eat our traditional food, you seem ready to accept that we introduce modern means in our hunting methods but when do you allow our economy to evolve by opening your markets for our products?
—Ingmar Egede, Greenlandic representative[2]

Since the early 1970s, the Inuit have been the target of anti-sealing campaigns waged by animal protection organizations in North America and Europe. These campaigns resulted in a ban on the trading of sealskins in both the United States (1972) and the European Union (EU) countries (1983). The international anti-sealing groups argue that only traditional hunters should be permitted to hunt seals. By traditional they mean someone who does not use imported technology of any sort and who does not sell such products for money. This point of view, which has been adopted by the EU in banning the trade of certain sealskins, has effectively and seriously undermined the market for all sealskins and sealskin products. The anti-sealing controversy remains unresolved. The main point of contention between Inuit groups and the anti-sealing protesters lies in the definition of a "traditional" hunting society.

The anti-sealing groups' protest against sealing was initially rooted in a concern for endangered species, in particular the harp seal. Later, when it became clear that harp seals were not endangered, the focus shifted toward all forms of sealing. This may appear odd if the purpose of the seal protest was to protect endangered species, but the anti-sealing issue had assumed much larger dimensions, well beyond an attempt to save the harp seals from possible extinction. Sealing had become a major public controversy and a important economic force funding other animal welfare (and some environmental) campaigns. "The seal" had become an icon for the animal rights movement.

The Inuit, up until the 1983 trade ban, were sympathetic to the protests against large-scale industrial harvesting of seal pups. The idea that animals were killed only for their pelts was in stark contrast to the Inuit's own use of the animals they hunt, for the Inuit use all parts of the seal (though the need for blubber has been reduced with the use of imported fuel oils for heating and cooking). Consequently, the Inuit initially agreed with the animal protection groups, because both agree that the use of renewable natural resources must be controlled and respectfully used. However, there is a difference between environmental groups and animal rights groups (see chapter 12).

The underlying reasons for Inuit concerns and the concerns of protest groups differ. The Inuit want to ensure their own cultural and economic survival, whereas the environmental protection groups are concerned with ensuring that the environment is not destroyed and with their own group's financial well-being. Inuit utilization of natural resources has to date not proven to be damaging to the environment. At the moment, the Inuit culture is under threat because their access to an important market for their limited produce has been closed. One might ask why the Inuit would need to sell seal pelts for money, since cash is not part of their traditional culture. This question is addressed below.

From Stone and Turf Dwellings to Wooden Houses

Until a few decades ago, it was customary for Isertomeeq households to move between summer and winter settlements for both hunting and social purposes. In the winter, extended families gathered in the well-insulated stone and turf houses, and in the summer they dispersed around the area in small tent camps. People would move between different places from year to year and not always return to the same site every autumn. A combination of yearly changing ice and hunting conditions and social relationships influenced the seasonal migration patterns.

By 1942 Isertoq had become a permanent settlement of six stone and turf houses, one of which doubled as a school and another as a church. The village became the exclusive place of habitation for local people in 1976, when the other settlements in the area were abandoned. Today the villagers live in wooden houses throughout the year, but the ruins of the traditional stone and turf structures are still visible and remind people of a not too distant past. The village now has a school (kindergarten to grade 9), a store, a post office and bank, a nursing station, and a municipal office.

Several sociocultural adjustments followed the shift from a seminomadic to a sedentary lifestyle. Mandatory school attendance limits extended hunting and gathering trips for those families who have school-age children. The deeply embedded custom of traveling at a moment's notice (to go hunting and fishing or to visit relatives) is waning. Another aspect of sedentary village life is the introduction of wage employment. People are dependent on the local environment for both their foodstuffs and cash, but current hunting and processing activities require a steady cash flow. Up until the recent sealskin-trade ban, cash could be made by selling sealskins.

With the establishment of a village, wage employment became another source of income. However, steady wage employment and full-time hunting are two activities that can be difficult to reconcile. Having a job in the village limits the time available for hunting, and it also limits the flexibility of the work schedule for both the hunter and his wife. To be successful, a hunting household must be able to take advantage of good weather and good hunting conditions that can occur at any time.

Current Events and Conditions

The conflicts created by the EU sealskin-trade ban can best be understood within the historic trade relations of the East Greenland Inuit, who have traded with the Danes since 1894, when a mission and a trading post were established in Ammassalik (now called Tasiilaq). Sealskins, polar bear skins, blubber, and shark liver were the main items of trade and source of cash.

Today, cash is earned from a combination of selling sealskins, earning wages, and receiving economic support from the Greenlandic home rule government (HRG). Greenlanders are able to earn cash from sealskins—despite the EU boycott—because the HRG subsidizes the purchase of skins. The HRG recognizes the value of sealskins and seal meat to the small villages and supports the hunt fully—despite international protest.

Naturally, we would have preferred that it was not necessary to subsidize the hunt-ers income; that sealskins once again could be sold in the world market for prices that make subsidies unnecessary. We do not know when that day comes. (Paviâraq Heilman, minister of fisheries, Greenland)[3]

The Isertomeeq household, which is the primary social unit, consists of a group of closely related individuals who share both the production activities and the resulting benefits through the distribution and consumption of country foods, cash, and store-bought goods. A sharing network, primarily involving country foods, links the households together. The sharing networks are a critical element of the social and cultural fabric of the society, for they not only maintain important social relations between large numbers of people, but also ensure distribution of a critical food source throughout the village. Thus, people who are not able to hunt themselves, or who do not live in the household of a successful hunter, will nevertheless have access to coveted seal meat and other country foods.

The Importance of Sealing Today

In Isertoq, seals remain important for a number of social reasons. For most households, seal meat is the main source of food, and sealskins remain an important source of cash. In addition, meat sharing serves as an important link between individuals and households. Today, as it was in pre-historic times, the main production activity in the village is seal hunting by the men, and skin and meat processing by the women. A typical Isertor-meeq hunter spends about 60 percent of his time away from the village on hunting trips (some fishing also takes place during this time). Women in an active hunter household spend about 75 percent of their time processing seal products.

Most Isertoq men possess the needed knowledge and equipment to go hunting. Nearly all households own a skiff and an outboard motor, and while all hunters have at least two rifles, many own more—for different types of hunting. Each hunter also maintains a team of from eight to twelve sled dogs. Since hunting from snowmobiles is prohibited by law (the noise from the machines frightens the seals), a dog team is essential for winter seal hunting. The cost of the hunting equipment and daily expenses, however, require a higher cash income than most households currently earn from selling sealskins. Without exception, people state that they cannot live solely from hunting. The needed cash is earned from three main sources: the sale of sealskins, wages, and government transfer payments (such as child care, pensions, and disability allowances). At least one member in each household receives wages or governmental support on a regular basis. Therefore, three conditions must be met for a household to be successful: a man who can hunt, a woman who can process the catch, and a cash income.

The ability to produce food from the local environment remains a necessity and also remains deeply embedded in the culture of the Isertormeeq today. The Isertormeeq belong simultaneously to a seminomadic past, when hunting was the main concern, and a socioeconomic present that calls for cash and imported technology. The problem is not just one of making a choice between two different lifestyles: the Isertormeeq are equally dependent both upon local foods and the cash required to produce this food. The reality of this type of mixed economy has created a major conflict between the Inuit and the anti-sealing lobby.

In the 1990s, seals remain the primary source of food for the Isertormeeq. They employ a combination of imported and locally produced technology and rely on cash and the purchase of imported goods. Thus, seals have three functions for this community: they are the main source of food; they are currently the principal source of cash from the local environment; and they are critical in the maintenance of cultural values and identity. To eat seal meat is to be an Isertormeeq.

Cultural Conflicts

Various socioeconomic, political, and cultural factors must be considered when trying to understand and resolve environmental problems. For example, deforestation can lead to the resettlement of a group of people, mining may do the same, or the depletion of fisheries resources can cause great problems for the people who depend upon them for their livelihood. The Isertormeeq case discussed here is not based on clear-cut environmental problems—such as depletion of resources, urbanization, pollution, or mismanagement—but rather on a value-laden social concern against seal hunting that has become an international cause. Legitimate environmental concerns, such as overharvesting of scarce resources, just do not apply in this case. A conflict has been created between anti-sealing groups and the Inuit that is based on differing views about natural resource use and livelihoods.

In the example being discussed here, anti-sealing groups have transferred their personal beliefs against killing animals to the Inuit people whose culture is founded on living directly from the living resources of the land and sea—which requires hunting animals. The two value systems are fundamentally opposed. This issue can be considered a serious cultural conflict between urban-based anti-sealing groups and indigenous arctic hunting communities.

The outcome of the anti-sealing protests, which include an ongoing sealskin-trade ban, can be characterized as an environmental crisis, for the anti-sealing protesters—although living far distant from the Arctic—nevertheless constitute part of the global environment that affects all Inuit and other marine mammal hunters (see chapters 10 and 12). Thus, the very culture and economy of the Isertormeeq, which depend on utilizing natural resources, are placed in peril.

Sociocultural Crisis

The argument against indigenous sealing rests on the idea of what is traditional. A basic premise in anthropology is that cultures are dynamic—they are not static or frozen in time. However, it must also be kept in mind that there are some critical cultural attributes which do not necessarily change, but instead, constitute the cultural core. What these essential aspects of culture are, will necessarily vary between cultural groups. For some groups, cultural identity is first and foremost connected to language, for others it may include how they utilize their environment, or how they constitute or value their family and community relationships. For the Isertormeeq, one critical cultural core value is the ability to utilize local resources, including seals. This means all aspects associated with hunting and related production activities, such as processing skins and consuming seal meat. To be an Isertormeeq today is clearly different from being an Isertormeeq hundreds of years ago, but any Isertormeeq would argue that he is Isertormeeq even though he now hunts with a rifle more frequently than with a harpoon.

This is important in the discussion about what constitutes a traditional seal-hunting household. An Isertormeeq's understanding and knowledge about the environment, which has been transmitted through many generations, is at present combined with the use of contemporary technology. Rifles, outboard engines, and synthetic clothing are all part of the contemporary Isertormeeq's tool kit. The acquisition and maintenance of such technology necessarily requires cash. Seal products are an obvious and, for some, a principal source of that needed cash. However, the accepted definition of a traditional hunting community for the anti-sealing movement does not include the sale of animal products for cash, nor does it accept that imported technology is needed in contemporary resource use activities. In fact, anti-sealing groups consider such technology a luxury and in conflict with traditional aboriginal life. It is on these grounds that indigenous hunters are being targeted by the anti-sealing protest. The problem is that this notion of traditional hunting is based on a romantic view of a pristine, primitive past, which is thought to be destroyed by the incorporation of outside elements such as rifles and a cash economy.

The reality of the situation in Isertoq contradicts this inappropriate analysis of the situation. In Isertoq, the seal-hunting households participate in a cultural and socioeconomic system that combines reliance on the use of local resources with a need for cash income. Through this mixed economy, they have multiple ties to external social, economic, and political institutions. That Isertormeeq hunters make use of firearms and Isertormeeq women make use of store-bought soap in processing sealskins are not recent phenomena; such trade goods have been in use for several generations. Their cultural and ethnic identity are connected not only to a past in which they relied wholly or in large measure on local resources for their hunting equipment and tools, but also to the present world economic and political system in which they participate at many levels.

The Isertormeeq themselves have formed and adjusted to this type of socioeconomic system. They have retained many traditional customs, modified others, or created new ones in response to changes in their social and economic environment. In short, traditions are kept, invented, and reinvented by the Isertormeeq but with a clear notion of what the traditional lifestyle used to be and what aspects of that lifestyle need to be retained or modified in order to remain Isertormeeq.

RESPONSE: STRUGGLES TO SURVIVE CULTURALLY

The Inuit Response to the Anti-Sealing Movement

Political groups such as the Inuit Circumpolar Conference (ICC) and Indigenous Survival International (ISI) have developed their own conservation strategy in response to the anti-sealing movement's criticism that Inuit seal hunting is not motivated by traditional needs but, rather, by market demands and economic wants. Their conservation policies focus on providing for Inuit subsistence needs through sustainable development—the responsible use of the resources through respect for the animals and an effective management of the local environment.

The gravity of the anti-sealing controversy is reflected in this pan-Arctic response by various indigenous groups. An ICC document, "Principles and

Elements for Comprehensive Arctic Policy," encompasses the major social, economic, and cultural concerns of the Inuit. It states, for example, that the Inuit should be involved in any decision making in regard to the management of natural resources:

In regard to the 1973 Convention on International Trade in Endangered Species (CITES), Inuit should continue to monitor and otherwise participate at CITES meetings. In this way, unjustified attempts to use the Convention to unfairly restrict native harvesting and trade may be effectively countered. (133)

Furthermore,

[T]he continuing significance of whales, polar bears, seals and other marine mammals to Inuit, as a coastal aboriginal people, must be appropriately recognized. A comprehensive national and international strategy is required concerning conservation of marine mammals and Inuit subsistence practices. (39)

One section spells out the significance of "subsistence" activities to the Inuit:

An Arctic policy must recognize that aboriginal "subsistence" is a highly complex notion that includes vital economic, social, cultural and spiritual dimensions. The harvesting of renewable resources provide Inuit with food, nutrition, clothing, fuel, shelter, harvesting equipment, and income. Subsistence means much more than mere survival or minimum living standard. It is a way of life that requires special skills, knowledge and resourcefulness. It enriches and sustains Inuit communities, in a manner that promotes cohesiveness, pride and sharing. It also provides an essential link to, and communication with, the natural world of which Inuit are an integral part. (36)

The Inuit are represented and involved in other international organizations, such as the United Nations Working Group on Indigenous Peoples, where the aim is to "shape international law so that it accommodates and reflects the fundamental values, perspectives, status, and rights of indigenous people."[4]

Some of the concerns expressed through the United Nations and other international organizations pertain to the anti-sealing lobby and the subsequent results of the sealskin trade ban. The Inuit consider it a human right to be able to hunt and utilize renewable resources, to choose the best method to do this, and to be able to sell parts of their catch.

At the 1992 United Nations Conference on Environment and Development held in Rio de Janeiro, ICC representative Ingmar Egede queried why indigenous peoples should have to choose between three particular options that others have specified: to return to their ancient ways, to assimilate, or to modify their lifestyle to combine old and new ways. He asked, "How did your Western culture develop? Not by returning to your old ways, nor by assimilation if you were not forced. A culture lives and develops by 'combining the old and the new in ways that maintain and enhance the identity while allowing their economy to evolve.' "[5]

A majority of the responses from the Inuit center on the notion of what is traditional. For the Inuit, tradition pivots on reliance upon seals—not on the type of technology employed in seal hunting. Their concern is the continuing importance of using seals and other marine mammals in their diet, their culture, and their economy.

Local Involvement in the Greenlandic Response

[We] find that not only do we have a right to live the way nature dictates living conditions in the Arctic, but we also have a right to market our products. We have experienced that entire nations deny us that right. This undermines our culture, because if we cannot market our products then we have no economy, and if we have no economy, people cannot go on living as hunters.

—Paviâraq Heilman, minister of fisheries, Greenland[6]

In Greenland, one response to the ban on the sealskin trade has been to arrange joint seminars for hunters and EU politicians in order to provide a forum for discussing the various relevant issues. Such discussions are seen as necessary because the market has been destroyed for the all sealskins— not only those specifically named in EU regulations—because consumers are unable to distinguish between the different types of sealskins and consequently have rejected all sealskin products. Topics discussed at the seminars usually include the economic and social costs and benefits of hunting, the government subsidies, and political agendas in support of the hunting culture.

For some Greenland hunters, discussions regarding seal hunting and the processing of skins focus on how to improve the conditions for the hunter and his wife. They are not addressing the question of whether these are traditional activities but instead are concerned with how Greenlanders, despite the loss of a market for skins, can still make hunting a viable profession. Other areas of discussion concern the sustainable use of natural resources and the increase in the understanding of the migratory patterns and the biology of the seals. In addition, the hunters' representatives feel that the Greenland Home Rule government must develop an effective way to respond to and to educate those who have a negative attitude toward sealing.

A dialogue is also continuing between hunters and their hunting-group leaders within Greenland and between the hunting-group leaders and the larger political organizations in the international arena. A recurring theme is the need for seal meat in the households of the different municipalities of Greenland. Ten percent of the Greenlandic population can be characterized as full-time hunters, and these hunters supply nutritious local foods to Greenlanders who do not hunt. Hunters therefore are seen as crucial to the overall well-being of Greenland's population.

FOOD FOR THOUGHT

The main issues in this chapter are the multilayered connections between the isolated East Greenlandic indigenous community and outside sociopolitical and economic events. The connections and events have a direct impact on this community and others like it elsewhere in the world. The debates between anti-sealing groups and the Inuit center on the definition of tradition. The animal rights, animal welfare, and environmental protection groups imply that the Inuit culture is frozen in time; the Inuit consider their culture to be dynamic and changing.

The anti-sealing controversy also illustrates the profound diversity that exists among different cultures and value systems. Seal hunting to some is crucial for cultural and economic survival; others regard it as unnecessary and even cruel. A lack of understanding and acceptance of cultural diversity can be detrimental to the well-being of any poorly understood or minority group such as the Inuit.

The Isertormeeq—and many other Inuit groups throughout the Arctic—still depend on the hunting of seals. This activity provides a culturally valued element of continuity with the past. Inuit society is also responding to a sociopolitical and economic world outside of the Arctic, which requires integrating with the cash economy, which represents a force for change.

Questions

1. How are seals critical in the maintenance of cultural values and identity among the Isertormeeq?

2. What do you think is meant by the statement that sharing seal meat serves as an important link between individuals and households in the village of Isertoq?

3. Many Inuit argue that sealing and access to a market for their products are their human rights. What are the arguments for and against this statement?

4. What do the terms "tradition" and "traditional" mean to you? How is tradition formed, and how does it change? Use examples from your own culture.

5. Discuss the ways in which the Inuit are connected to external sociopolitical and economic events. Make a comparison with the ways in which your own culture is connected to the rest of the world (e.g., the Internet, movies, and fashion).

NOTES

1. Remarks at the Conference on Sustainable Use, Whitehorse, Yukon, May 1998.

2. Remarks at the United Nations Conference on Environment and Development, Rio de Janeiro, 1992.

3. Remarks at the Conference on Sustainable Use.

4. Dalee Sambo, "Indigenous Human Rights: The Role of the Inuit at the United Nations Working Group on Indigenous Peoples," *Inuit Studies* 16 (1992): 27–32.

5. Remarks at the UN Conference.

6. Remarks at the Conference on Sustainable Use.

RESOURCE GUIDE

Published Literature

International Work Group for Indigenous Affairs. *Arctic Environment Indigenous Perspectives.* IWGIA Document 69. Copenhagen: IWGIA, 1991.

Inuit Circumpolar Conference (ICC). "Principles and Elements for a Comprehensive Arctic Policy." Montreal: Centre for Northern Studies and Research, McGill University, 1992.

Lynge, Finn. *Arctic Wars. Animal Rights. Endangered Peoples.* Hanover, N.H.: University Press of New England, 1992.

Nuttall, Mark. *Arctic Homeland. Kinship, Community and Development in Northwest Greenland.* Toronto: University of Toronto Press, 1992.

Wenzel, George. *Animal Rights, Human Rights: Ecology, Economy, and Ideology in the Canadian Arctic.* Toronto: University of Toronto Press, 1991.

Videos

Reclaiming Paradise, Color video. Mega Film, Klapparstig 25, IS-101 Reykjavik, Iceland (Fax: 354–1–624233.).

Survival in the High North, Color video. Mega Film, Klapparstig 25, IS-101 Reykjavik, Iceland (Fax: 354–1–624233).

Major towns in Greenland (with former Danish names beneath current names).

10

The Kalaallit of West Greenland

Richard A. Caulfield

CULTURAL OVERVIEW

The People

The people of western Greenland call themselves the Kalaallit (singular, Kalaaleq). In the West Greenlandic Inuit language, the world's largest island Greenland, is called *Kalaallit Nunaat*, or "Greenlanders' land." The Kalaallit share their island home with other Greenlanders, including the Inughuit of northern Greenland and the Iit of eastern Greenland. Most of Greenland's 56,000 people live in some 100 towns and settlements, ranging from 3,000 residents up to nearly 14,000 (in the capital, Nuuk), along the island's western coast on Davis Strait. Others live in dozens of smaller settlements with as few as two or three families. The livelihoods of people here are based largely on commercial fishing, hunting of sea mammals (especially seals and whales), sheep ranching, and government and service sector employment.

Most Kalaallit today identify themselves first and foremost as Inuit. As such, they have ties to fellow Inuit in Canada, Alaska, and Chukotka through history, language, and culture. Ancient peoples arrived in Greenland more than 4,000 years ago, and the ancestors of contemporary Kalaallit—the Thule Inuit—reached the island from the Bering Sea region of Alaska about 1,000 years ago. They were skilled hunters of whales and seals, and they brought with them the *qajaq* (kayak), the *umiaq* (skin boat), and the toggle-head harpoon. These enabled the hunters to secure food effectively from icy seas and to develop a flexible, pragmatic livelihood.

This pragmatic approach has enabled the Kalaallit and other Inuit to survive dramatic changes in the Arctic over time.

The Setting

Many people think of Greenland as a foreboding land of icebergs and glaciers inhabited only by a few hardy "Eskimos." Indeed, on the map, Greenland appears to be made up almost entirely of ice. Greenland's ice cap covers an area of about 772,200 square miles—about 85 percent of the entire island. Jets flying between North America and Europe frequently traverse this icy white expanse in the North Atlantic. From 35,000 feet in the air it can seem vast and utterly inhospitable—a place totally devoid of life or any means for human beings to survive.

For the Kalaallit, however, Greenland is much more than just glaciers, ice, and snow. Rather, the land and the sea make up a beautiful, rich, and productive homeland. The island is part of North America; at its closest point it is only 16 miles from Canada. Much of Greenland has an arctic climate, with temperatures reaching below −22°F in winter. However, its southern part is influenced by warmer North Atlantic Ocean currents. Summer temperatures here can reach 50–59°F, and arctic flowers and rich green vegetation carpet the inner fjords. In general, however, vegetation in Greenland is sparse, and there are almost no trees.

Traditional Subsistence Strategies

The first peoples of Greenland, some 4,000 years ago, were primarily hunters of muskox and other land animals. The ancestors of today's Kalaallit, who arrived about 1,000 years ago, were superb hunters of seals, whales, and other marine mammals. They had a remarkable array of specialized tools for life in the Arctic: sinew-backed bows, toggle-head harpoons, kayaks, skin boats, and dog sleds. These enabled them to hunt five species of seal, walrus, bowhead and other whales, and polar bear.

At about the same time (A.D. 985), Norse colonists arrived from Iceland and established two colonies in southern Greenland. Norse sagas and Inuit traditions both tell of trade and other contact between the Norse and Inuit people. By the fifteenth century, however, the Norse settlements had disappeared. Speculation continues to this day about whether deteriorating climate or other factors (including disease, starvation, or piracy) may have been the cause.

In the sixteenth century, Europeans "rediscovered" Greenland and began visiting in summer to catch whales or to trade with the Inuit. Later, in 1721, Norwegian-Danish missionary Hans Egede settled near Greenland's present-day capital of Nuuk and began seeking converts to Christianity. With the support of the Danish king, Egede expanded his mission and trading operations and solidified Danish colonial control over the island. After 1776 Denmark sought to insulate West Greenlanders from trading with other European nations. At the same time, the Danish king established the Royal Greenland Trade Company (KGH), which monopolized trade on the island for nearly 200 years.

Living conditions for many Greenlanders began to decline seriously in the mid-nineteenth century until a small group of Danes and Greenlanders, led by administrator Heinrich Rink, implemented changes that laid the foundation for greater indigenous political control. They developed representative councils (called boards of guardians) in which the Greenlanders themselves began again to have a voice in governmental policies. They developed a Greenlandic language orthography to foster literacy amongst the indigenous population. They also created a Greenlandic newspaper, *Atuagagdliutit*, which enabled Greenlanders in widely dispersed settlements to communicate more effectively. This contributed to a growing sense of a Greenlandic national identity and encouraged political mobilization.

In the early twentieth century, Greenlanders faced enormous challenges as changing climate conditions forced a society based largely on seal hunting to become heavily involved in fishing, especially for cod. A rise in ocean temperature caused seals to move northward and Atlantic cod to move in off western Greenland. This led to the development of a major cod fishery in the 1920s and 1930s. During World War II, Greenland was cut off from Denmark and was under Allied control. This ended the isolation created by Danish policies and opened Greenlandic society to new ideas and to the emerging postwar global economy.

Greenland's economy since World War II has become increasingly dependent upon commercial fishing, principally for shrimp, and on government subsidies from Denmark. Nearly 90 percent of Greenland's export earnings today are from one species: cold-water shrimp. Today, Greenland is seeking to diversify its economy based on market principles. Because of import bans on seal products in Europe and North America, Greenlanders have not been able to earn significant income from selling sealskins. Mining, which provided export earnings until the 1980s, is no longer a major income source. However, Greenland's government is now seeking to diversify the island's economy through a more effective use of fisheries and other living resources, exploration for hydrocarbons and minerals, and tourism.

Social and Political Organization

Greenland finally achieved Home Rule in 1979. As a result, Greenlanders now elect their own parliament (called the *Landsting*) and their own political leaders. Moreover, they enact their own laws with regard to economic development, education, language and culture, and health care. However, Greenland today remains a part of the Danish realm, and its population is subject to the Danish constitution. Foreign policy and the banking and justice systems remain under Danish control. In the end, Greenlanders had to settle for recognition of "fundamental rights" to natural resources—an as yet untested concept that fell short of an explicit acknowledgment of their aboriginal rights.

The social and political organization of the Kalaallit has been transformed radically over 200 years of colonization. Prior to European contact, the nuclear family was the most important social unit in peoples' lives; however, nearly all activities—hunting, traveling, and cooking—took place in conjunction with an extended family network. This extended family might consist of several generations of close relatives such as brothers, their wives, and children. Their bilateral kinship patterns showed considerable flexibility in organizing activities such as hunting or fishing.

In the aftermath of colonization, the nuclear family continued to be important but the extended family somewhat less so. Widespread sharing of foods and collaboration in hunting became less common, especially as people moved from settlements to larger towns where the limitations of housing often disrupted the role of the extended family.

Home Rule also had a profound effect on the social and political organization of the Kalaallit. Although Home Rule affirmed the distinct status of Greenlanders within the Danish realm and spoke to the aspirations of many for greater self-determination as a nation and as indigenous peoples, it also set in motion significant changes in political organization that incorporated both indigenous practices and Europeans institutions and processes. Among these was the emergence of Greenlandic political parties, which came to the fore in the 1970s and 1980s. Prior to Home Rule, Greenlandic politics was largely personal and regional; that is, one ran for office based upon personal qualities rather than any party affiliation.

The rise of a national identity under Home Rule contributed to the development of political parties. The most prominent party is Siumut (literally, "forward"), which was established as a moderate socialist party in 1977. In the early 1980s, the Atassut ("connections") party was formed to represent those seeking closer relationships with Denmark. The other major party, Inuit Ataqatigiit ("human fellowship"), was also established about this time by those seeking full independence from Denmark. Over time, these political parties have come to reflect growing social and economic differentiation in Greenlandic society. Coupled with these political developments is the growth of Home Rule political and administrative institutions, including municipal governments—each with a mayor and elected council—which have considerable influence over economic development, taxation, and social affairs. While indigenous Greenlanders control these institutions, the not insignificant role of imported administrators (principally Danes) is a persistent topic of political discussion.

These changes in social and political organization reflect dramatic changes in the world view of the Kalaallit over the past century. Profound changes in the environment, the economy, and society have led to the creation of new identities—hunters pursuing seals on the ice were forced to become fishermen in an economy dominated largely by industrial fishing and state subsidies. With this came significant changes in personal and regional identity—old allegiances to family and place are melded with a new identity as a Greenlander and as an indigenous person on the world stage. Differences in world view between the Kalaallit in small settlements and larger towns can be profound. Nuuk has a relatively cosmopolitan atmosphere, with wide representation of Danish and other cultural influences, a modern infrastructure, and well-established communications networks (including cable television and current films). People in the settlements live closer to the rhythms of nature in their daily lives and follow practices that express greater continuity with Inuit customs and traditions. The world view of the Kalaallit today incorporates both of these realities : in the words of one writer, they are "traditional people living in a modern world."[1]

Greenland's Home Rule status is of profound interest to indigenous peoples in the Arctic and throughout the world. It provides Greenlanders with an extraordinary degree of political self-determination and transforms Greenlanders' colonial dependence on Denmark into a more constructive and respectful relationship. Moreover, Home Rule has placed questions of language policy and cultural change back into the hands of Greenlanders themselves. Today, the West Greenlandic language, Kalaallisut, is widely used in educational settings, and illiteracy is almost nonexistent. The government supports an active publishing program in Kalaallisut, so one can read the works of John Steinbeck and Mark Twain, along with those of many talented Greenlandic authors and poets, in the indigenous language. Greenlanders also enjoy full health care coverage and free higher education, something sorely lacking in many indigenous communities around the world.

The quiet revolution that created Home Rule continues today. It is clearly a platform for nation building, for many if not most Greenlanders hope that Home Rule may one day become full political independence.

When I was born, my country, Greenland was a colony. . . . As an adult I have played an active part to establish Greenland as a home rule territory in a free partnership with [Denmark]. My experience shows that it is possible to change the world . . . so that we—without destroying the national states to which we belong—can take our independent and rightful place on the world scene, which in these years is changing and re-establishing democracy, freedom, and international cooperation.

We [as indigenous peoples] do not wish to break existing nations up. But we also do not wish to become assimilated into a culture, language, or lifestyle that is not ours. We are a specific people, even if we do not have an independent state. This must be accepted. . . . The key word is *self-determination.*[2]

Religion and World View

The ancestors of contemporary Kalaallit lived in close contact with the natural world. An uncertain and dynamic environment largely shaped their religious beliefs and world view. The Kalaallit believed that all animals and worldly things had a spirit, called an *inua* (literally, "its person"). It was important for the Kalaallit to respect the *inua* of animals to ensure hunting success. It was also important to show respect for such powerful spiritual beings as Sassuma Arnaa, the powerful "Woman of the Sea," who releases seals, whales, and other marine creatures to hunters who show proper respect.

With the advent of Danish colonialism in the eighteenth century, most Kalaallit gradually became converts to the Lutheran Church. Upon his arrival in 1721, Hans Egede challenged the local *angakkut* (shamans) and their spiritual beliefs. Initially, the *angakkut* resisted the missionaries, but imported European diseases like smallpox decimated the Inuit population, which weakened the authority of the *angakkut*, who were powerless to counter this scourge. Diseases caused enormous cultural disruption; as many as half of all Greenlanders died in a few short years.

Today, most Greenlanders are nominally members of the Lutheran Church. Under Danish law, there is no separation of church and state, and Lutheranism is the official state religion.

Greenlanders' world view has changed dramatically in recent decades as they have struggled to overcome colonialism and redefine their relationship to Denmark and the world economy. A change in the Danish constitution in 1953 ended Greenland's colonial status and sought to integrate it into the Danish realm. Greenlanders were to become "northern Danes." The Danish government planned to transform the island's economy into one based on industrial-scale fisheries. It attempted to do so by instituting two massive modernization plans based on shutting down smaller settlements, expanding commercial fisheries (especially for shrimp and cod), and building a new community infrastructure. However, as a result of these modernization plans, Danish construction workers flooded into Greenland, which created resentment among many Greenlanders. Many felt they were simply spectators in the development of their own land. This feeling was amplified when authorities shut down a number of small settlements and insisted that residents there move into large towns to work in fish-processing plants.

The turmoil created by these attempts at rapid, centrally-planned modernization contributed to a political backlash. Many Greenlanders began to push for a radical change in their relationship to Denmark. Said Lars Emil Johansen, then a young political leader and later Greenland's premier, "Greenlanders and Danes in Greenland must acknowledge the fact that they are two different peoples, and that we must not aim for integration of the two. Only on this basis can we achieve cooperation that builds on mutual respect."[3]

After much political agitation in the 1960s and 1970s—particularly by young Greenlanders—the Danish government finally agreed to consider greater autonomy for Greenland. It created a commission on Home Rule in 1975, consisting of seven Danes and seven Greenlanders. The commission's report in 1978 recommended that Denmark recognize Greenland as a "distinct community" within the Danish realm, and proposed a major transfer of jurisdictional power from Danish authorities to the island's indigenous people. In a speech, Johansen stated,

Despite the fact that Greenland is an island, and that we as Inuit always have been a majority on our island, we had to solve our land rights claim from Denmark through a compromise. . . . We accepted that the constitution of the nation state shouldn't be broken and thus that its territory couldn't be apportioned. In return, Denmark accepted the principle that the resident population of Greenland has the fundamental rights to the natural resources in Greenland.[4]

THREATS TO SURVIVAL

As Greenlanders look ahead to life in the twenty-first century, they face a number of major threats that could undermine the significant achievements of Home Rule. Among these are economic vulnerability, rapid social and cultural change, global climate change and Arctic environmental contamination, and animal rights challenges to sustainable use of marine mammals and other resources. The challenge for Greenlanders is how to avoid becoming victims of change and, instead, use Home Rule to promote sustainable development and a more cohesive, healthy society.

Economic Vulnerability

Resources from the sea have long been central to Greenland's economy and to indigenous culture and identity. In particular, subsistence hunting for species like beluga whale, ringed seal, walrus, minke whale, and caribou has made life possible in an environment that seems utterly inhospitable to outsiders. Fishing for cod, halibut, arctic char, and capelin also provides rich nutritional benefits and promotes enduring cultural beliefs and practices.

For us who live in Greenland, hunting and trapping are natural elements in our life, from cradle to grave. The people of Greenland have always been hunters. It is a way of life which has permeated our myths and legends for thousands of years, and has formed our attitudes toward hunting and the relationship with the natural environment. Our lives as hunters and trappers are at the very root of our identity. Our attitude toward nature and its resources is quite distinct from the attitudes of people in the industrialized world.[5]

Today, many Greenlanders continue to rely on a mixed subsistence and cash economy, in which the household procurement of wild foods, called *kalaalimerngit* ("Greenlanders' foods"), has an important nutritional, economic, and cultural significance.

However, while subsistence hunting and fishing remains important, Greenland's national economy is particularly dependent on two income sources: commercial fisheries, particularly for shrimp, and subsidies from Denmark. In 1995, for example, Greenland earned fully 94 percent of its export income from fisheries.[6] Seventy-eight percent of that came from shrimp alone. Biologists are increasingly concerned that shrimp and several other fish resources in Greenland are being caught at maximum possible levels. Moreover, Greenlanders know well how vulnerable these resources are to sudden and rather dramatic changes, for climate has long played a major role in shaping Greenlandic livelihoods.

Climate certainly played a significant role, in the eleventh and twelfth centuries, in the demise of Norse colonists who found they could not sustain their imported way of life under a regime of cooler temperatures and declining agricultural productivity. In the early twentieth century, rising ocean temperatures brought a massive influx of Atlantic cod into Greenlandic waters. This change caused the seals, upon which many Greenlandic hunters depended, to move farther north. Such changes forced many Greenlanders, particularly those in southern Greenland, to shift their livelihoods from seal hunting to the burgeoning cod fishery. In the 1970s and 1980s, changing ecological conditions and intense fishing activity, which led to the near disappearance of cod along Greenlandic coasts, contributed to yet another rapid change. Were Greenland's shrimp stocks to suffer the same fate as the cod, the island's economy could be devastated and its hopes for greater economic autonomy dashed.

Greenland is also highly dependent upon subsidies from the Danish state. Denmark provides 46 percent of Greenland's gross domestic product, (about US $500 million) each year in the form of block grants for government services and for activities of Danish authorities in Greenland (such as operating the justice system).[7] The significance of these subsidies increased in recent years because of a lagging economy. While the amount of these Danish subsidies is not expected to change dramatically in the short term, their prominence in the Greenlandic economy adds to the problem of economic vulnerability. Should Denmark decide to make significant cutbacks in these subsidies, Greenland's economy would almost certainly suffer. Moreover, the significance of these subsidies raises a critical question: Is it enough for indigenous peoples to have political self-determination without having a significant measure of economic autonomy? Greenlandic politicians are acutely aware of this question and are moving diligently to do all they can to diversify the island's economy.

Rapid Social and Cultural Change

Economic vulnerability goes hand in hand with Greenland's growing interaction with the global economy. This interaction leads to rapid social and cultural changes that can bring both opportunities and costs. Greenlanders now enjoy access to global markets and goods, new technologies, educational enrichment, and enhanced health care. However, interaction with the global economy also has had significant costs. Among these are pressures on the indigenous language (Kalaallisut), out-migration from small settlements to larger communities, changing gender relationships, new demands from wage employment, changing identity (especially for young people), and mass consumerism promoted by global media. These pressures have created, at times, uncertainty, anxiety, and serious social consequences.

In the years leading up to Home Rule in 1979, Greenlanders experienced a period of profound change over which they felt little control. Danish modernization programs of the 1950s and 1960s included shutting down many small settlements so that residents there could become workers in fish-processing plants in larger communities. However, many Greenlanders resented these efforts, arguing that these smaller settlements were the repositories of enduring Greenlandic cultural traditions and practices. The government's decision to move the 1,200 residents in the settlement of Qullissat in Disko Bay in 1971 caused widespread anger. It offered to sell the entire community. A newspaper at the time noted, "If you've always dreamed about buying an entire community, now is your chance. No sooner had the last resident left Qullissat . . . was the town put up for sale. This is the first time in Greenland's history that an entire town is available for sale. It will be exciting to see how much . . . will be paid for the town; we are undoubtedly talking about millions."[8]

The heavy-handed approach taken by the government in this and other situations soon came to symbolize the need for Home Rule. During the same period, use of Kalaallisut, the Greenlandic language, suffered while teachers emphasized teaching the Danish language in school as a means of integrating Greenlanders into the Danish realm. This too provoked a strong reaction; many younger Greenlanders felt their language and culture were being taken away without their consent.

Home Rule enabled Greenlanders to stop these extreme measures, and yet many Greenlanders continue to struggle with similar issues of rapid social and cultural change. Today, a slow shift of Greenland's population from smaller settlements to larger towns continues even though government policy is to maintain and support settlements. For example, the percentage of Greenlanders living in larger towns has increased from 58 percent in 1960 to 80 percent in the 1990s.[9] Today, almost half of the population lives in the three largest towns of Nuuk, Sisimiut, and Ilulissat. Those moving from smaller settlements to larger towns often must endure a move from a small, closely knit society to the more anonymous feeling of "city life." Often they no longer have access to subsistence resources that were close at hand in settlements. Moreover, finding housing in larger communities is not easy. Many are forced to move from a single-family dwelling into a large apartment complex that contributes to alienation from one's surroundings. Some families find they must wait years before they can secure a larger apartment or a home.

The growing urbanization of Greenlandic life also influences gender roles. Men who were used to being providers of subsistence foods for their family may find it more difficult to procure those foods near larger towns. And while opportunities to make a living as a small-scale hunter or fisher stagnate, wage employment opportunities—such as working on a fishing trawler—may require being away from family for extended periods. These realities can contribute to anxiety and alienation. In contrast, women are a growing part of the Greenlandic workforce; they find jobs in fish processing, in public administration, and in the service sector. Many end up double-shifting, they earn wages during the day and continue to be primary caregivers for children, processors of subsistence foods, and homemakers.

These changes contribute to the problems of alcohol abuse, domestic violence, and suicide, which occur at high rates in Greenland. While the health care system has improved significantly since the 1950s, deaths from accidents (especially involving alcohol), homicide, and suicide have increased. Life expectancy for women has increased significantly during this period but not for men, primarily as a result of increases in alcohol-related accidents and suicide. These nonnatural deaths account for more than 30 percent of the total for men—an extraordinarily high level compared with Denmark or other industrialized countries. The percentage of deaths by suicide has increased more than tenfold since the 1950s, and incidents of sexual assault against family members have doubled. Fortunately, per capita consumption of alcohol seems to be on the decline in Greenland, from a high of 23 quarts in 1987 to about 13.5 quarts in 1995.[10]

Global Change and Industrial Contaminants in Arctic Foods

Another major threat facing Greenlanders in the twenty-first century comes from global change and environmental contaminants in arctic foods. Global change issues include potential effects of global warming on Greenlandic communities and the impacts of increased ultraviolet radiation through ozone depletion. These changes are linked to greenhouse gas emissions and to the production of chlorofluorcarbons (CFCs), particularly in industrialized countries. While the seriousness of this problem is difficult to gauge, the Intergovernmental Panel on Climate Change (IPCC) believes that continued increases in global temperatures at current rates could raise the average global air temperature between 1.8° and 6.3°F by 2100. Should this occur, Greenlanders could experience melting of their enormous ice cap and an associated rise in sea levels. They may see changes in winds, water currents, and sea ice. Significant changes in sea ice could alter migration routes of bowhead whales, harp seals, and other animals. Unstable sea ice could also make ice-edge hunting more difficult and dangerous.

A thinning ozone layer raises concern about plants and animals (including humans) that could be damaged by increased ultraviolet (UV) radiation. As with climate change, the impacts of increased UV radiation are unclear. Studies suggest, however, that increased radiation could slow nutrient cycling in plants and perhaps damage zooplankton and fish.

Greenlanders are also concerned about increases in industrial contaminants in their foods, particularly wild meat and fish, which are renewable resources. These foods, rich in protein, vitamins, and essential elements, provide a substantial portion of Greenlanders' energy requirements and a healthy nutritional foundation for life in a demanding environment. Scientists believe the high consumption of fish and marine mammals by Greenlanders and other arctic peoples contribute to lower incidences of heart disease. These foods are also valued culturally; they are the focus of traditional hunting and fishing activities and of systems of sharing and exchange.

The sources of contaminants in arctic foods are almost entirely found in the industrialized countries of Europe, Asia, and North America. Of greatest concern are persistent organic pollutants (POPs); heavy metals, including mercury, cadmium, and lead; and radionuclides. These are often concentrated in organ meats of marine mammals and some fish and in the kidneys of terrestrial animals like caribou. Some Greenlanders have blood concentrations of methyl mercury that exceed levels at which toxic effects are thought to occur. Indications are that long-range transport and biomagnification of some of these in the Arctic contribute to contaminant levels as much as ten to twenty times that of people in temperate regions. Mothers, in particular, can pass these substances on to their embryos in the womb and to infants during breast feeding. Women in western Greenland and the eastern Canadian Arctic have particularly high levels of polychlorinated biphenyls (PCBs) and other POPs in their bodies, which raise concerns about fetal and childhood development and impacts on immune systems. The impact of these contaminants remains unclear, but scientists are focusing on long-term, subtle effects such as how they influence our ability to conceive and raise children, fight against diseases, develop mental functions, and avoid cancer.

Chronic exposure to radionuclides may lead to an increased risk of cancer. The most prominent example of recent radiation exposure is the 1986 Chernobyl nuclear accident in the Ukraine. A lesser-known source was a U.S. Air Force B-52 bomber carrying nuclear weapons that crashed on the ice near Thule Air Base in Greenland in 1968. Workers involved in the clean up have claimed that they suffer from radiation exposure.

In general, scientists believe that the benefits of eating wild foods in Greenland outweigh any possible risks. However, a recent study conducted under the Arctic Environmental Protection Strategy (AEPS) points to the dilemma that Greenlanders face in eating their traditional foods:

The current levels of exposure to persistent organic contaminants in the Arctic are clearly of great concern, but it is still not clear what public health measures should be taken. The dilemma is especially difficult in communities where traditional foods are vital to spiritual, cultural, and physical well-being. After weighing the uncertainty of some of the values for tolerable daily intake for POPs against the benefits of traditional food gathering and consumption, most Arctic jurisdictions still advise people to continue to eat as they have before.[11]

Greenlanders and other indigenous peoples continue to ask why they should have to bear the cost of industrial pollution that originates far to the south. Aqqaluk Lynge, a Greenlander and president of the Inuit Circumpolar Conference (ICC), a pan-Inuit organization that represents Inuit interests in Greenland, Canada, Alaska, and Russia, emphasizes that "the scientific evidence is in; certain POPs generated and used in the South are contaminating our food and threatening our health. Inuit look for rapid and effective action by states to reduce or eliminate emission of POPs."[12] It remains to be seen how the world's most industrialized nations will respond to this challenge.

Animal Rights Challenges to Sustainable Use of Marine Mammals

Another major threat to Greenlanders' livelihoods comes from animal rights organizations that object to sustainable use of marine mammals. Most seal and whale species in the Arctic are not considered endangered; nevertheless, the objections of animal rights groups are made not on biological grounds but on moral or ethical arguments about the appropriateness of marine mammal use. Since the arrival of the first humans in Greenland, people have survived by hunting. Large-scale agriculture is not possible in an arctic climate. Greenlanders believe that seals, whales, and

Pulling a narwhal ashore after a successful summer hunt, West Greenland.

other local resources can be managed for sustainable use and provide nutritional and culturally valued foods. As ICC president Lynge argues, the best way to protect the arctic environment is not to stop indigenous peoples from eating their traditional foods, but rather to encourage sustainable use of those valued resources: "The surest guarantee of long-term environmental protection and sustainable development in the Arctic is to have Inuit on the land hunting, fishing, trapping, and gathering . . . and acquiring and passing down traditional ecological knowledge and wisdom from one generation to the next."[13]

Such practices could include sustainable use of wildlife products, including sealskins and other products from nonendangered species. These provide cash for families in the smallest Greenlandic settlements, enabling them to buy gas for outboard motors, ammunition for hunting, and other needed items. However, trade barriers like the U.S. Marine Mammal Protection Act (MMPA) and the European Union's sealskin ban prohibit importation of such products. These preclude opportunities for trade in abundant marine mammal products which could form the basis for sustainable local economies in the Arctic. Greenlandic author Finn Lynge believes that the impact of such prohibitions is far-reaching: "The result of this trade barrier is painfully obvious to anybody who knows Greenland and northern Canada: disintegration of the small communities, social downfall, drinking, waves of suicides. This is no exaggeration. It has been documented many times over again and is there in front of anybody who wants to see."[14]

Indigenous peoples in the Arctic object to these trade barriers as a matter of equity and justice and as a violation of international law. When species are not endangered, they ask, why should people in industrialized countries dictate what resources they can use? Would we allow Hindus, who do not eat meat and consider cows to be sacred, to tell us that we cannot eat hamburgers? Greenlanders also point to an underlying hypocrisy of animal rightists: the biggest threat to Arctic wildlife is not hunting but the pollutants and the overconsumption of those living in industrialized countries to the south. In this situation, they argue that those concerned about wildlife protection have many larger offenders close to their own homes, so why not take issue with these much larger issues?

RESPONSE: STRUGGLES TO SURVIVE CULTURALLY

Home Rule and Self-determination

In many respects, Greenlanders are at the forefront of indigenous peoples globally in responding to threats to cultural survival. Rather than being simply victims of progress, they have struggled continually to secure control over their homeland, to protect their language and culture, and to ensure their rights to determine what course future development will take. The cornerstone for these efforts is the establishment of Home Rule itself. This form of government provides Greenlanders with a vital and dynamic vehicle for protecting their rights and for pursuing self-determination. The result of this quiet revolution is perhaps a hopeful example for other indigenous peoples seeking to overcome colonialism. Indeed, the process that led to the new Nunavut territory in Canada in 1999 mirrored in many respects that of Greenlanders in 1979.

Home Rule is a *process* rather than an end. Mistakes in governance have and will be made, and political conflicts even within Greenland will not disappear. But as one anthropologist has observed:

Despite several centuries of contact and colonial rule, Inuit in Greenland have shown resilience in lifestyle and identity. Much of this has been in the face of applied government policy. The Greenland Inuit have emerged in a position of self-determination which has allowed them a greater role in shaping their own social and economic development . . . the Greenland Inuit can perhaps make claims to be in the vanguard of indigenous rights.[15]

One of the many areas in which Greenlanders are using Home Rule as a means of cultural survival is in pressing for greater recognition of indigenous rights at the international level. Greenlanders have long been supporters of the ICC. The ICC participates actively in the newly formed Arctic Council, a body made up of the eight arctic nations. It is a strong supporter of the AEPS, which addresses issues such as industrial contaminants in the Arctic, conservation of arctic flora and fauna, and responses to oil spills in arctic waters. Moreover, Greenlanders continually press for greater recognition of the rights of indigenous people under international law. This includes provisions of Convention 169 of the International Labor Organization (ILO), which calls for governments to safeguard the rights of indigenous peoples to natural resources and their rights to participate in the use, management, and conservation of these resources.

Diversifying Greenland's Economy

Greenlanders are well aware that economic vitality, diversity, and autonomy are essential for meaningful self-determination. As Greenland's economic minister argues, "As an integrated part of the world market we will, in the years ahead, have to adapt our economic life to an international outlook to an even greater degree. The opening of the internal market within the European Community . . . provides an unambiguous signal that a closed and protected Greenlandic economy will not be able to survive."[16]

To move in this direction, Home Rule leaders are developing new fisheries; exploring for oil, gas, and mineral resources; improving Greenland's economic infrastructure (especially transportation); promoting sustainable use of renewable resources; and expanding tourism opportunities. While pursuing these objectives, they seek to increase the efficiency of Greenland's business, enabling them to be competitive in the world economy.

Greenland is exploring catches of new species and improving the efficiency of the existing fishing fleet. Recently, crab and Greenland halibut have been caught in larger numbers. Moreover, Greenland's major fish processor, Royal Greenland, is expanding its market globally. It now has plants and offices in Japan, Denmark, Sweden, Germany, the United Kingdom, France, Italy, Iceland, the Faeroe Islands, and the United States.

Greenland is investing heavily in exploration activities for oil, gas, and hard rock minerals. These resources, owned jointly by Greenland and the Danish state, are managed by a joint mineral committee in which each party has veto rights. Any revenues from production activities are to be divided equally between the parties up to 500 million Danish kroner (about US $75 million), beyond which a new agreement would be negotiated. Currently, mineral exploration activities are focusing on gold, lead, and zinc, as well as on resources in northern and western Greenland. Authorities continue to look at a possible zinc processing plant near Nuuk, Greenland's capital, that would use electricity from a nearby hydroelectric facility.

Oil and gas exploration is also under way off west Greenland in Davis Strait. Five oil companies have applied to explore in this area, even though previous exploratory drilling did not find commercial quantities of oil or gas. Interestingly, many Greenlanders strongly opposed exploration in this area, which is rich in fisheries, when the Danish government granted concessions in the 1970s prior to Home Rule. Now, however, Home Rule leaders agree that oil and gas potential in this sensitive region should be explored as part of the efforts being made to diversify Greenland's economy.

Greenlanders are also improving the island's economic infrastructure to promote development in local communities. This includes construction of seven new runways for fixed-wing aircraft, which are much cheaper to operate than the helicopters currently in use. Moreover, in 1993, Greenland completed construction of a large hydroelectric power plant near Nuuk that will reduce reliance on imported oil for electrical production and heating.

Home Rule officials are also working with hunters to promote sustainable use of renewable resources within Greenland—particularly wild foods caught by hunters and fishers in the island's smallest communities. This includes marine mammals like seal and whale, as well as seabirds, caribou, and muskox. Shoppers in grocery stores throughout Greenland today buy these locally produced products because they know they are fresher and more nutritious than imported foods. Moreover, their sale provides income to hunters and fishers in Greenland's smallest and most traditional settlements, where jobs are limited. These local markets are less geared to maximizing profits than to sustaining cultural relationships between communities and different sectors of Greenlandic society. If managed carefully, these small-scale markets for country food can continue to be an important part of sustainable community development. To ensure sustainable use of these resources, Greenland has joined other North Atlantic countries in forming the North Atlantic Marine Mammal Commission (NAMMCO). It also participates in the deliberations of international organizations such as the International Whaling Commission (IWC) and the Northwest Atlantic Fisheries Organization (NAFO).

A final element in diversifying Greenland's economy is tourism. Greenland is a place of extraordinary natural beauty. Home Rule authorities hope to expand tourism dramatically in the years ahead as a means of strengthening local economies and building on the island's extraordinary attractions. Of course, tourism—if poorly planned—can be detrimental to small communities and cultures. A challenge for the Home Rule government is to promote tourism in a way that benefits local people without disrupting their lives.

Countering Animal Rights Opposition to Sustainable Resource Use

The Inuit claims [to hunt seals and whales] are at the expense of an overlooked voice; the anguished cry of the sentient inhabitants of the deep. The whales find their own sustenance in the oceans; by what right do the Inuit expropriate the bodies of the whales to serve as their food?

—A. D'Amato and S. K. Chopra[17]

One of the most important struggles Greenlanders face in sustaining their culture is overcoming the misunderstanding of peoples outside of the Arctic about their way of life. Far too many people living in urban environments view hunting for seals and whales as a major threat to the arctic environment. These activities, closely tied to Greenlandic culture and economy, could—with careful management—provide a means of sustainable economic development for the island's most vulnerable communities. The sale of sealskins, blocked by legislation in Europe and the United States, could be a major source of income for families in these communities. Greenlanders fully appreciate that marine mammals are magnificent creatures. However, they believe there does not have to be a contradiction between appreciating them and eating them, as their ancestors have done for generations.

FOOD FOR THOUGHT

Through Home Rule, Greenlanders have achieved an extraordinary degree of political self-determination. Their struggles and their achievements provide hope for other endangered peoples seeking to overcome colonialism and to develop a new and productive relationship with the global community. Home Rule is an ongoing process. It provides Greenlanders with tools for deciding which path of development is most appropriate in the years ahead.

Home Rule is not a panacea for solving the issues of economic vulnerability, rapid social and cultural change, industrial pollution, or ill-informed opposition to sustainable resource use. Greenlanders seek to address these problems by diversifying their economy, sustaining cultural traditions and practices, and educating people in industrialized countries about distant impacts on arctic livelihoods. In so many ways, the greatest threats to the arctic environment and to the endangered peoples who live there come from those living in industrialized countries to the south. Solving these conflicts means addressing issues of greenhouse gas and CFC emissions and finding ways to reduce pollution from POPs, heavy metals, and radionuclides. Moreover, it requires greater appreciation in urban centers of cultural diversity—that sustainable use of marine mammals and environmental protection can go hand in hand.

Questions

1. What is Home Rule? To what extent does it provide Greenlanders with self-determination?

2. What was it about Greenlanders' history that made the struggle for Home Rule succeed?

3. Is it possible for indigenous peoples to have political self-determination without a strong economic base?

4. Is it possible for a hunting way of life to survive in the modern world? What factors have the greatest impact on this?

5. In what ways do the lifestyles and attitudes of people outside of the Arctic affect Greenlanders' livelihoods today?

NOTES

1. George Wenzel, *Animal Rights, Human Rights: Ecology, Economy, and Ideology in the Canadian Arctic* (London: Belhaven Press, 1991), 11.

2. Lars Emil Johansen, Opening Speech of the Year of the Indigenous Peoples at the United Nations, New York City, December 10, 1992.

3. Jens Dahl, *Arktisk Selvstyre* (Copenhagen: Akademisk Forlag, 1986), 50.

4. Lars Emil Johansen, Opening Speech at the United Nations Experts Meeting, Nuuk, Greenland, September 24–28, 1991.

5. Johansen, Opening Speech, 1992.

6. *Greenland/Kalaallit Nunaat 1997: Statistical Yearbook.* Nuuk: Statistics Greenland, 75.

7. Ibid, 67.

8. Dahl, *Arktisk Selvstyre*, 52.

9. *Greenland/Kalaallit Nunaat 1997*, 31.

10. Ibid., 106.

11. *Arctic Pollution Issues: A State of the Arctic Environment Report*, 1997, 177.

12. Aqqaluk Lynge, Remarks to the United Nations Commission for Sustainable Development on Behalf of the Inuit Circumpolar Conference, United Nations, New York City, April 15, 1997.

13. Ibid.

14. Finn Lynge, *Arctic Wars: Endangered Animals, Endangered Peoples* (Hanover, N.H.: University Press of New England, 1992), 99.

15. Mark Nuttall, "Greenland: Emergence of an Inuit Homeland," in *Polar Peoples: Self-Determination and Development* (London: Minority Rights Publications, 1994), 27.

16. Quoted in Richard Caulfield, *Greenlanders, Whales, and Whaling* (Hanover, N.H.: University Press of New England, 1997), 6.

17. A. D'Amato and S. Chopra, "Whales: Their Emerging Right to Life." *American Journal of International Law* 85, no.1 (1991): 59.

RESOURCE GUIDE

Published Literature

Arctic Monitoring and Assessment Programme. *Arctic Pollution Issues: A State of the Arctic Environment Report.* Oslo: AMAP, 1997.

Berthelsen, C., I. H. Mortensen, and E. Mortensen. *Kalaallit Nunaat/Greenland Atlas*. Nuuk, Greenland: Pilersuiffik, 1990.

Caulfield, Richard. *Greenlanders, Whales, and Whaling*. Hanover, N.H.: University Press of New England, 1997.

Damas, D. *Handbook of North American Indians*. Vol. 5, *Arctic*. Washington, D.C.: Smithsonian Institution, 1984.

Greenland Home Rule Government. *Greenland 1997: Statistical Yearbook*. Nuuk, Greenland: Statistics Greenland, 1997.

Lynge, Finn. 1992. *Arctic Wars: Endangered Animals, Endangered Peoples*. Hanover, N.H.: University Press of New England, 1992.

Films and Videos

Greenland: A Wealth of Opportunities, 1994. In English. Available from the Mineral Resources Administration for Greenland, Slotholmsgade 1, 4, DK-1216 Copenhagen K, Denmark.

Greenland: Land of Challenge, 1995. In English. Available from Isak Kleist, Box 917, 3900 Nuuk, Greenland.

Yes, but Seal Is "Our Daily Bread," 1993. In English. Available from Ivars Silis, DK 9620 Qaqortoq, Greenland.

Internet and WWW Sites

Greenland Home Rule Government
http://www.gh.gl/

Greenland National Library
http://www.katak.gl/

Greenland Travel
http://www.greenland-guide.dk/default.htm

High North Alliance
http://www.highnorth.no/Default.htm

Radio Greenland
http://www.knr.gl/

Royal Greenland A/S (fisheries)
http://www.randburg.com/gr/royalgre.html

Organizations

Greenland Home Rule Administration
Tusagassiivik/Information Department
P.O. Box 1015
DK-3900 Nuuk, Greenland
Telephone: 299 34 50 00
Fax: 299 32 86 02
E-mail: homerule@gh.gl

Inuit Circumpolar Conference
Box 204
DK 3900 Nuuk, Greenland
Telephone: 299 32 36 32
Fax: 299 32 30 01
E-mail: iccgreen@greennet.gl

11

The Kaska of Canada

Patrick Moore

CULTURAL OVERVIEW

The People

In their own language Kaska refer to themselves, and to neighboring Athabaskan groups, as "Dene." Their traditional territory is in the drainage of the upper Pelly and Liard rivers in the southern Yukon and northern British Columbia. The term "Kaska" was originally the name of McDame's Creek in British Columbia and was used to refer to the Kaska people of that region at the time of the Cassiar gold rush of the 1870s. This term was gradually extended to refer to all speakers of the Kaska language, in accordance with the European ideology that the term for a group of people should identify all the speakers of one language. The Kaska language is also closely related to other Northern Athabaskan languages, including Beaver, Slave, and Tutchone. The relationship is similar to that existing between French and Spanish, or between English and German.

The Setting

The Kaska homeland is characterized by seasonal extremes of temperature, with summer temperatures in the valleys reaching as high as 86°F while wintertime low temperatures of −58°F are not uncommon. The climate and vegetation vary widely with altitude. There are permanent glaciers in the Itsi Mountains and also on Keele Peak and on some of the other nearby Mackenzie Mountains. The higher mountains throughout the Kaska region are treeless at high altitudes. Most of Kaska territory is characterized

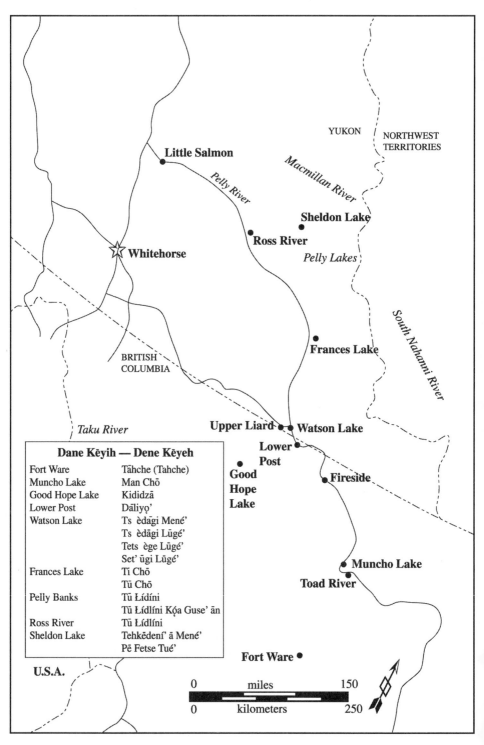

Kaska communities in Yukon and British Columbia, Canada. Courtesy of Kaska Tribal Council. Reproduced by Nighthawk Design.

by narrow valleys bounded by hills and mountain ranges. The Liard Plateau is covered with a commercially valuable forest of spruce, pine, and other species.

Precipitation, which is generally moderate, averages less than 23 inches annually in many areas. South-facing hillsides in these areas are often treeless and covered with sage and other shrubs and grasses. Since higher elevations receive more moisture, many alpine areas are covered with lush vegetation during the brief summer growing season.

Caribou and moose are the most common big game animals. Mountain sheep, mountain goats, grizzly bears, and black bears are also killed by hunters, and there are many other furbearing species including wolf, wolverine, marten, otter, lynx, beaver, and muskrat.

The major rivers of this region are generally swift flowing and punctuated by rapids that are difficult for larger boats to navigate. Early traders were forced to portage freight around the rapids on the Liard, Pelly, and Frances rivers. Only the Dease River, which was free of dangerous rapids, was a convenient trade route.

A network of major highways, including the Alaska Highway, the Robert Campbell Highway, the Stewart-Cassiar Highway, and the Canol Road, now traverse Kaska territory and connect the major settlements. There are also numerous logging roads, mining roads, and tote roads which are used seasonally.

Traditional Subsistence Strategies

The Kaska traditionally used a wide variety of food plants and animals. Plant foods, such as edible roots, berries, and the cambium of lodgepole pine, were harvested seasonally and dried or preserved for later use. Berries and other plant foods were most commonly collected by women and children, and small game animals, such as rabbits, gophers, marmots, and small game birds, such as grouse and ptarmigan, were killed by men, women, and children.

Traditionally fish of all kinds were an important source of food. Salmon were especially important in the Pelly River and its tributaries, and most families camped along the river in July and early August to catch and dry salmon. Salmon were traditionally caught in fish traps set in shallow water, or they were gaffed by men using long gaff poles. In recent times, people have used twine nets for salmon and other fish. John Dickson, a Kaska elder, recalled that his family used to catch over a thousand salmon in fish traps for their own consumption and to feed their large dog teams. Before twine nets became available, fish were also caught with hooks and nets made either of sinew or willow bark.

Large game such as caribou, moose, and sheep were pursued and killed with bow and arrow, or they were snared along game trails. Dickson described how people used to set snares for mountain sheep on the bluffs overlooking the upper Liard River:

People were living there at the head of this river [Liard River]. There is a sheep lick way out there, and they set a snare there. Sheep were coming down to the lake; they wanted to drink. There was a lake up there and beside it was a sheep lick. The mountain was really steep. In the morning the people got up and there was a mountain sheep hanging down from the snare. There was just one snare as there was only one place that was really good. When people got up, something white was hanging down. That was the place they say. (translated from interview with author, Upper Liard, August 7, 1994)

To capture caribou, people constructed a fence or surround to funnel animals into snares concealed at the end of the corral. Kaska elder Mary Charlie described how people gathered bundles of brush to place along the sides of the caribou fence: "People know that lick and they cut off that tree or willow, any kind of poplar tree or buckbrush. They cut down lots. They put them together like that. They pack it down to that lick. . . . Little tree they line it up like that, up alongside the mountain from that lick. I don't know how many miles, two miles I guess. They put them just like that on both sides" (translated from interview with author, Ross River, July 23, 1995).

The populations of many animals fluctuated dramatically, and people sometimes starved during periods of scarcity in the last century. During such times, people ate anything that they could find to keep food in their stomachs. Dickson described this situation in one story about a girl in the last century: "No one could walk around they were so hungry. They went looking for mushrooms which were stored away in squirrel caches. The people all spread out looking for mushrooms. People were not strong enough to travel around very far. They scattered all over. At that time there weren't even any whiskey jacks. There weren't any ptarmigan. No grouse. Not even any kind of berries. There was nothing. The earth was good when it was first made, but this time there was nothing" (translated from interview with author, Upper Liard, August 8, 1994).

Social and Political Organizations

All Kaska belong to one of two matrilineal clans: *Mésgâ* raven and *Chíyōné* (wolf). The raven clan is more commonly called "crow" in English. People traditionally married members of the opposite clan, and individuals who married into Kaska families from other groups, including white people, were assigned a clan affiliation opposite that of their spouse. Traditionally Kaska lived in small local residence groups whose adult members included members of both clans. Hunting or trapping partners were often brothers-in-law and therefore from different clans.

Clan affiliation structured many aspects of peoples' behavior. For instance, it was *ái*, or taboo, for a man to speak directly to his mother-in-law, or for a woman to speak to either her older brother or father-in-law. The children of one's mother's sister were called by the same term as siblings, but the children of one's father's sister were called by different terms. Older people were generally deferred to, as elders were considered to be both more knowledgeable and more spiritually powerful.

When someone died, the Kaska gathered for the burial and for a funeral potlatch which consisted of a feast, speeches, and dances. Memorial potlatches would also be held the year after a death, which is now often the time when a fence or headstone is placed on the grave. Membership in a clan also determined the events that took place during a potlatch. According to Lena Charlie,

They had a big potlatch when a Crow (member of the Crow Clan) died, Crows gave them a big potlatch, eh. If a Crow died they gave away mooseskin and everything. My mother and aunt used to do that as well. When Crow people died then Crow people ate and the Wolf people would just sit. After a while someone would give one Wolf person something to eat. They gave food to one Wolf and then finally the other members of the Wolf Clan all ate.

Local residence groups were closely related to the members of adjacent local groups; people traveled widely in the past and often married individuals from outside of the region where they grew up. In this way, many individuals were related to families who lived in other parts of Kaska territory, and even beyond.

Political leadership involved influential individuals who advised people from their local group—and others who might travel to see them—concerning social and political concerns. Political solidarity among the Kaska has increased in response to the strong role appropriated by non-natives in Kaska territory, for example, when the government proposed the institution of registered traplines, a process which often resulted in non-native trappers taking over traditional native traplines. Political awareness has increased as a result of the land claims process and disputes over control of forestry and mining in Kaska territory.

Religion and World View

In the Kaska world view there is a proper way to do things, called *Dene k'eh* ("people's way"), and there are things that are improper, which are *ái* or taboo. The term *ái* is apparently derived from *á* ("don't"). All living things were to be respected according to their nature, and therefore children, who were raised traditionally, were not allowed to play with any living thing.

Women and children also did not touch certain things belonging to men, such as their hunting equipment, fish traps, drums, or medicine bundles. Women were isolated during their menstrual periods and underwent a special training period at puberty. The practice was still widespread when Poole Field, a trader in Ross River, Yukon, made the following observations in the early 1900s: "When a girl first comes to the age of puberty she was made to go away about a quarter of a mile from the main camp and camp alone in a skin tent. She wasn't allowed to cook anything. Food was sent by a woman from her father's camp and no male was allowed to see her or pass close where she was stopped for if he did it was supposed to bring him bad luck either by sickness or in his hunting."[1] The practice of isolating girls at puberty largely stopped in the 1940s.

Kaska believe there are consequences for the violation of prohibitions. A hunter who does not bury the guts of a mountain sheep might encounter severe weather in the high mountains. A person who fails to respect the head of a bear may be attacked by bears, or game may avoid that person. There are many stories about the consequences that have befallen those who did not show proper behavior. Mary Charlie told one story about a girl who disobeyed the conditions of the puberty seclusion in the past:

Her mother went to where her daughter was camped in puberty seclusion while her husband and son went hunting for sheep on the mountain. She told her daughter not to look on the mountain. "Don't ever look up there, just sit there" she said. A long time ago strange things happened, that's why she said that. After her mother told her this she left her daughter. Her daughter thought, "Why shouldn't I look up on the mountain?" Where she was sitting was just like a tent tied up (puberty hood). She opened this and looked up the mountain. She spotted the hunters and they became still, they turned to rock. The son was pulling their dog behind with a rope so that the dog wouldn't chase the sheep. He was walking along behind his dad. The dog became still and turned to stone. The rope that was around his neck, the one the boy was holding, also turned to stone. (translated from interview with author, Ross River, August 1995)

Some individuals, both men and women, were recognized as being especially knowledgeable about spiritual matters. These individuals, who were known as *nédet'é*, or "dreamers," had special songs and helped cure people. Some of these individuals also observed special food taboos or restricted their activities because of their powers. Lena Charlie recalled one man from Ross River, Yukon, who ate only when others were not present: "They called that kind of a person dene nédahdéhi 'person who swallows a spirit.' They said he could swallow people's spirits. He would go without food during the day. He starved himself they say. Early in the morning he got up and he would eat. Then all day he didn't eat or drink anything."

Traditionally most Kaska, both men and women, had visions of the spirits of natural phenomena including plants and animals, and most kept a medicine bundle relating to their personal experiences. Some spiritual leaders were well known for their visions and prophecies about the future, some of which combined elements of traditional beliefs and Christian beliefs.

THREATS TO SURVIVAL

The History of Language Change

Over the last two centuries, the Kaska speech community and the use of the Kaska language within that community have changed. The role of Kaska and other languages in the Kaska speech community in this century can be inferred from written accounts by non-native explorers, big game hunters, and miners, and from the accounts of Kaska elders. It is also reflected in the language skills of older speakers and how they use English, Kaska, and in some cases other native languages. For earlier periods there are fewer written records, but the Kaska language itself provides some indications of the changes taking place.

In the earliest period, before 1820, there was no direct contact with speakers of English, but there is evidence of fairly intense trade with the Tlingit. Tlingit words for some common trade items such as *sunĕ'* (flour), *tāk'átl* (needle), *únē* (gun), and *etūtĕ* (bullets) were adopted as loanwords in Kaska. When white traders with the Hudson's Bay Company reached Kaska territory, the Kaska had already been supplied with guns by Tlingit traders, and lead ball, lead shot, and gunpowder were sought-after trade items. The Tlingit presence in the interior is thought to date from the period of Russian colonization in the 1790s, but it may be even earlier.

After the arrival of white fur traders, there was some contact with speakers of English and French. Kaska loanwords from French such as *lidí'* (tea) may date from this period, or these words may have entered Kaska indirectly through the native trade language known as Chinook Jargon. In any case, contact with English- and French-speaking traders was limited, since Kaska came to the trading posts only for short periods, and the women and children often stayed behind. There was likely a high rate of bilingualism involving neighboring Athabaskan languages and Tlingit, but Kaska narratives indicate that Kaska in the period from 1850 to 1898 had only limited facility in English. Mary Charlie told about one man who took meat to traders at Pelly Banks: "He was worried about those whitemen who lived down at the trading post at Pelly Banks. Unfortunately it was impossible for him to understand English. . . . For this reason he never really spoke to those whitemen, but still he felt sorry for them" (translated from interview with author, Ross River, July 14, 1993).

The Cassiar gold rush of 1873 brought several thousand miners to the region, and at least some of the Kaska in the region, such as Albert Dease, became fluent in English. Dease later worked extensively as a boat crew foreman and big game guide. Kaska in other regions were more isolated from the English-speaking miners and traders and had little fluency in English at that time.

Another indication that few Kaska were fluent in English is that some traders at Ross River and Pelly Banks, learned to communicate quite well in Kaska. The Klondike gold rush of 1898, which brought thousands of miners to the Yukon, had less effect on the Kaska than on other groups because they were not situated on the most commonly used route to the Klondike, and no major gold deposits were found in the Kaska region in this period.

The Klondike gold rush resulted in a general increase in exploration and trade throughout the Yukon. Some miners traveled up the Stikine and Liard rivers and then down the Pelly and Yukon rivers to Dawson City. There were also minor gold finds near Ross River and along the South Macmillan River. Beginning in the early 1900s, some Kaska men found employment on boat crews, as big games guides, and as special constables assisting the Royal Canadian Mounted Police. Some men learned English while working in these jobs. Older Kaska men who learned English as a second language often use both Kaska and English, depending on the audience. John Dickson, who worked as a guide and special constable, was typical in the way he mixed English with Kaska. When addressing an audience that did not understand Kaska, including some of his own children who had been educated in the Lower Post Residential School, he used English. When addressing a mixed audience or one that was bilingual in Kaska and English, he often switched back and forth between the two languages, translating for himself to echo key passages in both Kaska and English. He was also quite capable of narrating a story completely in Kaska for individuals who were fluent in Kaska. The passage below shows this mixing of Kaska and English from a story about a girl who is turned into a salmon. The passage is translated into English below.

Shāl, shāl, łūge, têgedeleh, łūge têgedeleh. That's why *metá'elīn. Łūge tésegīn, ten. Iyéh meyéhłigé' łūge ahgan,* salmon. *Iyéh dedi* last one, she take, cut his head. She cuts his head. Never cut, *"Gās, gās, gās." Kułīni et'āás:* chain. (interview with author, Upper Liard, October 21, 1989)

They were taking fish out of the fishtrap. They were taking out fish. The girl's father packed fish up, ten of them. Then his wife dried those fish, those salmon. Then she took the last one and tried to cut its head her knife made a scraping sound, "Gas, gas, gas." She couldn't cut it. She had cut into something: the girl's necklace chain. (author's translation)

Women who were raised in this period had few opportunities for employment in situations where English was used; consequently, they continued to use Kaska almost exclusively. While some of these women did learn English, especially after World War II, they continued to use Kaska among themselves.

Displacement of Kaska by English: 1942–Present

World War II brought major changes to the Kaska which resulted in a rapid shift to the use of English. Prior to World War II, there was only a small white population in the Yukon and northern British Columbia. The non-native population declined steadily for many years following the Klondike gold rush. There may have been fewer than twenty white people, many of them men married to native women, who were living in Kaska territory just prior to World War II. Kaska children learned Kaska as their first language in this period.

This changed dramatically in 1942 when tens of thousands of military personnel and construction workers came to work on the Alaska Highway and the Canol Pipeline and Highway. Both of these highways passed directly through Kaska territory. During this period many Kaska came to live in settlements located on the highways during at least part of the year. It was also a period of social disruption as people, including many young children, died from epidemics of measles, diphtheria and influenza, and alcohol consumption increased dramatically.

The residential school at Carcross, which had opened before the war was expanded, and a Catholic residential school was built at Lower Post, and a Baptist residential school was established in Whitehorse. Following the war, students were forced to attend mission schools where they were forbidden to speak their own language. Prior to the establishment of the residential schools, Kaska was the first language of virtually all Kaska children, but this situation changed rapidly. Most of the fluent speakers, those who learned the language as children, are now more than forty years of age. By the late 1950s, almost all Kaska children were learning English as their first language. This dramatic shift in a period of only sixteen years was undoubtedly facilitated by the residential schools, where only English was used. The impact of the residential school experience is also evident in the language skills of many thirty- and forty-year-olds who are able to understand Kaska well, but never speak the language. They learned the language as children before being taken off to school but never spoke the language after they entered mission school, even when they returned to their families in the summer.

Prior to World War II and the establishment of residential schools, there were some regional differences in the rate at which Kaska was being displaced by English, which likely reflects the relative isolation of some regions of Kaska territory prior to World War II. However, mandatory attendance at residential schools later resulted in virtually all children shifting to using English between 1942 and 1958.

English language media, especially television, is often cited as a factor in the language shift; however, the dramatic shift to English in Kaska territory occurred at a time when there were no television broadcasts in the Yukon. English print media became a factor in the displacement of Kaska only after large numbers of people became literate in English while attending residential schools.

RESPONSE: STRUGGLES TO SURVIVE CULTURALLY

Early Documentation of the Kaska Language

From 1942 until 1958, the period in which English replaced Kaska as the first language of children, there was little response to this threat to the language. Non-natives were firmly in control of all public institutions including the schools. Native children in the Yukon were excluded from public schools during this period and educated exclusively in residential schools. Between 1958 and 1976, native children began to attend public schools, but there was still very little response to the displacement of Kaska and other Yukon native languages by English. Some documentation of the Kaska language had been accomplished before 1976 by traders, explorers, missionaries, and anthropologists, but no systematic work to document the language was undertaken until after the Yukon Native Languages Project was established in 1976.

Yukon Native Languages Project

In 1976 the first institutional response to the displacement of Yukon native languages by English occurred. The linguist-director of the project, John Ritter, had previous experience with other Yukon native languages and soon began to work with Kaska as well. In 1978 a Kaska language course for elementary students was initiated in Watson Lake with Clara Donnessey and Joanne Johnson as the first instructors. A similar program was started in Ross River in 1986, with Grady Sterriah as language teacher and Pat Moore as linguist. The Yukon Native Languages Project, which later became the Yukon Native Language Centre, was established with a two-part mission: to document Yukon native languages and to train teachers to teach the languages in the public schools. Documentation of Kaska continued through the last decade, and language programs were added in the schools in Lower Post and Good Hope Lake in northern British Columbia.

In the Yukon, women have taken a leading role in language programs.

All the Kaska language instructors in the Yukon are women, as are many of the Kaska interpreters. One of the functions of the Native Language Centre was to develop a writing system for Kaska and other languages. These writing systems could then be used by language teachers to write teaching materials. There are now native language programs in the public schools for seven of the eight Yukon native languages, and there are practical writing systems for all eight languages.

Use of the Language by the Media

Efforts were made to use native languages in the broadcast media starting in the 1980s. Native language programs were designed to meet the needs of a native audience and also to promote the use of the native languages. A native radio station, CHON FM, trained a number of speakers of native languages, including Jim Atkinson, a speaker of Kaska, to work as broadcasters in the 1980s. Native-controlled television broadcasting in the Yukon first began with the native television program *Nedaa* in the 1980s. Following the establishment of a native television network, Television Northern Canada, which serves all of northern Canada, a second program was added, *Haa Shagoon*, which featured elders speaking in Yukon native languages.

Political Initiatives by Yukon First Nations

The growing awareness of native languages in the Yukon occurred in both a context of greater awareness of these issues in Canada generally and in the context of Yukon Native Land Claims. The Yukon Native Brotherhood, which later became the Council of Yukon Indians (CYI) and then the Council of Yukon First Nations (CYFN), was founded in 1970 to negotiate a land claim settlement for Yukon First Nations. An umbrella final agreement was negotiated between the federal government, the territorial government, and the Council for Yukon Indians in 1989, with provisions for the completion of final agreements for each individual Yukon First Nation.

By 1998, six Yukon First Nations completed land claims and eight did not. The two Kaska First Nations in the Yukon have not signed final land claims settlements. The Kaska First Nations in British Columbia are also actively negotiating land claims. Kaska elders have been particularly skeptical about the value of land claims and often voice their opposition to any settlement of claims that would restrict their traditional rights or alienate traditional lands. The long and intensive process of land claims negotiations has heightened awareness of native political issues generally. Language rights are specifically mentioned in the proposed land claim agreements for the two Kaska First Nations in the Yukon.

Protection of Language Rights in Canada

Another contributing factor to the growing awareness of native language issues has been the successful recognition of French language rights in Canada as a result of constitutional negotiations and the threat of the separation of Quebec from Canada. Native political leaders are aware of the constitutional recognition of French language rights and the high level of funding for French language programs. In the Yukon, funding for French language programs is one order of magnitude greater than the funding for native language programs. There is a separate French School Board and both French first language programs and French immersion programs from grades K–12, but there are no native language equivalents.

The Kaska have a strong desire to control their own programs, especially their lands and their cultural heritage, including language. Limited funds for cultural documentation, and for the identification of heritage sites, became available as part of land claims research starting in the 1970s. Until 1990, however, virtually all funds for native language research and programming were controlled by the Yukon Native Language Centre and the territorial Department of Education. In 1990 an agreement was reached between the territorial and federal governments to provide funding for Aboriginal Language Services (ALS), an agency of the territorial government which would provide services paralleling those provided for French-speaking Yukoners. The Northwest Territories took a slightly different approach in declaring six aboriginal languages, as well as French and English, to be official languages. The Yukon chose instead to provide services in native languages without declaring them official languages.

Kaska have taken advantage of the federal government funding for language services to have interpreters at practically all public meetings. They have also recognized the need for more printed materials in Kaska. The Yukon Native Language Centre published a set of basic Kaska lessons in 1993 and has since published some elementary school reading booklets. The Kaska Tribal Council published a Kaska, Sekani, and Mountain Slavey Dictionary in 1997, and they are currently preparing an extensive collection of Kaska narratives for publication.

The Kaska Approach to Language Renewal

The Kaska have taken a very inclusive approach in conducting their own language projects. The Kaska noun dictionary, for example, includes not only entries from six dialects of Kaska, but also from Sekani and Mountain Slavey, which are minority languages spoken within the area administered by the Kaska Tribal Council. The Kaska Narratives Project is a two-week camp with elders and Kaska interpreters and language teachers held at

Frances Lake, a traditional Kaska meeting place. Approximately 100 Kaska participated in the two-week camp, where the stories of sixteen elders were written in Kaska and translated into English by Kaska language professionals. Efforts were made to maximize the involvement of Kaska of all ages and to have representation from all the Kaska regions. Marie Skidmore, who administered the Frances Lake camp, commented on why she chose to invite such a large group of elders:

It was an elder who told me that it was important to invite all the elders. Sometimes the elders don't remember the whole story. However, the elders help each other and encourage each other. Each family grouping has its own versions of each story. It is important for younger people to realize that so that they understand when they hear the stories told in different ways. (personal communication, March 1998)

This approach of involving interested Kaska of different ages in language projects has fostered a strong sense of ownership. Leda Jules, a Kaska interpreter, described why it was important for her to listen to and record the stories: "That's the only way we pass down our traditions, our laws. That's how we know we are people. We say, 'Dene lēst'ē' [I'm Kaska]. It's very important for our young people to know their ways and that we are a little different from the other groups. They should be proud of who they are" (personal communication, March 1998).

The Kaska have gone beyond simply including the narratives of a large number of elders and hence allowing them to have a voice through their publications. At the Frances Lake camp they created, or re-created, a community context in which the stories could be properly performed. In addition to the elders and the many translators and their families, there were many people who came just to listen and participate in the daily activities of the camp. The organizers and participants created an instant settlement of wall tents set up along more than a half mile of beach front. Marie Skidmore, Kaska administrator, made some observations concerning the camp: "We were in our natural environment which was something the elders were used to. There was nothing formal about it . . . no formal structure: no place where people had to be, or were not allowed to be—no children in the corner. Everyone was free to interact. We didn't separate people" (personal communication, March 1998).

FOOD FOR THOUGHT

Unfortunately, the language programs in the schools and the language documentation conducted by the Yukon Native Language Centre and the Kaska Tribal Council have failed to reverse the language shift from Kaska to English. While Kaska is now heard in schools, at public meetings, and

Kaska elder Clara Donnessey demonstrates moose-hide tanning at a Kaska language workshop, 1998.

on radio and television, there are no younger people with a high level of fluency. No children are learning Kaska as their first language, and the second language programs in the schools do not give students a high degree of fluency.

Native people have only begun to appreciate how difficult it is to develop programs that will successfully bring about language revival. Children require extensive exposure to the language and continual practice to become fluent. Further, the language must be used extensively in the community, at home, or in the workplace, so that people will continue to use it as adults. The attitudes of native people and the larger society are now more supportive than they were in the postwar era, but the level of language awareness and concerted action is still less than, for instance, that found in French-speaking communities throughout Canada.

The possibility of providing immersion instruction in Kaska in either day-care facilities or in the schools has been discussed, but these programs do not yet exist. One major obstacle to initiating such programs is the lack of certified native teachers who are fluent in native languages. A second obstacle is the lack of teaching materials in Kaska; only a handful of very basic materials is currently available. The awareness of language issues is quite high in the Kaska communities at present, and major steps may be taken in the future to redress the language shift from Kaska to English.

Questions

1. What factors resulted in the different effects interaction with English speakers had in different time periods: 1820s–1850, 1897–1900, and 1942?
2. What was the role of Kaska women in maintaining the spoken language, and what roles are Kaska women taking in contemporary language revitalization efforts?
3. What factors exist in a place like Israel which make the revitalization of Hebrew as a spoken language possible which do not exist for Kaska?
4. One of the major controversies in language revitalization efforts, including those with Kaska, is the proper age group to target for language teaching. Some have advocated encouraging the use of Kaska at home or in day-care facilities; others have pressed for school programs. What are the advantages and disadvantages to each of these approaches?
5. In the Yukon there is a K–12 French language school in Whitehorse as well as K–12 French-immersion programs for English-speaking students. Anyone who wishes to access government services in French will be served in French. Should Kaska and other native groups seek similar services in native languages? Would this affect the use of the language? Would it increase the fluency of younger people?

NOTE

1. Poole Field Letters manuscript, National Museum of Man, Ottawa, Ontario, Canada.

RESOURCE GUIDE

Published Literature

Campbell, Robert. *Two Journals of Robert Campbell, Chief Factor, Hudson's Bay Company, 1808 to 1853; Early Journal, 1808 to 1851; Later Journal, Sept. 1850 to Feb. 1853.* Seattle: Shorey Book Store, 1958.

Dawson, George. *Report on an Exploration in the Yukon District, N.W.T. and Northern Portion of British Columbia 1887.* Ottawa: Queens Printer, 1898.

Honigmann, John. *Culture and Ethos of Kaska Society.* New Haven, Conn.: Yale University Publications in Anthropology 40, 1949.

———. *The Kaska Indians: An Ethnographic Reconstruction.* New Haven, Conn.: Yale University Publications in Anthropology 51, 1954.

———. "Kaska." In June Helm, ed. *Handbook of North American Indians.* Vol. 6, *Subarctic*, 442–51. Washington D.C.: Smithsonian Institution, 1981.

Hunter, Fenley. *Dawson 1887, Hunter 1923.* Long Island, N.Y.: Flushing, 1924.

Kaska Tribal Council. *Guzagi K'úgé, Kaska, Sekani and Mountain Slavey Noun Dictionary.* Watson Lake, Yukon: Author, 1997.

McClellan, Catharine. *My Old People Say: An Ethnographic Survey of Southern Yukon Territory*. 2 parts. Ottawa: National Museum of Man, Publications in Ethnology 6, 1975.

Wheelock, Angela, and Patrick Moore. *(Dene) Gédéni: Traditional Lifestyles of Kaska Women*. Ross River, Yukon: Ross Dena Council, 1997.

Internet and WWW Site

Yukon Native Language Center
www.yukoncollege.yk.ca/language

Organizations

Aboriginal Language Services
Government of Yukon
Box 2703
Whitehorse, Yukon Y1A 2C6
Canada

Council of Yukon First Nations
11 Nisultin Drive
Whitehorse, Yukon Y1A 3S4
Canada

Kaska Tribal Council
Box 2806
Watson Lake, Yukon Y0A 1C0
Canada

Yukon Native Languages Centre
Yukon College
Box 2799
Whitehorse, Yukon Y1A 5K4
Canada

12

The Whalers of Lofoten, Northern Norway

Arne Kalland

Whaling is among the most important skills relied upon to make a living in Lofoten . . . It is indeed important that we do have people with the special knowledge necessary in several sectors. We have specialists on sealing and whaling, on longlines, jigging, gillnets, Danish seines, etc., etc.

—Government fishery adviser[1]

In 1982 the International Whaling Commission (IWC) voted for a temporary moratorium on commercial whaling beginning in 1986, allegedly as a precaution until new stock abundance estimates were available and a new management regime for whales (the so-called revised management procedure [RMP]) had been developed. Norway objected to the moratorium, which means that the country, according to international law, is not legally bound by that decision. Nevertheless, the Norwegian government decided to halt whaling from 1987 but launched at the same time an extensive research program in order to estimate the abundance of marine mammals in the northeastern Atlantic and to investigate the roles these mammals play in the marine ecosystem. By 1992 it was clear that the stock of minke whales could sustain a modest harvest, and the IWC's scientific committee had successfully developed a robust RMP that would allow a harvest to take place without endangering or depleting the whale stock. When the IWC still refused to lift the moratorium, Norway commenced minke whaling in 1993 amidst strong protests from several foreign governments and environmental organizations.

Today minke whaling is slowly recovering, but the whalers still feel

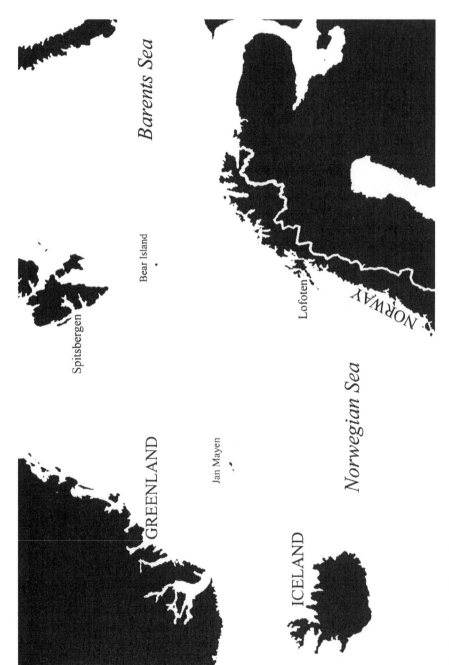

Northeastern Atlantic Ocean.

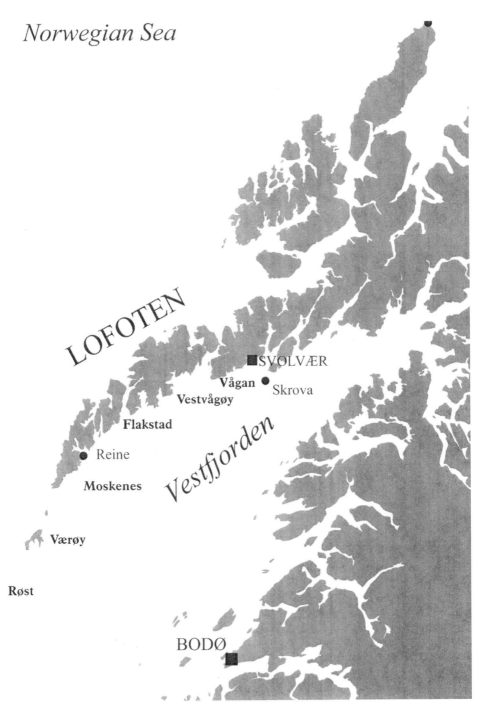

Norwegian Sea

LOFOTEN

SVOLVÆR

Vågan

Skrova

Vestvågøy

Flakstad

Reine

Vestfjorden

Moskenes

Værøy

Røst

BODØ

Lofoten Islands, Northern Norway.

threatened in several ways. The campaigns against whaling continue, and the IWC is now dominated by antiwhaling nations. The Norwegian government, moving cautiously in order not to provoke antiwhaling governments unnecessarily, has introduced severe restrictions on whaling activities, including a ban on the export of whale products.

CULTURAL OVERVIEW

> The coastal people have the fantastic ability to learn from another, who again talk to a third. And so it has been carried on. This is the coastal culture, whether it is fishing or hunting.
> —Norwegian whaler, interview with author, July 1990

The Setting

Lofoten is a 124-mile-long string of islands running from Hinnøy in the east to Røst in the west, with the lighthouse on the skerry, or rocky isle, of Skomvær even farther out in the sea. Located north of the Arctic Circle, Lofoten has a surprisingly mild climate thanks to warm ocean currents. The mean temperature at Skomvær in the coldest month (March) is 38°F whereas the average temperature in August is 52°F. Farther east, however, the winter temperature drops below the freezing point.

The islands are filled with steep mountains carved out by glaciers; the highest peak towers nearly 3,800 feet above sea level. The Lofoten Islands are divided into six municipalities: Røst, Værøy, Moskenes, Flakstad, Vestvågøy, and Vågan. Vågan includes the main island of Austvågøy where Svolvær, the Lofoten "capital," which had 4,125 inhabitants in 1997, is situated, as well as the small island of Skrova where most of the whale meat is processed. In 1988 the total population of Lofoten was 24,384 showing a slow but steady downward trend from 29,699 in 1950.[2]

Traditional Subsistence Strategies

Only about 5 percent of the land area is arable, and that only for grass to feed the animals. Most of the inhabitants live in fishing villages along the narrow southern coast and in the four outer municipalities of Røst, Værøy, Moskenes, and Flakstad where about one third of the population is engaged in the primary sector (fishing with some raising of sheep). Another third is engaged in the public sector; the remaining are employed in various industries, construction work, transportation, and trade. Trade and the public sector are more important in Vestvågøy and Vågan. Only Vestvågøy has extensive land for farming; 10 percent of its area is arable. This is also were most of Lofoten's 4,000 cattle are to be found. The farmsteads in Flakstad, Værøy, and Røst give only subsistence for a few sheep each. In recent years tourism has become another important source of income, but the season is short and the weather is unpredictable.

Fishing has always been the most important source of income on the islands. The value of the 1993 fisheries was 570 million kroner (about US $75 million).[3] In recent years aquaculture has become an important new enterprise in several municipalities. The industrial sector in Lofoten is dominated by fish-processing plants which account for 67 percent of the industrial sector.[4]

Most of the minke whalers live in small outlying settlements of a few hundred inhabitants each, which are often located on remote, rather barren islands where conditions for agriculture are poor. The Lofoten archipelago, which today has the highest number of whalers, consists of a string of rugged islands north of the Arctic Circle, whose inhabitants have always relied heavily on marine resources, of which cod has long been the most important. The rich cod fishery which takes place from January through April, has in the past attracted fishermen from distant parts of the country. For the rest of the year, the Lofoten fisheries are far less favorable.

For centuries the people in Lofoten were able to exploit what may be termed "generalized niches," that is to say, niches composed of several resources as opposed to "specialized niches" consisting of one or a very few resources. This strategy enabled them to switch to other resources if one failed. Typically, a fisherman owned a cow and perhaps five or six sheep which made the family self-sufficient in milk, meat, and wool. Many people collected eggs and eiderdown on the skerries and hunted birds, particularly ptarmigan and puffin; driftwood and peat provided them with fuel. Working in the fish-processing plants provided both men and women with cash, and children earned money by cutting cod tongues, which are still regarded as a delicacy. The typical adaptation was that of a *fiskerbonde* (a fisher-farmer).

During the winter months, the fishermen were fully occupied, but they had less to do during the summer and autumn. This is the context in which the development of minke whaling, carried out from May through September, must be seen. The introduction of new technologies—particularly powered, decked boats and cheap harpoon guns previously used in bottlenose whaling in the North Atlantic—enabled the fishermen in the early 1930s to outfit their boats for whaling with only modest additional investments. Within a few years, the new technology had spread along most of the Norwegian coast. Until the early 1950s, almost half of the minke whales were caught in Vestfjorden (south of the Lofoten archipelago), and this area developed as a major catching ground, where many of the boats were registered, and became the most important center for processing whale meat.

Whereas whaling at first was an activity that filled relatively idle periods during the summer, whaling became a cornerstone of the local economy, and many fishermen in the early 1980s derived between 50 and 70 percent of their income from whaling. Whaling, unlike fishing, represents a very predictable source of income. "It is like having money in the bank," is a typical local saying. Whaling guarantees the economic viability of many households when other resources that make up their ecological niche cannot be harvested or are subject to low market prices.

Organization of Whaling

Two important features of Norwegian minke whaling are that it has remained owner operated and that none of the boats are designed exclusively for whaling. The size of the boat is a compromise between the requirements for whaling and fishing. Averaging sixty-five feet, carrying crews of fewer than five people, and made mostly of wood, the boats are frequently owned by a group of fishermen, usually by brothers or by a father with his sons. The core of the crew consists of a group of relatives, and others are recruited only to fill vacancies. The owner holds key positions on broad as a gunner or a skipper or helmsman.

A 50 or 60 mm caliber harpoon gun is mounted at the bow some boats have a second harpoon gun mounted at the rear. After the whale is killed, it is hauled onboard by means of a winch and an outrigger, and it is immediately flensed, or stripped of blubber. The meat and blubber are cut in large chunks and laid on racks to cool for at least twenty-four hours. The smallest of the boats, some forty feet in length, deliver their catches within a couple of days, but the larger boats can store the meat and blubber in ice on the boat and can operate at sea for up to a month at a time. The main catching grounds for these larger vessels are the Barents Sea, including the areas around Bear Island, Spitsbergen, and Jan Mayen.

Most of the meat and blubber is landed in northern Norway where it is marketed through the fishermen's own sales organization, Råfisklaget. More than half the meat and blubber is processed on Skrova in Lofoten, a small island with about 300 inhabitants. In the heyday of whaling as many as 200 people found employment in the five processing plants located on the island. Not all the meat reaches the commercial market, however. Each whaler takes home between 175 and 220 pounds of meat, some of which is given to relatives, friends, and neighbors. In Lofoten, whale meat became a part of an informal economy, called *kliring* (clearing). Occasionally a plumber was paid by a piece of whale meat, or one exchanged some whale meat for a piece of lamb or some fish. Whale meat was thus one object in a wide noncommercial economic system that linked people and households together in a wide social and economic network.

With the owners working onboard the whale boats, much of the day-to-day management on land is left to the wives, who constitute the land-based "ground crew." Many women found work processing the whale meat and

Whaling boat at Reine Harbor, Lofoten.

recently have taken on a more active sociopolitical role. Beyond the local community, the wives are integrated into a national community of whalers, and they are at times surprisingly well informed about their colleagues who live at the other end of the country. Whaling is thus a family enterprise where the aim is to secure household and community viability, rather than to maximize profit on investments.

Norwegian minke whaling is thus typically based on a household mode of production, and it shares more features with subsistence aboriginal whaling than with industrial whaling formerly conducted by a number of nations in the Antarctic. It is based on relatively small-scale, simple technologies; work is organized around kinship or friendship with little difference between the work tasks or social status of the owners and crew members; and there is a widespread sharing of costs, risks, and benefits. Whaling is also well-integrated in their belief system. Being Lutherans and members of the Norwegian State Church, they have a pragmatic, anthropocentric approach to natural resources. In their view nature was created for the benefit of human beings who remain superior to animals. They also see themselves as stewards of nature, but few believe that their own fishing and hunting activities is too small-scale to pose a threat to the resources. On the other hand, their own success depends on the observation of a number of taboos that may vary from crew to crew. Few would start a journey on a Sunday; and a few would take a rest on that day even at the open sea. Some would not bring umbrellas and rucksacks onboard, and as in fishing communities throughout the world, there are naming taboos: farm animals should particularly not be mentioned. It is also a widely held belief that sexual intercourse shortly before the commencement of a voyage will enhance its success. When whaling is challenged by outsiders, much more than a livelihood is therefore at stake; it is a question of a way of life being threatened, of cultural survival itself.

THREATS TO SURVIVAL

If you imagine the rainbow, it is as if one color suddenly disappears.
—local journalist[5]

By the mid-1960s, it had become obvious that the IWC had failed to prevent the depletion of many of the world's whale stocks, and a new, more restrictive management regime was adopted in 1974. This change did not prevent a rapid growth of the antiwhaling movement, particularly in the Anglo-Saxon world. Many new nations, most of them very small, were recruited to the IWC with the sole purpose of bringing about the required voting majority to stop all kinds of commercial whaling, whether sustainable or not, a purpose that violates the aim of the international whaling convention, which is to secure a sustainable and orderly development of the whaling industry.

A Temporary Norwegian Moratorium

Responding to international pressure and scientific uncertainty concerning the whale population numbers, the IWC gradually reduced the quota for northeastern Atlantic minke whales from 1,690 in 1983 to 325 in 1987. It nevertheless came as a shock to the whalers when in 1986, apparently after strong pressure from the United States, the Norwegian government announced a moratorium on catching minke whales beginning the following year. One whaler commented, "We have completely lost control. It is the Americans who make the decisions for our country. Our politicians are so frightened of the Americans that when they cough, our politicians pee in their pants."[6]

The moratorium put several crews out of work. An estimated 246 man-years were lost: 115 man-years in whaling inself, 85 in processing, and 47 in related activities. Since whaling and processing are seasonal activities, these losses resulted in a large number of people losing what used to be the most secure part of their annual income.

When whales were removed from the fisher-whalers' niche—deleting one color from the rainbow—the affected fishermen were brought closer to occupying a single-species niche, which results in a greater vulnerability to environmental changes that may occur in the future. This was one more step in the process toward "mono-cropping"—a process which started years ago when people began to rely more heavily on the market for consumer goods. Since World War II, the policies formulated by the central authorities located in Oslo have worked to separate the fisherman from the farmer, and to place new restrictions and licensing requirements on fishermen which cause them to specialize further. Bringing the number of whaling licenses down from 378 in 1949 to 53 in 1987 was another step in this process of increased specialization—and increased vulnerability to unforeseen future environmental changes.

It was not easy for the whalers to compensate for this loss by intensifying their exploitation of remaining resources or by taking up new fisheries. Many of their fisheries were already facing overexploitation and overcapitalization and, consequently, were tightly regulated by quotas and licenses. Moreover, most of the whalers did not have the financial means to invest in new gear, and such investments would only add to the damaging overcapitalization already existing within those fisheries. It would also take time to acquire the needed skills to handle new and sophisticated fishing equipment.

Many households and communities were severely affected economically by the moratorium, but the threat was more than economic. The whaling moratorium challenged the individual whaler's self-image in several ways. For example, self-respect was undermined when the loss of an important source of income prevented these individuals from fulfilling their expectations and obligations as providers for their families. Moreover, their way of life was now questioned and their values were often ridiculed; even their neighbors began to question the value of whaling. Their wives suffered from a loss of prestige and were unable to socialize their children into a culture of which they had been proud. Some women lost welcome income when the processing plants closed; others found themselves loaded with extra burdens in continuing to provide for their husbands and families. "I live off my wife," declared one whaler.[7]

When whaling resumed in 1993, several older license holders were not able to outfit their boats, which had been scrapped, sold, or converted to other uses, but the number of participating boats has slowly increased to thirty-four in 1997, thirty-five in 1998, and thirty-six in 1999. Although the whalers are more optimistic today than they were ten years ago, they know that the final battle has not yet been won. The IWC moratorium on commercial whaling is still in force, and the whalers are facing a number of threats to their way of life, ranging from violence and boycotts to trade restrictions and ridicule.

Trade Restrictions

Resumption of minke whaling does not mean that life for the coastal whalers is back to normal. Since the early 1970s, a number of countries have prohibited imports of whale products. Norwegian catches of bottle-nose whales, for example, came to an end when the United Kingdom banned imports of whale meat for pet food in 1972, and the 1969 Endangered Species Conservation Act and the 1972 Marine Mammal Protection Act both prohibited imports of whale meat into the United States. In 1981 the European Community introduced licenses for importing whale products into the community. The IWC has adopted several resolutions to limit trade in whale products. However, the main obstacle to international trade in whale products is the listing of all whale species—whether threatened or not—by the Convention on International Trade in Endangered Species (CITES). Such a listing in practice means that international trade is prohibited. Although Norway objected to the listing of the minke whale and is therefore not legally bound by that decision, the government has so far refrained from allowing exports of whale products to avoid provoking the international community.

The impact of the restrictions on international trade is most severely felt in regard to blubber. In Norway only the red meat is used for human food, and it has been difficult to find a domestic market for the blubber. From the late 1970s, much of the blubber was exported to Japan where it is regarded as a delicacy. Today, however, Norway and Japan have suspended this trade for fear of economic sanctions from the United States which, more than once, has been willing to use coercion and threats against whaling nations. Under U.S. domestic legislation, specifically the 1971 Pelly Amendment to the Fisherman's Protective Act, the U.S. president is authorized to prohibit all import of sea products from a country that "diminishes the effectiveness of an international fishery or wildlife conservation agreement." As a consequence of this policy, processing plants in Norway are running out of storage space for blubber, which encourages whalers to dump the blubber at sea. To the whalers, it is ironic that so-called green politics let valuable human food deteriorate in one country or be thrown away, while there is a high demand for that nutritious food in another country.

The Antiwhaling Movement

It is terrible. It is the radicals who are heard. They play on emotions which easily carry people away. They believe that whalers simply are murderers, that they kill whales only for fun. But nobody thinks it is funny to kill animals.

—Norwegian whaler (interview with author, December 1991)

The antiwhaling movement is made up of a number of nongovernmental organizations (NGOs), from environmental organizations like Greenpeace and the World Wildlife Fund (WWF) to animal welfare and animal rights' organizations like the International Fund for Animal Welfare (IFAW) and the Humane Society of the United States. These organizations often collaborate; while some are lobbying politicians in Washington, D.C., and Brussels, others are organizing boycotts and engaging in demonstrations and terrorism. At times as many as eighty antiwhaling NGOs attend the annual meetings held at the IWC.

The most militant of the NGOs is undoubtedly the Sea Shepherd Conservation Society based on the West Coast of the United States. Its leader, Paul Watson, brags about having destroyed several fishing and whaling boats around the world. His first act of sabotage in Norway was the attempted scuttling of the whaling boat *Nybræna* in Lofoten during Christmas 1992. This organization has also claimed responsibility for other attacks on Norwegian whaling boats, and Watson has promised large monetary rewards to those who destroy whaling boats. This, he hopes, will increase insurance fees and make whaling unprofitable. Although the activities of Sea Shepherd fall squarely within the common definition of terrorism, the United States—the self-proclaimed champion against international terrorism—has refused to take action against Watson or his organization.

Greenpeace is another NGO known for its militancy, and Greenpeacers have on several occasions boarded whaling boats both at sea and in harbor. They have also tried to prevent the unloading of whale meat. Probably one of the least successful actions was Greenpeace's attempt to stop whaling in the North Sea. Videos of the more than 2,000-ton Greenpeace ship *Solo* carrying a helicopter and chasing a tiny, forty-foot whaling boat reversed the David versus Goliath image Greenpeace created so skilfully when its rubber inflatable(s) confronted steel whaling ships in the Antarctic.

Several NGOs have launched campaigns against Norwegian products and services. After Norway announced its decision to resume whaling, boycott campaigns were organized in the United States, United Kingdom, and Germany. Although these campaigns seem to have had an insignificant effect—foreign earnings from fish and tourism both showed record figures in 1993—boycott campaigns often feel threatening to producers and exporters alike.

In the long run, perhaps the greatest threat to whaling comes from the changing attitudes of a general public constantly exposed to new ways of looking at whales. The mass media (particularly television) feature romantic images of whales and the sea. Even in Lofoten, children have been exposed to cartoons depicting whalers as barbaric villains and whales as lovely and innocent creatures. Some NGOs see their task as an educational one. When foreign NGOs put their efforts into a whale-watching project in Andenes just north of Lofoten, "educating" people was one of their stated aims. Consequently, whale watching has been strongly opposed by most of the whalers in Lofoten.

Making Whaling Nonviable

It is people in the big cities who decide. It is not people up here. And the sea is our field and when we are not allowed to harvest, it goes extinct. And it goes extinct fast, I think, all of the existing hunting culture.
—whaler's sister during the Norwegian whaling moratorium[8]

That antiwhaling organizations have exerted considerable influence in some nonwhaling countries is clearly reflected in the actions taking place at IWC meetings. When it became difficult to justify the IWC moratorium using credible, scientifically based arguments, various other strategies were used to make whaling difficult, if not impossible. One such strategy was to set exceedingly conservative standards in the RMP, in order to set quotas so low that whaling is no longer economically viable. However, when whale population sizes were found to be larger than expected, it became necessary to abandon the RMP altogether—despite it earlier having been accepted by an IWC resolution—and replace it with an entirely new revised management scheme (RMS). The RMS includes restrictive and costly measures for inspection and control of whaling operations, including demands that all whaling operations be monitored by international inspectors—some delegates have requested two on each boat to enable them to work in shifts—as well as satellite-monitoring of whaling and DNA testing of meat from each whale to deter illegal hunting and smuggling.

Such demands are problematic for several reasons. One such reason is the problem of space on the many small whaling boats. A trained veterinarian already works as an inspector on each Norwegian whaling boat, and the larger boats may also at times carry scientists. To replace Norwegian inspectors with international ones with extensive powers raises troubling and complex legal questions regarding the jurisdiction on Norwegian boats operating in Norwegian waters, a situation no other fishery nation would ever allow in its own offshore waters. By such tactics, involving lengthy debates and introducing entirely new controls, any decision by the IWC on lifting the moratorium becomes indefinitely postponed.

These increasing demands in connection with the ever-changing RMS introduces the problem of costs. It is expensive to have inspectors on each boat, and satellite tracking and DNA samples will add to this cost burden. The IWC seems unwilling to share the expenses, and the whalers cannot cover these costs themselves—at least not as long as they are not allowed to sell whale products on the international market. So far the Norwegian state has paid both for the inspectors and the DNA databank which has been established in Bergen, but it is questionable whether the public will be willing to pay this cost indefinitely. Another aspect is that minke whaling is in the process of becoming the industry under the closest surveillance with an infringement on privacy that is not generally tolerated in democratic societies. "Am I not allowed to pee in private?" one whaler asked indignantly at an IWC meeting held in Lofoten in 1995. What damage this kind of monitoring and questioning (with the implication of dishonesty and untrustworthiness) does to people's self-respect and cultural identity remains to be seen.

RESPONSE: STRUGGLES TO SURVIVE CULTURALLY

The whalers and the state authorities have responded in various ways to the antiwhaling campaigns, ranging from attempts to accommodate the demands of their adversaries to political mobilization. In order to understand these responses, the distinction between ecological, animal welfare, and animal rights arguments should be kept in mind. The ecological argument, which is concerned with the environment as a *system*, seeks to make secure both species' habitats and biodiversity. Its proponents accept that species are utilized as long as this can be done sustainably. Animal welfare advocates are concerned with humankind's treatment of animals, including how the animals are killed, but they do not deny that animals may be killed to provide for human needs. Animal rights advocates, on the other hand, oppose killing animals because they believe that animals have an intrinsic value greater than peoples' needs for any animal-derived products that require killing or confining animals.

Whalers and their supporters have tried to establish a dialogue with the first two groups in order to find solutions that reduce animal suffering to a minimum and are economically and ecologically sustainable. However, it has been most difficult to establish any dialogue with animal rights advocates because the gulf between each side's perceptions and values appears to be too great (see chapter 9).

Appeasing Their Adversaries

Taking the international whaling convention, which provides the legal mandate under which the IWC is supposed to operate, at face value, and believing that the initial opposition to whaling was rooted in uncertainties concerning the sustainability of the hunt, the Norwegian government has spent a large amount of money on research to provide scientific evidence that whale resources of direct interest to Norwegian whalers were not depleted and could sustain controlled harvests. Sighting surveys have been an important part of this research, and whalers and their boats have been used extensively in this task.

Only when this research clearly indicated that the stocks of minke whales in the northeastern Atlantic could sustain a harvest—a view supported by the IWC's scientific committee—*and* the IWC still refused to lift the moratorium, did Norway resume whaling. By that time it was obvious to most Norwegians and many other observers that the voting majority in the IWC was not guided by ecological considerations, as required by the whaling convention, but by other issues, such as animal welfare and animal rights concerns, or the need to maintain a favorable "green" image in their home constituencies. It might appear that the research effort has been futile; however, there is no doubt that the massive scientific evidence that has been assembled has given legitimacy to Norwegian whaling—both at home and abroad.

Norway has also tried to address the problem of animal suffering. The animal welfare and animal rights advocates have painted a bloody picture of whaling. In 1975, therefore, the IWC took up the challenge to review killing methods in an effort to improve them. In the following years, a series of recommendations was adopted, and the IWC Working Group on Humane Killing was established in 1983 and has thereafter met on a regular basis. Norway has contributed to the activities of the working group by initiating a research program in 1981 which has involved testing a number of killing methods. When it was demonstrated that an explosive penthrite grenade is the most efficient and humane method for killing whales, this technology was made mandatory for Norwegian whalers from the

1984 season onward. Following this, in 1993, Norway introduced compulsory shooting tests for all the gunners in an attempt to improve their performance and reduce the killing time. Work to develop more reliable grenades and improve the whalers' skills continues. Norway's (and Japan's) requests for scientific studies comparing the suffering of hunted whales with sufferings caused by modern farming practices and game hunting have, on the other hand, fallen on deaf ears in the IWC.

Symbolic Importance of Whaling

Despite the effort whalers and their supporters have made to respond to issues raised by individuals and organizations opposed to whaling, the IWC moratorium is maintained. Findings and recommendations of the IWC scientific committee have increasingly been ignored, and some IWC member states attempt to reinterpret the whaling convention in order to justify their efforts to render the whaling moratorium permanent. Many whalers have been at a loss as to how to interpret and give meanings to these developments, but today most of them regard the antiwhaling efforts not only as a threat to their livelihood but also as an assault on their culture. What we are facing are radically different value and symbolic systems, each firmly embedded in and conditioned by historical processes in the cultures where they prevail. To the international anti-use movement, whales have become symbols of great importance: they symbolize purity, innocence and nature. To the whalers, whaling has come to symbolize their culture as well as their rights to self-determination.

The Lofoten whalers, as well as the Norwegian authorities, make use of several global discourses to defend whaling. Foremost of these is the one on ecology and sustainable use. This portrays whalers as stewards of green values, and whaling is not only seen as sustainable but as an important means to preserve balanced marine ecosystems. One whaling skipper pointed out that "the violation of the rain forest is done by capitalists, not the Indians who live there. The same is true here. We don't destroy the whale stocks. The danger is big capital. We are limited by the quotas. We have to live within them. This is our home."[9]

To Norwegian whalers, state authorities, and scientists, whaling has become a symbol for the principle of sustainable utilization of natural resources and the need for enlightened resource management based on sound scientific knowledge. This is one reason why Norway continues to spend so much time and energy on the whaling issues despite its insignificance for the country's economy. Whaling is seen as part of a much larger issue, namely the right to exploit natural resources sustainably—particularly marine resources which amount to one of Norway's most important exports, second only to oil. According to one director of the Fishermen's Association, "Whaling is basically an extremely important front line issue about ecology, resource management and international law. For a nation with such a great dependence on harvesting the sea, it is necessary to use all ecological niches in a responsible way. . . . If we lose the right to whale, I fear that other sections of our fishing industry will suffer in the future. We will get a sort of domino effect, if you like."[10]

Another useful global discourse is related to the issue of cultural diversity. Cultural arguments in support of continued whaling are accepted by the IWC when they are presented by Alaskan Inuit and Greenlanders, but Norwegian whaling is not considered to have any legitimate cultural significance. Gradually cultural arguments have replaced old arguments about levels of unemployment and economic hardship. In this rhetoric, Norwegian minke whaling is traditional, and it is imbedded in coastal culture. At another level, whaling has become a tool to separate us from them. In this process, eating whale meat has gained new meanings. It has become both an act of protest—as when a large whale barbeque party was held in Svolvær Loften, on the Fourth of July—and a way to communicate belongingness to the Norwegian tribe and thus signify an essential difference from others. Preserving cultural diversity is a strategy for securing the right of local groups to control their own development. Phrased more simply, it states that people have a right to be different. To some Norwegians, whaling symbolizes the nation; to fishermen, it also symbolizes the right to self-determination and to have influence over the resources on which one's life depends. The antiwhaling campaign is regarded as an infringement on these rights and is therefore perceived as a form of cultural imperialism.

Becoming Organized

We simply couldn't sit around up here watching the International Whaling Commission and dozens of anti-whaling organizations from all over the world playing pingpong with our lives. We had to do something. . . . We could at least offer an alternative view of what the whole Commission is supposed to be all about, namely whaling.

—member of High North Alliance, an international whalers' support group[11]

Whalers and their supporters have defended the right to harvest natural resources in various ways. At the national level, the police and coast guard have been forced to protect whalers against militant NGOs, and information about the hunt is restricted to prevent attacks on whalers and their property. Dissatisfaction with the IWC led to the establishment of the North Atlantic Marine Mammal Commission (NAMMCO) in 1992, with the Faroe Islands, Greenland, Iceland, and Norway as contracting partners and with Canada, Denmark, Japan, and Russia as observer nations. So far, NAMMCO has involved itself primarily with management questions not covered by the IWC, including the management of small cetaceans and seals, but it is certainly a warning, and it may eventually be a real alternative to the IWC.

The whalers have tried to work through old as well as new organizations. All the whalers have become members of the Nordland Small-Type Whaling Association (Nordlands Småkvalfangerlag), which started out as a regional association to unite northern Norwegian coastal whaling interests. The whalers are also members of the Fishermen's Association (Norges Fiskarlag). Both these associations are represented on Norwegian delegations to the IWC.

The whalers' and fishermen's associations are examples of traditional political organizations established in the manner of labor organizations to effect cooperation and negotiations within a particular national setting. However, the international antihunting movement has forced these organizations to assume new roles for which they are not designed or have experience in filling. Therefore, new NGOs have been established for these new international undertakings. One of the most successful attempts to create a more effective resistance is the High North Alliance (HNA) with an office in Reine, Lofoten. Initiated in 1990, it now organizes fishermen, sealers, and whalers in Canada, the Faroe Islands, Greenland, Iceland, and Norway. The HNA is fighting the antiharvest movement on a broad front; it is active during CITES and IWC meetings (where it publishes the *The International Harpoon*), organizes a number of public hearings and debates, and has a wide international network that provides lobby assistance in Brussels and Washington, DC.

The Norwegian whalers have joined the World Council of Whalers, an international organization with its secretariat on Vancouver Island, British Columbia. The World Council of Whalers aims to create solidarity among whaling peoples and provide educational services to whalers and the general public. It has an executive board with members from the Arctic, North Atlantic, North Pacific, Caribbean, and South Pacific regions.

The Friends of the Harpoon (Harpunens venner), which was established by housewives across Vestfjorden after the attempted scuttling of the fishing-whaling boat *Nybræna*, is much more limited in scope but testifies to the grave concern women also feel for their children's and, hence the coastal communities', future existence. Another example is Mayday (Nødrop), a women's group organized in Reine, Lofoten, in 1984.

Together these efforts may bear fruit.

FOOD FOR THOUGHT

In the whaling debate, two conflicting views on humankind's relationship with the natural environment are apparent. The *preservationists* seek to protect species and habitats, and they argue for the establishment of national parks and sanctuaries. Whales are important icons for this group. The *conservationists*, on the other hand, argue that natural resources may be used if this can be done sustainably. In Norway whalers hold this second view. Related to this is the conflict between the global and the local levels. During the last decades, attempts have been made to redefine whales as a global resource, a common heritage of mankind. The central arena for this attempt has been the IWC. At the same time, today it has become a widely held notion that natural resources are best regulated if the local communities that depend on these resources are directly and centrally involved in managing these resources.

This principle of self-management is laid down in two international covenants associated with the Universal Declaration of Human Rights. According to these internationally accepted norms, "all peoples may, for their own ends, freely dispose of their natural wealth and resources. . . . In no case may a people be deprived of their means of subsistence." The IWC recognizes these rights as they apply to indigenous people, but not when they are applied to Norwegian whalers. On the contrary, most IWC member states are working to impose a permanent ban on commercial whaling in violation of the Whaling Convention and of these international human rights statutes.

Questions

1. With perceptions of nature varying between cultures, to what extent (if at all) should one cultural group be allowed to force its views upon another?

2. How can the global and local interests in resource management be reconciled?

3. To what extent should concerns about animal welfare and animal rights be allowed to play a role in the management of natural resources, or should science be supreme?

4. Is it reasonable to protect the rights of an indigenous people more than those of another local community people living under similar conditions with similar cultural needs? If so, why?

5. Is it acceptable that signatories to international conventions and treaties openly work against the letter and the spirit of these conventions? Should they employ other means to achieve their political goals?

NOTES

1. Personal communication to author.
2. *Regionalstatistikk* (Nordland 9/98) and author's field notes.
3. *Fiskeristatistikk 1993–1994* (Oslo: Statistics Norway, 1997), 66.
4. Geir Thorsnaes, *Store norske Heksikon*, Vol. 9 (Oslo: Kunnskapsforlaget, 1997), 618.
5. Interview with the Norwegian Broadcasting Corporation, February 8, 1991.

6. International Study Group on Norwegian Small Type Whaling, *Norwegian Small Type Whaling in Cultural Perspectives* (Tromsø: Norwegian College of Fisheries, 1992), 111.

7. Personal communication to author.

8. Interview.

9. International Study Group, 110.

10. Ibid., 114.

11. Ibid., 116.

RESOURCE GUIDE

Published Literature

Broch, Harald Beyer. "North Norwegian Whalers' Conceptualization of Current Whale Management Conflicts." In Milton M. R. Freeman and Urs P. Kreuter, eds., *Elephants and Whales: Resources for Whom?* Basel, Switzerland: Gordon and Breach Publishers, 1994.

Foote, D. C. "Investigation of Small Whale Hunting in Northern Norway, 1964." *Journal of Fisheries Research Board of Canada* 32 (1975): 1163–89.

International Study Group on Norwegian Small Type Whaling. *Norwegian Small Type Whaling in Cultural Perspectives.* Tromsø: Norwegian College of Fisheries, 1992.

Mønnesland, J., S. Johansen, S. Eikeland, and K. Hanssen. *Whaling in Norwegian Waters in the 1980's.* Oslo: NIBR Report 1990–14, 1990.

Videos

Bigger Than a Whale, 1998. Color video. Knut Skoglund, Strandveien 95, N-9005 Tromsø, Norway (Fax: 47–77 60 04 20).

Reclaiming Paradise?, 1993. Color video. Mega Film, Klapparstig 25, IS 101 Reykjavik, Iceland (Fax: 354–1–624233).

Sealers: Killers or Hunters?, 1996. 52-minute color video. Knut Skoglund, Strandveien 95, N-9005 Tromsø, Norway (Fax: 47–77 60 04 20).

Survival in the High North, 1989. Color video. Mega Film, Klapparstig 25, IS 101 Reykjavik, Iceland (Fax: 354–1–624233).

Internet and WWW Sites

High North Alliance
www.highnorth.no

International Whaling Commission
http://ourworld.compuserve.com/homepages/iwcoffice/

Man in Nature
http://website.lineone.net/~s.ward/MIN/index.html

World Council of Whalers Website
www.island.net/~wcw

Organizations

High North Alliance
Box 123
N-8390 Reine i Lofoten, Norway
E-mail: hna@highnorth.no

International Whaling Commission
The Red House
135 Station Road
Histon, Cambridge, UK CB4–4NP
E-mail: iwcoffice@compuserve.com

North Atlantic Marine Mammal Commission
c/o University of Tromsø
N-9037 Tromsø, Norway
E-mail: nammco-sec@nammco.no

World Council of Whalers
P.O. Box 291
Brentwood Bay, B.C. V8M IR3
Canada
E-mail: wcw@island.net

13

The Saami

Hugh Beach

CULTURAL OVERVIEW

The People

The Saami, or Lapps as others have called them, are the indigenous people
of the Russian Kola Peninsula and northern Norway, Sweden, and Finland.
There is no reliable population census for the Saami people, and the matter
of defining who is a Saami is problematical; nonetheless, according to current estimates, there are about 40,000 Saami in Norway, 17,000 in Sweden,
6,000 in Finland, and from 1,500 to 2,000 in Russia. The Saami who
earlier (and with good cause) sought to avoid public admission of their
ethnic roots for fear of stigmatization now take new pride in their ethnic
membership. Saami spokesmen have campaigned for the replacement of the
term "Lapp" (considered by many to be derogatory) with their own name
for themselves.

Although Saamiland was divided by national borders following the colonization of the North, the Saami emphasize that they are "one people in
four countries." They have their own language, their traditional styles of
dress, their own distinctive handicraft work, and their own unique form of
singing—*joiking*—actually, in the words of the Saami author Johan Turi,
"a way to remember."

Although the Saami did not possess a written language before contact
with Christian missionaries, their oral tradition is extensive, and Saami
authors have produced written classics. The Saami language is divided into
a number of major dialects with variations so marked that a northern
Saami and a southern Saami in Sweden might speak to each other in Swed-

ish in order to communicate more easily. The early Christian missionaries of the 1600s and 1700s formulated their own Saami alphabets based on the dialect spoken in the region of their mission stations, and it is only relatively recently that a common writing system has been accepted widely, though by no means unanimously, by all Saami dialect groups.

There have been numerous theories regarding the origins of the Saami. It was once thought that they might have wintered over along an ice-free land strip of the North Sea coast during the close of the last ice age. Cultural anthropologists emphasize the characteristics that link the Saami eastward to other northern and reindeer herding peoples in Asia. Linguists have tried to determine the antiquity of the Saami as a distinct ethnic group by studying the amount of divergence in Saami dialects from a so-called proto-Finnish language. Physical anthropologists have examined the genetic traits—such as blood groups—of the Saami. There has been little agreement among experts working in these various fields of research. This has led some researchers to conjecture that the appropriate question to ask is not where the Saami came from, but rather when the various peoples in the north coalesced into Saami with a self-perceived common Saami identity. The conjectures of the past have been set in turmoil by modern DNA analysis which indicates that the Saami are probably the oldest population in Europe. They share a genetic history distinct from other Europeans, and they are without any known close genetic connections with any other peoples.

The Setting

Because Saamiland is situated at a relatively high latitude, it experiences great seasonal variation. The famous midnight sun circles the horizon at the peak of summer but turns bashful in the winter, at times never climbing above the horizon and providing only a few hours of pale daylight. The geographical positioning of Saamiland, crossing many degrees of latitude, adds further climatic and ecological variability. This is compounded by the considerable differences in altitude from the coasts and wide lowland forests to the high mountains extending along the border between Norway and Sweden and curving across the top of the Scandinavian Peninsula into Russia. Along the Norwegian North Sea coast the mountains meet the water abruptly, and long fiords reach into the steep-sided mountain valley. Inland, behind the mountains, in that part of Norway that crosses over the top of Sweden and Finland, lies the so-called Finnmark *vidda*, a relatively flat tundra zone with small scattered scrub birch forests. In Sweden, the mountains to the west slope gradually through a wide taiga (area south of the tundra that supports trees and more varied vegetation) forest belt cut by many powerful rivers down to the Baltic Sea. The forests of Finnish and Russian Saamiland are dotted with numerous lakes and marshes.

Saami herder stops the reindeer caravan during the December move of his herd and searches for reindeer carcasses left by predators, near Jokkmokk, Sweden.

An increasingly dominant human presence has, over time, significantly altered the northern flora and fauna. The once common wild reindeer exist today only in small areas of Norway and Finland and not at all in Sweden. The beaver, once trapped to near extinction in Saamiland, has only recently begun to reappear. The European elk (moose), however, seems to have increased in number both to the joy of hunters and to the chagrin of motorists, for whom they are a danger on the roads, and to forest land owners, upon whose newly planted saplings they thrive.

The number of semidomestic reindeer has increased dramatically with the rise of full-scale reindeer herding, especially with its transition from the more traditional subsistence to a modern, market-oriented form of livelihood. This in turn has led to changes in vegetation caused by reindeer grazing and also the elimination of reindeer predators—notably the wolf. Major environmental change has also resulted from the massive damming of waterways for hydroelectric power, by large-scale lumbering, and by heavy and increasingly motorized tourism.

Traditional Subsistence Strategies

Traditional Saami subsistence strategies have been well adapted to the climatic and geographical diversity of Saamiland, but throughout the historical process of colonization and the continuing appropriation and administrative control of their lands by the national governments, the Saami have had to readapt these strategies.

Along the northern coast of Norway, many Saami have, by tradition, been engaged in saltwater fishing. In the interior regions, hunting and fresh-water fishing have formed a major subsistence livelihood since time im-memorial. Dotting the landscape, in strategically located mountain passes, are the remains of laboriously constructed systems of pits for trapping wild reindeer, indicating a scale of collective social activity which later decreased with the development of full-scale reindeer pastoralism.

The large-scale, intensive herding of tame reindeer as a dominant form of livelihood for some—but by no means all—Saami probably did not develop until the 1500s in Saamiland, but it is commonly this activity for which the Saami are best known to the rest of the world.

It should be noted that although different environmental conditions placed varying degrees of emphasis on different subsistence activities, these activities were frequently pursued in a seasonal combination that required considerable movement between settlement areas. Similarly, trading rela-tions were developed with settled non-Saami peoples to the south and along the coasts. The Saami language carries numerous terms imported during pre-Christian times from neighboring people. Saami reindeer milking ter-minology is predominantly Norse in origin, suggesting that the large-scale reindeer milking and cheese making of the Saami in the intensive herding era was learned by them through contact with other peoples' livestock prac-tices.

The best survival strategy in the Arctic has been to spread risk by utilizing a wide range of locally available resources. Thus, along with hunting and fishing, Saami have also herded and farmed; however, over time, access to resources and the manner by which they may be utilized has become rig-orously regulated by the northern national governments. In Sweden, for example, the integration of reindeer herding and agriculture would have been far more prevalent had it not been for laws insisting on their sepa-ration. It could happen that Saami families possessing more than five goats were denied the right to continue herding on the grounds that they were no longer true reindeer pastoralists. Even long before this, the development of full-scale reindeer pastoralism itself may be the result of the depletion of wildlife from taxation pressure imposed by the various states declaring sovereignty over sections of Saamiland. Of course, each nation-state has followed its own Saami policies, some of which are similar, and others different, from those of its neighbors.

Reindeer herding is a broad term for a livelihood which has undergone and continues to undergo tremendous development. Long before the rise of full-scale pastoralism, the Saami kept some tame deer to use as decoys when hunting wild reindeer. Saami families also kept a small number of tame deer for transport purposes, for both packing and pulling sleds. There are even major distinctions within the pastoral framework; for example, one can base one's pastoral economy upon the use of the deer primarily for milk or for meat, and that choice largely determines the kind of herding one pursues.

Today, modern means of transportation link Saami herders to a wide international market where reindeer meat brings a high price. Now that foodstuffs and clothing can be purchased, and the sale of meat can provide the funds for such purchases, milking has disappeared, and the herds are used basically for meat production. This change was accompanied by changes in the size, age, and sex composition of the herds, as well as the methods of herding. Reindeer are also used to satisfy the household's own need for food. When one pays income tax on the sale of meat, it makes good economic sense (and meets cultural maintenance and taste satisfaction needs) to eat one's own reindeer.

Social and Political Organization

Researchers hypothesize that, with the rise of pastoralism, the early so-called *siida* form of social organization, which brought Saami together into winter camps, splintered with the need to disperse into smaller family groups so as to find sufficient grazing for the stock of tame reindeer and also to guard them adequately against predators. The *siida* or *sita* form of social organization—a loose community of related families who used collective resources, shared according to need, and dispersed and regrouped seasonally—is thought to be the basic pan-Saami form of social structure. This form of organization is most closely followed today among the Skolt Saami (a Saami group with their original homeland in the border area of Finland and Russia). It is not agreed how pan-Saami this form of social organization really was, or to what extent the winter villages may have been influenced in their concentration and localization by outside trade relations.

The term *"siida"* also has a modern and somewhat different meaning in the herding context: it signifies a group of herders with their families who tend their reindeer together, work together, and move together. It refers to a small group who care for their reindeer intensively as a separate herd usually in the autumn and winter seasons.

Traditional Saami society was not characterized by hierarchical structures of political or ritual power, and inheritance of property may occur through either or both parents. This is not to say that the Saami lacked respect for their elders or people of exceptional influence, only that these characteristics were earned through individual ability and performance, rather than by birth or public election.

Saami handicrafts were previously a necessary part of household work. Reindeer hides and furs were sewn with reindeer sinew for clothing. Herding gear, tents, sleds, knives, and a wealth of other utensils were made from the materials at hand and acquired, over the centuries, a distinctive Saami form and decorative style. Access to the wider market economy has freed Saami from the necessity of creating their own wares, it has brought Saami handicraft to world attention and appreciation, and it has transformed many utilitarian objects into objects of art, created with traditional feeling and pride. Men commonly work in antler and wood; women work with leather, pewter thread, roots, and fabrics. With the introduction of modern materials and the transition to a more settled lifestyle, many of the old handicraft skills began to disappear. Basket weaving with roots, for example, has only barely been rescued from oblivion. Saami handicraft work has become of considerable economic importance, not only to those few who have become full-time Saami handicrafts artists, but also to reindeer herders, for whom it can provide seasonal work and much-needed supplementary income.

Today, reindeer herders constitute a minority within the Saami minority. Nonetheless, despite an economic tradition based on non-herding as well as herding, and despite regulations driving many Saami from herding, reindeer management is still enormously important in defining the legal status and the culture of most Saami. In much of Saamiland, reindeer herding rights are all that remain in practice of special Saami rights; in effect, reindeer herding legislation has come to embody the main part of state policy toward its indigenous people.

Religion and World View

Christian missionary activity paralleled and formed a part of the gradual encapsulation of the Saami. The Saami pre-Christian world view was unconcerned with personal salvation. It was animistic and used shamanistic techniques and ecstatic trances to contact and negotiate with the spirit world. The *noaide* (shaman) was similar to that of many other circumpolar peoples. A shaman could beat on his magic drum and, in a condition of trance, release his spirit to travel to other worlds, often in the form of another spirit animal. The shaman could cure the sick or tell of events in far-off places.

The Apostle of the North, Stenfi, in A.D. 1050, was the first to attempt to Christianize the Saami. Further attempts were made and a few churches were built in northern locations during the next few centuries, but there were no resident Christian missionaries in the region. More regular missionary activity, and the settlement of churchmen at northern stations, began along the coasts but had spread inland by the mid-1500s. The Skolt and Kola Saami to the east came under the religious influence of the Russian Orthodox Church. The major transition of the Saami to Christianity, however, occurred in the 1600s, but shamanism persisted in places hundreds of years later. Christianity has still not eradicated all elements of the Saami pre-Christian world view.

The communication of the Saami shaman with helper spirits was considered by early missionaries to be a discourse with the devil. Shamanistic activity was harshly suppressed, and even *joiking* was dubbed sinful. Accounts of the Saami pre-Christian religion have come to us largely by way of these early missionaries, so naturally they must be read very critically. It is significant that the missionaries did not see themselves merely as spreading enlightenment among superstitious people. In their accounts, the missionaries frequently marvel at the supernatural powers of the Saami shamans, and they saw themselves as struggling against a real and powerful devil with whom the shamans consorted.

Much of the colonial administration was facilitated by the Church, which kept records of marriages and births. The early markets, held once a year in fixed places—usually at churches and on religious holidays—were also occasions when the Saami registered themselves and paid taxes to the Crown. The Church also played a prominent role in Saami education. At this time, since the northern borders between kingdoms were unspecified, missionary activity was also a means for a king to establish sovereignty (with tax rights) over a territory. This in turn meant that the Saami policies of the early kings were often quite Saami-friendly, for if the tax burden was too high or their rights infringed upon too greatly, the Saami might simply attend another church, register there, and pay tax to another king.

Much later, in the 1830s, a puritanical movement started by Saami Lars Levi Laestadius gained a strong following in Saamiland, and it did much to overcome the terrible social problems caused by alcohol. It is still a vital force today among Saami and non-Saami alike, and it has also spread to other countries.

The Organization of Saami Herding

The well-defined territorial herding zones existing today in Fennoscandia (the region occupied by Norway, Sweden, and Finland), so-called *districts* in Norway, *samebys* in Sweden, and *paliskuntas* in Finland, define social units, the groups of people whose reindeer are permitted to graze in these zones. The evolution of these herding zones has been heavily influenced by legislation and administrative policy in each of these countries.

Sweden

Although the herding zones were designated in 1886 with many accompanying regulations, they were basically composed of the old Saami *sita* entities. In 1971 the Swedish authorities replaced the original name (*Lappbys*) with the current name (*Samebys*) but did not change their physical or social borders.

While all herding in Sweden is reserved for those of Saami descent (with eligibility granted to others who marry herders), this does not mean that all reindeer owners must be Saami. However, all reindeer in Sweden must have a herder. Any non-Saami owner must employ the services of a Saami herder and gain permission to do so by the appropriate *Sameby*, as every Saami must be a member of a *Sameby*. Only *Sameby* members can exercise the Saami rights to herd, hunt, and fish, which has caused a serious division to occur between herding and non-herding Saami.

Norway

In Norway, the herding districts, which correspond mainly to summer grazing use areas, have also been patterned largely according to Saami traditional use. As in Sweden, the Saami herders in Norway tend to splinter into smaller, *siida* entities during the autumn and winter. A small area in the southern part of Norway's herding zone is open to herding by non-Saami. The number of herders is carefully regulated by permit. By no means could all Saami in Norway (or in Sweden) practice their herding right, even if they so desired.

Finland

Finnish non-Saami can own and herd reindeer as long as they live within the reindeer-herding area. This area, which is divided into fifty-eight herding districts (*paliskuntas*), covers most of Lapland province and the northern part of Oulu province. The Finnish Reindeer Act came into effect in 1932, although it has been revised several times since then. The *paliskunta* is a type of economic cooperative which served in part as a model for the Swedish *sameby* reorganization in 1971. A *paliskunta* has a communal treasury to which members pay according to the number of reindeer they own. Each of these countries has a well-developed governmental herding administration with a number of provincial offices.

Russia

Unlike the other three nations where the Saami live, Russia contains many different traditional reindeer-herding peoples. In the Kola Peninsula today, for example, where Russian Saami live, herders can be Saami, Komi, Nentsi, Pomors—or even Russians, Ukranians, or other immigrants from the south for whom reindeer herding is not an ancestral tradition. During the Soviet era, reindeer herding, along with other productive enterprises, was collectivized. A program of forced centralization was imposed whereby many Saami were relocated to larger towns. Private ownership of reindeer was basically abolished, and reindeer-herding kolkhozes, or collective farms, were established where the workers themselves owned and worked collectively on large farms and shared their produce. Later, many reindeer-herding farms in the Soviet Union were reorganized under the sovkhoz form, in which the state owned the reindeer, and the workers were wage earners paid by the state.

The recent dissolution of the Soviet Union and ensuing turmoil of the Russian economy have had profound effects on the Saami of the Kola Peninsula. The Russian government has terminated the old state-owned reindeer farms (sovkhozes) in which many of Russia's Saami worked as salaried employees. In effect, although new terms for herding cooperatives are employed, herding on the Kola Peninsula has in many respects reverted to the old kolkhoz form where responsibility for production and finding market partners is no longer the responsibility of the national government. Nonetheless, the internal administration of the herding cooperatives remains highly centralized, and the herders themselves work in much the same way and see little real change from their old situation.

The changes that occur today, stem not from business reorganization so much as from the collapse of the Russian economy. As the herders themselves comment, it makes little difference to them which form of organization is unable to pay them anything. With prices soaring, and the Russian ruble subject to runaway inflation, herding enterprises must rely completely on foreign export and currency. On the Kola Peninsula, the struggle has been desperate to build a modern slaughter facility that will qualify for European Union (EU) certification and permit the export of reindeer meat to Europe.

For most herding families, the new political and economic freedoms have proven disappointing. The dissolution of state control, coupled with economic collapse, has meant that foreign investors in pursuit of the exploitation of local nonrenewable resources, can practically dictate their terms for establishing their own operations. Local interests can be readily sold out by corrupt officials. One herding range heartland has, for example, recently been leased by a mining company under a twenty-five-year exploration and exploitation contract, something that has evoked bitter protest from the Lovozero Saami Association.

On the other hand, new freedoms have enabled the Kola Saami to organize themselves politically. Russian Saami have established firm connections with their Saami neighbors to the west (cultural and educational exchange programs, for example) and have even joined the Nordic Saami Council (Sámiráđđi), first as observers, but by 1992 as full voting members (causing the term "Nordic" to be removed from the name of the organization).

THREATS TO SURVIVAL

Contested Rights to Saami Lands and Land Use

The vast majority of the people in the countries where Saami live know little about the Saami, and what they think they know is frequently wrong. Ignorance about the Saami is often matched with a sympathetic attitude toward them and the recognition that they have been mistreated by the colonial powers; however, this mistreatment is thought to be something that occurred only long ago. Few people understand that some of the most blatant injustices committed against the Saami are quite recent and are, in fact, ongoing. Matters of injustice and discrimination regarding the Saami have been subject to legal contests in both national and international courts of law.

Do the Saami own the lands they inhabit, or does their traditional presence (that opponents claim is seasonally variable and lacking in intensity) only give them a strong right to *use* the land, but not to *own* it? What evidence does the historical record provide? Did the early kings regard the Saami as taxpayers for lands they owned—or was this tax only a form of rent for the use of Crown lands? If Saami immemorial rights are judged to confer only rights of land utilization (rather than land ownership), is it still within the rights of the state to regulate which Saami can—and which cannot—practice their rights of utilization? Since reindeer herding is a well-recognized element of Saami culture, does international law support state-imposed regulations that exclude a majority of Saami from this particular livelihood?

These and similar questions are still largely unresolved. When considering current threats to Saami cultural survival, the discussion is necessarily based upon the existing legal framework, although this legal framework probably constitutes the greatest threat of all. The wide array of threats facing the Saami include some that have existed for decades; others are more recent. These threats may be grouped as follows: land encroachments, confiscation of Saami small-game hunting rights, the Sveg Case (by which Swedish Saami lost winter grazing utilization rights), and globalization and the question of Saami "eco-morality."

Land Encroachment

Traditional Saami livelihoods depend upon the maintenance of a northern environment in which fish, game, and wildlife thrive. Reduction of the grazing territory results in fewer reindeer and hence pressure to reduce the number of herders. Saami cultural maintenance, through its strong connection to the herding livelihood, would suffer from such a reduction. Infringement on grazing lands cannot be calculated only quantitatively; herders vary the reindeers' use of the grazing resource on a seasonal basis, conserving the pasture in one time and place to compensate for grazing pressure occurring elsewhere. It is therefore not appropriate to consider the loss of grazing lands merely according to the extent of the area being lost. For in reality, the *location* of the grazing infringement (not just its size) is of vital importance to the herds as they move their herds in a strategic fashion from place to place.

Those industries that compete with reindeer herding for land resources include farming, mining, logging, hydroelectric development, and tourism. Farming in the north has waned, as have mining and the building of hydroelectric power dams, since almost all of Sweden's natural waterways have now been dammed. These different forms of land encroachment, however, are highly integrated; for example, a mining project requires large amounts of electricity which in turn requires a dam, which requires a road to be built for the transport of heavy machinery to the dam site. Later the existence of this road provides the timber industry with an access route to forest regions which would otherwise be too expensive to log. All of these industries together at one time provided long-lasting jobs in the north for a sizable non-Saami population. This non-Saami population almost everywhere—including in the Saami so-called core area—is now far more numerous than the Saami population itself. The many northern city dwellers engage in various recreational activities in what they consider to be an untouched wilderness. In only a few municipalities in the north (and none at all in Sweden) do the Saami maintain a viable political voice.

Confiscation of Hunting Rights

The same legislation that granted the Swedish Saami their much-desired Saami parliament (Sameting) with one hand struck at their vulnerable resource base with the other. Government Proposition 1992/93:32 asserts that the state possesses hunting and fishing rights on Crown (state) lands that are parallel to that of the Saami. This part of the proposition was passed by the Swedish parliament without consultation with either Saami groups or the government's own Ministry of Environment. The Saami were simply given the option to support the establishment of a Saami parliament together with the new hunting regulations, or they would obtain neither. This occurred, despite a prior Swedish supreme court decision that confirmed that, in the areas demarcated by the land survey, Saami hunting and fishing rights were exclusively theirs. Immemorial rights have legal precedence over newer laws and these cannot invalidate immemorial rights without due process or just compensation; nevertheless, this is precisely what has occurred.

The opening of small-game hunting to everyone may threaten sustainable use of small-game resources, yet for the Saami this is far from the only issue at stake. When the *Samebys* were in control of hunting activities, these could be managed so that they did not conflict in time or place with herding activities taking place in the same area. Now, however, hunters with dogs traverse regions where herders are trying to gather their herds. Moreover, the new regulations have caused a division between herding and non-herding Saami. Non-herding Saami, with clear immemorial rights to the land they inhabit, have continually petitioned the government for the recognition of their hunting and fishing rights on *Sameby* territory. However, some of them have ceased their efforts to attain justice and have not joined the herders in their efforts to overturn the regulations because they are now able to enjoy small-game hunting on these lands with a license from the state, not based on their rights as Saami, but just like any other citizens of the nation.

The current position of the government is that, although it regrets that the new regulations were ushered in as they were, it would cause far more upheaval and social tension between Saami and non-Saami groups if the regulations were to be removed. Instead, the environmental effects of the new hunting regulations and the disturbance they might cause to herding have been subjected to a major investigation. The state is willing to concede that some adjustments in the regulations might be called for when the needs and desires of all parties are considered. Of course, for the Saami, once an issue has been removed from a context of their basic legal rights and re-framed into a context of social good for the greatest number, the battle is lost. The remaining leverage the Saami have comes from Swedish ratification of international declarations and covenants for the protection of minority people and the preservation of minority cultures.

The Sveg Case

In a highly controversial verdict, the lower court of Sveg in Jämtland province ruled in 1996 that the five southernmost *Samebys* in Sweden did not hold any grazing rights based on sustained and immemorial use of the lands for winter grazing. In effect, the court ruled that the traditional use of these lands by the Saami was of shallow historical depth, highly variable, and sparse, and their use did not occur in the area prior to utilization and habitation by non-Saami people. The case had been brought against the *Samebys* by private land owners in the region who were disgruntled over the consideration they were required to show herding interests, especially in recent times when reindeer numbers were high. The private land owners demanded legal clarification of existing land rights in the area, and the burden of proof to demonstrate sufficient use since time immemorial was placed upon the Saami.

This case focused on archaeological evidence; however, the archaeologists differed in their opinions as to whether the material remains were Saami, so the court would not concede that the evidence supported the Saami position. Historical evidence of the Saami presence, of course, fared no better in the court because the historical evidence was based on written records made by the Swedish settlers who were not in the least interested in documenting prior Saami habitation.

This is not to say that the Saami are automatically the first inhabitants wherever they put their feet, or that the private land owners could not conceivably have a case. It is only to observe that, given the terms under which the case was tried and the burden of proof being demanded, there was little chance of a Saami victory. Aided by hindsight, some commentators have reflected that the Saami would probably have fared better had they set up their courtroom strategy around their early tax payments to the Crown for use (or ownership?) of their *Sameby* territories for herding purposes, a herding that presupposed that their reindeer were grazing *somewhere* in the winter and this use should therefore have indicated that they also had the right to do so at that time.

Over the centuries, it is apparent that the state has shifted in its policies toward the Saami, at one time respecting their rights, but at another time defining these rights as mere privileges, secondary to the rights of farming settlers. Both sides—settled land owners as well as Saami herdsmen—can point to historical documents that indicate government support for their claims. Sorting legal priorities down through the various layers of legislation and regulation becomes an exceedingly time-consuming and expensive undertaking. In the final analysis, resource conflicts and social tensions will hardly be improved by a total legal victory of one side over the other. Many Saami and non-Saami alike feel it is incumbent on the state to sort through the legal uncertainties and forge a viable settlement out of court, with compensation paid to any party given false assurances of rights which must now be annulled with the recognition of the prior rights of the other party.

To date, however, the matter remains in the courts. The Saami side owes more than US $1 million in debt from its defeat in the lower court but continues with an appeal to higher courts. All national legal processes must be exhausted before the Saami are able to submit their case to international courts. Meanwhile, buoyed by the private land owners' victory in the lower court of Sveg, other land owners have now filed similar suits against the *Samebys* of their own regions.

Globalization

The limited self-determination in herding matters which the Saami have been able to maintain is now under threat, not as before—from the competition of farmers and settlers—or by the rationalization programs of the welfare state, but rather from the consequences of globalization, especially as these involve urban-based environmental values.

Arguments waged in favor of preserving a viable wolf population in the reindeer-herding area are based largely on Swedish participation in global programs aimed at preserving biodiversity. The issue of reindeer overgrazing is now a concern for all environmentally conscious Swedes. Moreover, large tracts of reindeer range are being incorporated into a so-called world heritage area. As mentioned earlier, small-game hunting has been opened not only to local non-Saami hunters with their own subsistence needs, but also to wealthy trophy hunters from other countries. The entry of Sweden into the EU is also a matter of utmost significance for the Saami, as it has imposed yet another layer of regulation designed by decision makers far removed from the local context.

At the same time, international conventions and EU membership mean new forms of protection and new sources of subsidy and regional aid for the Saami. Such elements of globalization are not always detrimental to Saami interests, nor are they perceived this way by the Saami. However, the terms of debate and the strategies involved by the various Saami and non-Saami lobby groups are now significantly altered. Saami have recently been portrayed as ecological criminals, and new state regulations have been prescribed for sustainable development and protection of biodiversity in Saamiland with little attention given to whether these programs are compatible with rational herd management.

Yet, globalization can mean greater recognition of Saami rights on an ethnic basis, when backed by international conventions and integrated fourth-world unity. The threats to herding encourage Saami to seek solidarity and strength in other forums, although this is not without accompanying fears from the herding Saami, who feel their limited resources cannot be stretched to support the demands of all ethnically defined Saami.

Indigenous politicians, invoking a so-called eco-morality argument against the governments of industrialized nation-states, assert that industrialized nation-states have ravaged the global environment to the extent of exterminating many species and threatening the survival of humankind. They further assert that indigenous peoples have lived in harmony with nature and therefore should be entrusted with the care of their ancestral lands at the very least. Those opposed to indigenous peoples' empowerment generally counter this argument by saying that if indigenous peoples had adhered to a way of life less damaging to the environment than that of industrial man, it is not due to any moral superiority on their part, but rather to their primitive traditional technology. Now that they are in possession of modern technology, the argument goes, they are as liable to be "eco-criminals" as the next person.

For the Saami who are a minority, and for the herding Saami—a minority within a minority—moral arguments are essential. It is one thing to have a legal right, but another to keep it. If the Saami are unable to maintain support for their special resource rights with the majority population, it is very likely that (as in the case of small-game hunting) these special rights will be further limited.

Conflicting Urban-based Views of Nature

Herders today are attacked on many fronts: they are blamed for the decimation of scarce species (reindeer predators such as wolves) and their use of high-technology equipment (such as motorbikes) which is said to destroy the tundra. Not only do modern herders destroy the tundra with motorized vehicles, it is claimed, they now keep too many reindeer which overgraze and trample the sensitive ground cover. Government administrators have long been involved with the problem of high reindeer numbers, but previously the concern was to avoid overgrazing and to promote the long-term sustainability of the herding industry. Today, however, attention is directed more toward protecting the mountains as a part of both the national and world environmental heritage and keeping them natural for the benefit of tourists. From the Saami perspective, the wilderness, which Swedish environmental policy wishes to preserve, is their own back yard: it is not untouched Nature, but a cultural landscape created through centuries of Saami stewardship.

The Saami are caught in a dilemma. On the one hand, it is essential for their livelihood, now integrated with the market economy, to be as profitable or rational as possible to sustain at least a minimal number of Saami with a decent living standard. This, however, means modernization and the use of high-technology equipment, elements which detract from the willingness of non-Saami to permit special Saami resource rights (seen as special privileges) in order to preserve the unique Saami cultural heritage. Naturally, majority support of the special Saami resource rights is further eroded by overly simplistic assertions by some members of the environmental lobby that the Saami are in fact destroying Arctic ecosystems.

Of course, environmental lobby groups may be justified in regard to some of their concerns, and some parts of their criticism of Saami herding are not completely erroneous. Moreover, the Saami and the environmentalists share many common goals in opposing the actions of certain land-encroaching industries. New, globally popular environmental protectionism, while burdening the Saami with yet another layer of regulations, might in the long run shield Saami traditional livelihoods more effectively than Swedish national policies.

Yet there is the fear of what many Saami regard as the most recent form of colonialism—"eco-colonialism," in which simplistic ecological arguments for increased regulation of Saami livelihoods are proposed for questionable purposes. In some cases, even with the best of environmental intentions, an imperfect understanding of ecology—one that fails to appreciate the complex and enduring relationship between the natural environment and social needs—comes to dominate policy. This is the perspective that first permits massive exploitation of northern natural resources, forcing herding into ever diminishing confines, and then blames small-scale Saami livelihoods, first for threatening what is left of the natural environment and second for no longer being ecologically sustainable.

Competition with Other Herding Peoples

The Saami of the Russian Kola Peninsula are not the only traditional reindeer herding people now living in that area. While the Saami can make the historical and prehistorical claims to be the indigenous people of Kola, the Russian government has declared that this is a claim they must share with others. At the beginning of the twentieth century, large numbers of reindeer herding Komi spread westward into the Kola Peninsula, and a small number of Nentsi herders in their employ accompanied them. As the original Komi grazing lands had become insufficient for their purposes, the government sought to confer special resource privileges upon these up-rooted people, and as their indigenous status entailed certain special hunting and fishing rights, the government decided to extend indigenous status to the Komi and the Nentsi people. Today, there is considerable resource competition and tension between the Komi and the Saami of the Kola Peninsula. In Kola, therefore, Saami goals are not likely to be attained simply by contesting indigenous versus nonindigenous resource rights.

RESPONSE: STRUGGLES TO SURVIVE CULTURALLY

The Saami are attempting to employ every means available to secure their resource base and ensure that the Saami people pursuing Saami livelihoods maintain and develop their culture and attain at least a modicum of internal self-determination. Of course, political realities in the different countries in which they live provide the Saami with different means and different constraints; additionally, their past successes and failures influence their choice of current strategies.

Political and Legal Strategies

In Finland (as in Russian Saamiland), reindeer herding is not an exclusively Saami livelihood, and even Saami herders may combine a herding economy with farming or logging to an extent hardly permitted in Sweden. Under such circumstances, political alignments and strategies take a different course to those more commonly found in Norway and Sweden. However, Saami responses to threat in Finland, Norway, and Sweden also share elements that have evolved from common histories and similar modern developments.

Finland had been integrated into the Swedish kingdom by the early 1600s and was lost to Russia only in 1809. Sweden and Norway were unified from 1814 until 1905. Consequently, these countries have many legal and political similarities, and they have ratified many of the same international declarations and covenants. Moreover, they have well-established relations with each other—for example, through the Nordic Council—and, very important, they have made a concerted effort over the past fifteen years to harmonize their Saami policies. In fact, as early as 1751, Norway and Sweden had entered into a bilateral international agreement with respect to their Saami policies. Thus, when the Norwegian-Swedish border in the northern districts was finalized in 1751, a codicil to the border treaty was made specifying that the Saami would be able to continue to migrate without hindrance across the land now divided by a border. This codicil of 1751 has been termed the Saami Magna Carta. The terms of this agreement have been renegotiated numerous times since then, so that Saami and reindeer movement across the border is not completely free, but the codicil is still in effect. However, when Norway attempted to bar a group of Swedish Saami from utilizing their immemorial grazing right in Norway, the Swedish Saami took the issue to court and won an unprecedented victory with the so-called Altevatn verdict of the Norwegian Supreme Court in 1966. In effect, the immemorial right of Swedish Saami had won confirmation in Norway when at the same time it was hardly recognized in Sweden.

The 1966 legal victory in Norway inspired the Swedish Saami, with Saami ombudsman Tomas Cramér as legal counsel, to open another legal confrontation to test Saami land rights, this time in Sweden with the so-called Taxed Mountain Case. This case lasted fully fifteen years from the district court, to the court of appeal, and finally through the supreme court in 1981. While the Swedish government does not recognize any general Saami ownership of land, and did not regard Saami utilization of the specific Taxed Mountain area as sufficient to establish *ownership*, the Swedish supreme court did confirm that Saami reindeer-herding rights constitute a special form of property right based upon ancestral use since time immemorial. Moreover, even the immemorial ancestral land use of Saami nomads could lay a foundation for true ownership over specific tracks, if, the court ruled, such usage—besides being from time immemorial—was intense enough, applied to well-demarcated areas, and was not encumbered by the contesting claims of others.

Yet Saami ancestral right, which supersedes any requirement of *Sameby* membership and which is based on continuity of usage through the descent of individuals, is hardly recognized in the series of Reindeer Acts legislated by the Swedish government since 1886. The government insists that all Saami ancestral rights are completely regulated in the current Reindeer Act. This act supposedly upholds the reindeer-herding right of all Saami. However, in reality, only certain Saami—those who are *Sameby* members—have the right to practice their herding right.

Recent research on the legal rights of the Saami in Finland during the period of Swedish rule has had a major effect on Finnish Saami policy and will probably also impact policies in Sweden and Norway. This research, on tax records, shows that the Swedish/Finnish government recognized that Saami people *owned* their lands. This recent research demonstrates that Saami land use in certain areas probably fulfills the criteria for land ownership itemized by the Swedish supreme court. However, the high cost of litigation, the demand that national legal proceedings be exhausted before cases can be heard in international courts, and the fact that the Saami in Sweden have no political power and are weakened politically by factionalism (herding Saami as opposed to non-herding Saami) and now suffer serious threats from the environmentalist lobby have caused progressive Saami policies in Sweden to slow and, in many ways, even to regress.

In Finland, the Finnish Saami Rights Commission was established in 1978 by the Advisory Board on Saami Affairs to evaluate which natural resources rights currently administered by the state should be transferred to the Saami. A few years later, a Norwegian Saami Rights Commission was established, and shortly after that, a Swedish Saami Rights Commission was established, but it was dismantled in 1991. The Finnish commission proposed the reinstitution of Saami collective ownership to the so-called state forests formerly owned by them, and although the proposition was greeted favorably by many, the government has not yet acted. In Finland, a so-called Finnish Saami parliament has been operating since 1973.

The Saami Rights Commission in Norway was created in the wake of the massive resistance of the Saami and conservationists to the construction of the Alta hydroelectric dam in Norway. The Norwegian commission was mandated to analyze Saami resource rights in Norway, a task necessitating a thorough historical study.

The Swedish commission, however, confined its legal perspective on Saami rights mainly to the minimal requirements of international law. In the spirit of Nordic harmonization, the work of both of these commissions led to the establishment of Saami parliaments in their respective countries. While many Saami had hoped for more from these commissions—for example, a veto on land encroachments injurious to Saami land use practices—great hopes are pinned upon the fledgling Saami parliaments. Despite their differences, the various national Saami factions can now speak with one voice and cannot easily be ignored by the government. In fact, these parliaments are created as government departments (a construction with both positive and negative points). Representatives from the three Saami parliaments have already taken initial steps toward the founding of a unified Nordic Saami parliament.

The Potential of International Action

Besides ongoing negotiation with respect to national Saami policies and confrontation in national courts, the Saami when possible have taken their concerns into the international arena. The nations encompassing Saami populations do not recognize the Saami as "a people" according to the accepted terms of international law set down in various United Nations conventions. Legal avenues open to the Saami internationally lead to either the United Nations Human Rights Committee or the European Court. However, not only must national court processes be exhausted before a case can be appealed to an international court, but the case is subject to a complex legal process of admissibility. Because of the technicalities of admissibility, Sweden, for example, has narrowly escaped international investigation of its regulation barring Saami who are not *Sameby* members from exercising their herding and hunting rights (basic to their culture) and for its confiscation of exclusive Saami small-game hunting and fishing rights.

The Saami of Norway, Sweden, and Finland have become members of the World Council of Indigenous Peoples (WCIP). They maintain close contact with the United Nations Working Group for Indigenous Populations in Geneva, the United Nations Conference on Environment and Development, and other international bodies. The Saami Council has nongovernmental organization status within the United Nations, and Saami representatives frequently serve as experts on the national delegations from Norway, Sweden, and Finland to the United Nations. The Saami, together with the Inuit and Russian indigenous groups, enjoy permanent membership on the eight-nation Arctic Council. At this time, the Saami have not yet been granted membership in the Nordic Council.

Appealing to the Public

When Saami causes are not adequately served by policy negotiation and fail to win respect in national courts, or cannot even be heard in international courts, the only recourse for the Saami is to appeal to public opinion. During the height of the protest over the damming of the Alta River, Saami activists appealed to the public by emphasizing the inequalities of power—but also their common interest with the dominant population—by erecting a Saami tent as a base for operations outside the Norwegian parliament building in Oslo. In their attempts to bring their case to worldwide attention, the Saami have become adept at lobbying, both from platforms reflecting their own ethnic identity and also from the platform of indigenous peoples in general.

FOOD FOR THOUGHT

How the individual identifies as Saami has dramatically changed over the past ten years. This has been the result of new state regulations as well as changing individual motivations and actions. Problems of discrimination, neglect of legal rights, pressures for assimilation, and straightforward conflicts with the majority population over natural resources still exist for many Saami. However, these are not the only issues that determine the current interaction between Saami and non-Saami, the formulation of Saami personhood, or the negotiation of Saami landscapes. Moreover, as recognition of "Saamihood" shifts gradually in emphasis (especially for the majority populations) from reindeer herding to larger ethnic criteria as well, a major adjustment is also occurring in the relations between herding Saami and non-herding Saami. Identities are reshaped, and landscapes are imbued or reimbued with new Saami values.

Specific land encroachments, court verdicts, and parliamentary laws detrimental to Saami interests are generally quite easily identified. Yet the most pressing threats to the maintenance of Saami culture and livelihoods lie often hidden in larger mechanisms where government policies, the economy, and public opinion interact. The attempt by herders to supplement their meager incomes by developing hunting and fishing businesses under Saami control has resulted in indignation over the purportedly high prices charged, public outcry, and eventually the confiscation of exclusive Saami small-game hunting rights in Sweden. Efforts to forge a strong reindeer-herding economy, based upon government-supported rationalization programs that encourage the use of modern technology, have led to conflict with environmentalists, public disapproval, and further legal constraints on herding. The more that herding comes to ressemble Swedish animal farming, the more it loses majority support for its moral claim to special indigenous rights.

Recent developments, including the creation of Saami parliaments in both Norway and Sweden, have brought about the resurgence of Saami identity and rights based on ethnicity, rather than simply on the practice of the herding livelihood. The ethnic dimension of Saamihood is also increasingly visible in state policies and subsidy programs for Saami language, theater, and handicrafts. In Sweden, for example, there is much discussion about expanding the economic potential of the *Samebys* by permitting various non-herding activities, and there is talk of opening the *Samebys* to non-herding Saami membership. While such developments are to be applauded, they contain the seeds of serious threats to herding and, through it, to all Saami culture.

This can lead to a dangerous situation in which cultural elements such as language and art are greatly supported, but the cultural elements that involve access to and utilization of natural resources (e.g., herding) that conflict with non-Saami land-use schemes are neglected. Although it can appear that the state is strongly supporting the Saami, in fact this support is extended only to those elements that do not conflict with non-Saami interests. Herding is caught in a bind: if given financial support (even if only to the same degree as provided to other branches of Swedish agriculture) and its Saami monopoly as an indigenous livelihood maintained, loud complaints are heard that herding is little more than a "nursing home for the handicapped," or a hobby play school for Saami cultural "imposters." On the other hand, if the Saami legal monopoly on herding (as in Norway and Sweden) is removed, and herding is evaluated merely in terms of how much money it earns and how many people it employs, it could hardly maintain a strong position with respect to land utilization when its large land needs and small generated profits are compared with those of heavy extractive exploitation.

Given these mechanisms, it would seem that the Saami herding livelihood and culture are in danger of becoming artificially preserved to serve the tourist market. This dismal development can be avoided if the dominant majority comes to learn that Saami interests and environmental interests are far more similar than divergent, that Saami culture cannot be maintained as a static entity, that this ever-changing cultural continuity demands Saami self-determination rather than fickle government patronage, and that the fate of the Saami and indigenous peoples as a whole is a precursor to the fate of humankind.

On a more mundane level, and lest "the reindeer starve while its grazing rights are negotiated," the Saami are engaged on many fronts: to stop Saami language decline, to promote Saami handicrafts, to counteract the spiral of increasingly high-technology reindeer herding and the increasingly high costs of management, to reaffirm Saami livelihoods as ecologically responsible and viable, and to gain a meaningful voice in the development of northern industries so that they may grow with consideration for Saami livelihoods.

Questions

1. How does Saami immemorial right to land compare and contrast with the right of land ownership?

2. Why do so many Saami in Sweden believe that the state has deprived them of their reindeer-herding livelihood and cultural traditions when, according to the Swedish Reindeer Herding Act, all those of Saami ancestry have the right to herd reindeer?

3. How does the government justify the legislation that prohibits the Swedish *Samebys* from engaging in any economic activity other than herding?

4. In what ways can increasingly global environmental consciousness and legislation be a threat to Saami rights when the Saami themselves are so dependent upon maintaining natural systems free from heavy exploitation?

5. What are the essential differences between, on the one hand, the Saami parliaments—most recently established in Norway and Sweden—and, on the other hand, the political organizations of the Saami that previously existed and that are still active?

RESOURCE GUIDE

Published Literature

Bäckman, L., and Å Hultkrantz. *Studies in Lapp Shamanism*. Stockholm Studies in Comparative Religion. Stockholm: Acta Universitatis Stockholmiensis, 1978.

Beach, H. "The Saami of Lapland." In Birgitta Jahreskog, ed., *Polar Peoples: Self-Determination and Development*. Atlantic Highlands, N.J.: Humanities Press; Stockholm: Almqvist and Wiksell International, 1994.

———. *A Year in Lapland: Guest of the Reindeer Herders*. Washington, D.C.: Smithsonian Institution Press, 1993.

Collinder, B. *The Lapps*. Princeton, N.J.: Princeton University Press, 1949.

Jahreskog, B., ed. *The Sami National Minority in Sweden*. Legal Rights Foundation, 1982.

Konstantinov, Y. "Field Research of Reindeer-Herding in the Kola Peninsula: Problems and Challenges." *Acta Borealia* 2–1996, 13, no. 2: 53–68.

Paine, R. *Herds of the Tundra: A Portrait of Saami Pastoralism*. Washington, D.C.: Smithsonian Institution Press, 1994.

Sámi Instituhtta. *The Sami People*. Karasjok, Norway: Davvi Girji O.S., 1990.

Siuruainen, E., and P. Aikio. *The Lapps in Finland: The Population, Their Livelihood, and Their Culture*. Helsinki: Society for the Promotion of Lapp Culture, 1977.

Thuen, T. *Quest for Equity: Norway and the Saami Challenge*. St. John's, Newfoundland: Institute of Social and Economic Research, Memorial University of Newfoundland, 1995.

Films

An Invisible Enemy, 1987. 52 minutes. Disappearing World Series, Stock no. 51247. Pennsylvania State University, 118 Wagner Rd., University Park, PA 16802–1003. (Documents the threat to the economic and cultural survival of the Saami after the Chernobyl nuclear accident and the challenges to young Saami contemplating their futures)

The Sami: Four Lands, One People, 1978. 24 minutes. National Film Board of Canada, Catalogue no. 113C-0178-506. (Shows how Saami in the four countries are trying to find a way between the old traditions and new developments)

Sami Herders, 1978. 28 minutes. National Film Board of Canada. (Award-winning film follows the Mikkel Haette family on their annual migration in northern Norway)

Internet and WWW Sites

Nordic Sami Institute (provides links to English Web sites)
www.montana.edu/sass/sami

Swedish Sami Parliament
www.samefolket.se

Organizations

Nordic Sami Institute
N-9520 Kautokeino
Norway

The Norwegian Sami Parliament
N-9730 Karasjok
Norway

Sami College
Hannoluohkka 45
N-9520 Kautokeino
Norway

The Sami Council
FI-99980 Utsjoki
Finland

The Sami Parliament in Finland
PL 39
FI-99870 Inari
Finland

The Swedish Reindeer Herders Association
Brogatan 5
S 903 25 Ume°a
Sweden

The Swedish Sami Parliament
Geologgatan 4
S 981 31 Kiruna
Sweden

14

The Yupiit of Western Alaska

Ann Fienup-Riordan

The Yupik people of western Alaska are, in many ways, unique among northern peoples. They struggle against many of the same forces that beset other indigenous peoples, both in the past and the present. Yet their isolation and relatively late encounter with the non-native world have meant that they retain much that was lost elsewhere. The efforts of many Yupik men and women today focus on carrying the best of their past with them into the future. Today major issues that animate Yupik people as well as other Alaska natives are regaining control of their land, resources, and local affairs; improving economic conditions; and maintaining the Yupik language and values. Although these issues are not new, they focus public debate to an unprecedented degree.

CULTURAL OVERVIEW

The People

We call ourselves Yupiit or "Real People." In our language, yuk means "person" or "human being." Then we add pik meaning "real" or "genuine."
—Paul John (personal communication, 1985)

The name "Yupiit," or "Yupik Eskimos," is the self-designation of the people of western Alaska. They are members of the larger family of Inuit cultures that extend from Prince William Sound on the Pacific coast of Alaska to both sides of the Bering Strait and from there 6,000 miles north and east along Canada's Arctic coast into Labrador and Greenland. Within

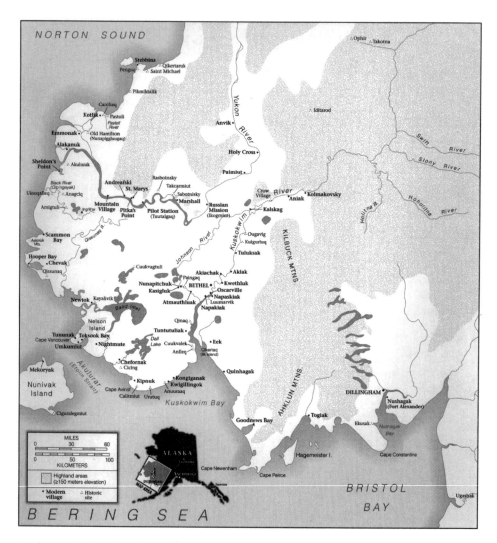

Southwest Alaskan Yupiit communities.

that extended family, they are members of the Yupik-speaking, not Inuit/
Iñupiaq-speaking, branch.

Following the population decline that resulted from the epidemics of the
nineteenth and early twentieth centuries, improved health care and the decline of infant mortality during the last seventy years have allowed the
population to surpass its aboriginal number. Today, nearly 20,000 Yupiit
live in western Alaska, scattered among seventy small communities of from
150 to 600 inhabitants each. All these modern villages have both elementary and secondary schools, a city government or traditional council, a
health clinic, a church or churches, an airstrip, electricity, and, in a few
places, running water and flush toilets. The traditional residential separation of men and women has been abandoned in favor of single-family
dwellings, and children divide their time between public school, video movies, and playing basketball in high school gymnasiums, not listening to
elders tell stories in the *qasgi* (communal men's house). Conversations between the generations still take place, in homes and special youth-elder
conferences, but these opportunities are more limited than in the past.

The Setting

The coastal landscape the Yupiit call home consists of a broad, marshy
plain, the product of thousands of years of silting action by the Yukon,
Kuskokwim, and Nushagak rivers. The sea is shallow and the land is flat,
criss-crossed by innumerable sloughs and streams which created the traditional highways of its native population. Although dubbed a frigid, barren
wasteland by many a non-native visitor, the subarctic tundra environment
nourishes a rich array of plants and animals, and the Bering Sea coast
supports rich fauna. An impressive variety of animals and fish appears and
disappears as part of an annual cycle on which many Yupiit continue to
this day to focus both thought and deed.

The Yupik people built on this rich resource base, developing a complex
cultural tradition prior to the arrival of the first Euro-Americans in the
early 1800s. Sometimes referred to as the "cradle of Eskimo civilization,"
the Bering Sea coast traditionally supported and continues to display a
cultural diversity and vitality unsurpassed in the Inuit world. As many as
15,000 people may have lived on the Yukon-Kuskokwim Delta in the early
1800s.

Traditional Subsistence Strategies

The abundance of fish and game in western Alaska allowed for a more
settled life than in other parts of the Arctic. Like the northern Inuit, the
Yupiit were nomadic but because of the rich environment they could remain within a relatively fixed range. Each of at least a dozen regional

Alan Hanson and Joseph Smith of Alakanuk prepare a place for a blackfish trap, 1982.
Copyright © James H. Barker. Used by permission.

groups moved freely in self-sufficient areas throughout the year in their quest for food.

Along the coast, harvesting activity focused on seals, walrus, beluga whales, ocean-going and freshwater fish, migratory birds, small animals, berries, and greens. As people moved inland and upriver, sea mammals decreased in importance and salmon increased in importance. Upriver hunters also pursued larger animals, including moose, caribou, and bear. Trade between groups ensured that upriver residents were well supplied with seal oil, and coastal residents had caribou skins for clothing.

Social and Political Organization

The extended family, including as many as thirty persons, was the basic social unit. Spanning from two to four generations, including grandparents, parents, and children, the group might also include siblings of parents or their children. An overlapping network of family ties, both real and fictive, joined people in a single community. In larger villages, most marriage partners came from within the group.

Extended families lived together most of the year in winter villages divided residentially between a communal men's house and smaller sod houses occupied by women and younger children. The winter villages ranged in size from one extended family to 300 people. Married couples or groups of hunters often moved to outlying camps for fishing and trapping during spring and early fall, gathering again after "freeze-up."

All men and boys older than five years of age ate their meals and slept in the *qasgi*, the social and ceremonial center of village life. When not away hunting, they spent their spare time there talking, carving, and making and repairing tools.

Good hunters were richly rewarded. The *nukalpiaq* ("good provider") was a man of considerable importance in village life. Social status and power accrued to those who could afford to give to others. Although the prowess and generosity of the *nukalpiag* were a primary focus of both political and economic integration in the community, the council of elders, who not only advised when to harvest but when distribution was appropriate, mitigated his authority.

Religion and World View

In the early decades of the 1900s, the Yupiit gathered after freeze-up in winter villages where they enjoyed a varied and elaborate ceremonial season. Each ceremony emphasized a different aspect of the relationship between humans, animals, and the spirit world.

The Bladder Festival, along with related ceremonies, ensured rebirth and return of the animals in the coming hunting season. During the Feast for the Dead, people elaborately fed and clothed living namesakes as a way to provide for and honor the souls of their departed relatives. The great Feast for the Dead served the same function within human society as the Bladder Festival did within animal society, expressing and ensuring continuity between the living and the dead. The intra-village Petugtaq and the inter-village Messenger Feast played on, exaggerated, and reversed normal social relationships between husband and wife, and between host and guest. The Messenger Feast also served important social functions, including displays of status, social control, and redistribution of wealth. At the same time, it provided a clear statement to the *yuit* (persons) of the animals, that the hunters were once again ready to receive them. Finally, the masked dance performed during Agayuyaraq dramatically re-created past encounters with spirits in order to elicit their participation in the future.

Together, these ceremonies embodied a cyclical view of the universe whereby right action in the past and present reproduced abundance in the future

THREATS TO SURVIVAL

To understand culture change and survival in Alaska today, it is necessary to understand how the Yupik people have responded to changing conditions during the last two centuries. This historic period can be understood to comprise six overlapping stages in the relationship between the Yupik people and those who came to live among them: coexistence, population disruption, attempted assimilation, global incorporation, dependency, and empowerment.

Coexistence

Significant Euro-American settlement did not occur in western Alaska until the end of the nineteenth century. Though rich in the resources necessary to support a scattered and seasonally nomadic population, the Bering Sea coast is notoriously lacking in the commercially valuable resources—gold, sea otters, bowhead whales—that first attracted non-native adventurers and entrepreneurs to other parts of the Arctic. Because of its geographical isolation and dearth of commercial resources, the Yukon-Kuskokwim Delta was virtually ignored by outsiders during the first three-quarters of the nineteenth century. A handful of Russian traders and Russian Orthodox priests migrated inland along the delta's major rivers beginning in the 1830s, but the people living along the Bering Sea coast between the Yukon and Kuskokwim rivers did not experience extended contact until nearly 100 years later.

Population Disruption and Attempted Assimilation

The arrival of Catholic and Moravian missionaries in the 1880s dramatically altered village life. These two missions made a much more sustained bid to convert the "baptized heathen" to whom the Russian Orthodox missionaries had laid claim. Moreover, both churches made concerted efforts to alter the Yupik way of life, especially along the Yukon and Kuskokwim rivers near their mission stations.

The year 1900 marked a major demographic shift in the region. The influenza epidemic that arrived that year with the annual supply vessels killed half the native population in just three months. Although coastal communities were not as severely affected, numerous winter villages were abandoned. At the same time the native population declined, the region's white population increased as a result of the Nome gold rush which spawned a concerted effort to locate mineral deposits along the upper Yukon and middle Kuskokwim rivers.

The Yupik people supplied fish and cordwood to miners and steamship captains and participated in an expanding fur trade, all of which brought about substantial changes to their domestic economy. In 1916 the regional superintendent for the U.S. Bureau of Education, John Henry Kilbuck, wrote with satisfaction that most Yupiit living along the Kuskokwim now lived in log cabins heated with cast-iron stoves, ate home-grown turnips and potatoes from graniteware dishes, possessed at least some Western clothing (which they mended on treadle sewing machines), and received education, health care, and Christian teachings from federal employees and missionaries.

Much had changed in western Alaska by 1959, when Alaska was granted statehood, but much remained the same. The continuities between past and present were as significant as the innovations. Most Yupiit continued to speak the Central Yupik language, enjoyed a rich oral tradition, participated in large ritual distributions of food items and other goods, and focused their lives on extended family relations that were bound to the harvesting of fish and wildlife. They never converted to gardening or reindeer herding, regardless of sustained missionary and federal encouragement to do so. The coastal population had declined dramatically, but its geographical isolation and commercial insignificance had inhibited change. The seasonal cycle of activities remained much the same as that of their ancestors. Most important, for the time being, they continued to be masters of their own lives.

Global Incorporation and Dependency

During the decade after statehood, Alaska natives generally were viewed as extremely disadvantaged, and the Yupiit of the Yukon-Kuskokwim

Delta region was one of the most impoverished groups among them. Relative to other areas of rural Alaska, the availability of Western material goods was minimal, modern housing nonexistent, educational levels low, and tuberculosis—as destructive as earlier influenza and smallpox epidemics—rampant.

In the 1960s, the Great Society dispatched scores of Volunteers to Service in America (VISTA) to the region as soldiers in President Lyndon Johnson's War on Poverty. Programs emphasized equal opportunity and full participation; however, as with the more blatantly assimilationist policies of the first half the century, the implication was still that non-native society was the goal toward which the Yupiit were striving.

Events in the 1970s began a new era in the Yukon-Kuskokwim Delta and throughout rural Alaska. Passage of the Alaska Native Claims Settlement Act (ANCSA) in 1971 transformed land tenure in the state, and it is still the major determinant of land status in Alaska today. It extinguished aboriginal land claims statewide, giving in return fee-simple title to 44 million acres of land and nearly $1 billion to twelve regional and one nonresident profit corporations and more than 200 village corporations. These organizations administer the land and money received under ANCSA. The Calista Corporation (literally "the worker") was established to manage the corporate resources of western Alaska.

ANCSA paved the way for the construction of the trans-Alaska pipeline, and the state's share of the oil profits gushed into public works projects and social programs. Supported by ANCSA village corporation activity and state services, the coastal communities of western Alaska experienced steady growth during the 1970s and 1980s. Villages burgeoned in both population and modern facilities, and employment income and cash provided support for local subsistence harvesting activity.

The regional economy shifted radically as the Yukon-Kuskokwim Delta's population settled at permanent village sites. Along with the continued importance of subsistence harvesting activities, the most significant feature of village economy in western Alaska today is its dependence on government. Commercial fishing and trapping, craft sales, and local service industries provide only a small portion of the total local income. As much as 90 percent flows through the village economies from the public sector, including both wages and salaries and various state and federal transfer payments.

Men and women in contemporary communities participate in a mixed economy, where both transfer payments and wages are used to pay for the snowmobiles, skiffs, motors, ammunition, and fuel required by modern harvesting activities. A man needs money to hunt and fish, and his success at the traditional acts of harvesting animals is directly tied to his ability to harvest cash. As the market economy of western Alaska continues to be marginal at best, hunting and fishing are activities that many find difficult to afford.

RESPONSE: STRUGGLES TO SURVIVE CULTURALLY

Western Alaska can be seen to represent an extreme example of both the positive and negative consequences of 200 years of cultural encounter. During the 1980s, increased state spending (coincident with the oil boom) accelerated the rate of change in this region. Though only 100 miles separate the two Yupik villages presented here—Toksook Bay on Nelson Island and Alakanuk at the mouth of the Yukon Delta—their responses to change have been markedly different. The discussion centers around two very different issues: game regulation on Nelson Island and Alakanuk's recent suicide epidemic. These two issues illustrate the tremendous importance for community and the personal well-being of having one's feet firmly grounded in the past when attempting to reach into the future.

Threats of Resource Use in Tooksook Bay, Nelson Island

One of the most important issues facing Nelson Islanders over the last ten years has been their relationship with their land and resources. In the past, this relationship was not one of possessive ownership. Humans took fish and game by virtue of proper attitude and action. People viewed animals as nonhuman persons that possessed immortal souls as well as an awareness comparable to that of humans. By this view, hunting and fishing could not directly deplete animal populations. Rather, human activity influenced the numbers or availability of animals through the reactions that human behavior caused in the animal world: animals and fish would always be available as long as they were given the proper respect.

One controversial issue on Nelson Island today is goose hunting. During the last ten years, the rapid decline in populations of several species of geese has resulted in a prohibition on hunting them during the early spring as well as during summer nesting and molting seasons. Although Nelson Islanders have cooperated with federal wildlife managers by limiting their hunting of selected species, their attitudes toward the issue dramatically contrast with those of the biologists and game managers responsible for federal oversight of the coastal waterfowl population.

Nelson Islanders readily admit that they do not see as many geese in the spring as in years past. Many are unwilling, however, to attribute this change to overkill, either through their own actions or those of hunters in California and Texas who harvest from the same populations during winter migrations. They maintain instead that fewer geese are in evidence because the birds are not receiving proper treatment and respect.

Moreover, the majority of Nelson Island hunters oppose the activities of the biologists who have set up observation platforms in the wetlands north of Nelson Island to provide accurate counts of waterfowl returning in spring. Many hunters believe that the scarcity of geese can be directly attributed to the general lack of respect shown the birds during the crucial nesting season, rather than to overkill. The Yupik explanation of hunting success and failure depends on proper social relations between humans and animals. This contradicts the idea that animal populations can be managed by selective hunting. Although they grudgingly limit their kills to comply with federal regulation, many Nelson Islanders remain unconvinced that this limitation really strikes at the core of the problem. Rather they believe that offenses against the birds are the cause of their "hiding themselves from our sight," and only when such inappropriate behavior ceases will the birds return.

Another resource conflict revolves around the herring fishery. In 1974 on Nelson Island, residents were firm: they did not want a commercial fishery in local waters. In the 1980s, however, the waters adjacent to Nelson Island were opened to commercial fishing, and although the local people were apprehensive, they also recognized that new sources of income had to be found to support the island's growing population. Regulations initially limited the fishery to local use. However, restrictions on certain types of fishing gear were lifted to increase the productivity of the fishery, and this allowed the entry of outsiders into the fishery.

Here again, the issue is not only economic but also moral and ideological. The non-native fishermen think that each man has as much right as any other to harvest the herring. After all, they say, the Yupik fishermen do not own the fish. Nelson Islanders, however, believe that rights to the fish do in fact belong to them in the sense that they have relied on the herring for generations and have a social relationship with them, not to mention moral obligations to them. For Nelson Islanders, rights to the herring are inalienable, conferred by knowledge and prior use.

What we can hope for is increased knowledge and awareness among both native and non-native leaders and policy makers in western Alaska of the organization of social relations in general, and of human and animal relations in particular, according to different cultural perspectives. Without such mutual understanding, fisheries development (both commercial and sport) and game management conflicts will continue. This is particularly true as declining revenues promote increased reliance on these resources. Although economic in character, these conflicts highlight cultural differences as much as the problem of disparate material circumstances. Their resolution is essential to cultural survival on Nelson Island.

Also, in looking to the past to help us better understand the relationship between humans and animals on Nelson Island today, it is important to realize that new ideas are also being accepted. Thus, today, some Nelson Islanders express the view that the geese suffer from overkill. Although they continue to affirm the need to respect geese as essential nonhuman persons, they have embraced the Western view of wildlife as a limited resource subject to management through selective hunting. Such attitudes signal a fundamental change in cultural understanding. It remains to be seen if and when this particular interpretation will become widely accepted by Nelson Islanders.

Alakanuk, Yukon Delta

Not all villages have been as successful as those on Nelson Island in retaining the cultural vitality for which coastal Yupik communities are known. Recent rapid social and economic change have had tragic consequences in the village of Alakanuk. In 1978 Alakanuk seemed different from the Nelson Island village of Toksook Bay in several important respects. None of the young people spoke the Yupik language. Also, although villagers pursued subsistence harvesting activities, they spent much less time and energy hunting and fishing than did the people of Nelson Island. Many older hunters held a traditional view of subsistence, but the majority of young men neither understood nor acted according to the view of the relationship between humans and animals described for Nelson Islanders.

These differences mark Alakanuk's history, which has been very different from that of Nelson Island. Its location along a major waterway meant that it was in contact with non-natives and their commercial economy much earlier. The extreme social disruption associated with epidemic diseases also came early to the community, and the orphans from these epidemics were gathered in mission schools where they were discouraged from using Yupik language and traditions.

In 1982, on the average, one person in every household had cash employment, thirty new houses were under construction, and the village government was both aggressive and successful in obtaining state funds for capital projects and other forms of municipal development. On the other hand, although villagers continued many seasonal harvesting activities, their overall reliance on local resources was less than that of neighboring coastal communities. Young men especially were less active in subsistence pursuits than their Nelson Island counterparts and were not training to be skilled hunters. This was in part due to the high cost of subsistence harvesting, requiring thousands of dollars to purchase and maintain needed hunting equipment, a sum few young men could afford.

In 1987 the village was in a serious economic recession, with a slow but steady increase in unemployment, more reliance on transfer payments, and (not surprising when one considers costs) a substantial decrease in subsistence harvesting activity. Although the village birthrate had increased, few new households had formed since 1982.

But something much more disturbing than a housing shortage or a decline in annual household harvesting activity had taken place. An alarming number of violent deaths had occurred between 1982 and 1987. Eight villagers (seven men and one woman) had committed suicide during a sixteen-month period in 1985 and 1986. Another nine attempted suicides were reported, and additional attempts probably went unreported. These suicides and attempted suicides occurred among young adults between the ages of eighteen and thirty. All the suicides were believed to be related to alcohol and drug use.

The suicide epidemic among this group of young adults affected members of all socioeconomic groups. Although several of those who died were unemployed at the time, at least two of the eight had significant incomes. Some came from families with few close relatives within the community, but just as many came from large extended families. Although some came from households heavily involved in subsistence activities, others did not.

All suicides occurred in the twenty-to-thirty-year-old age group. This group represents the largest sector of the population—105 men and women out of a total village population of 522. The impact of the suicide epidemic on Alakanuk's community structure has been compared in magnitude to the explosion of one of Anchorage's six high schools—leaving no survivors. Also, it is the members of this group who are normally looked to as the core of new households and future employment growth. However, present employment opportunity in the village is shrinking, and although children are being born at a rapid rate, new households have been much slower to appear.

Adolescents and postadolescents typically fare worst in periods of rapid culture change. Young adults are in the process of forming their personal identity—their basic orientation toward life. The formation of a strong identity requires continuity between the values and identifications learned in childhood and the roles available to them as adults, where those learned values can be expressed. Finding ways to realize Yupik values in the context of Western culture, which has shaped the significant goals available to young adults, is hard enough. When even these means of realizing personal identity are lacking, extreme frustration and confusion can result.

The mass media and Western consumer culture barrage village Alaska with diverse and unintegrated values, making it difficult for young adults to choose a future course. In the 1950s, anthropologist Margaret Lantis noted that "the new people with their new standards have nearly overwhelmed the Eskimo, not in numbers but in wishes and wants."[1] With the introduction of cable television—installed in Alakanuk in 1983—and increasing exposure of young Yupik men and women to American popular culture, it can easily be appreciated how much more intense this encounter is today.

Along with death through suicide, Alakanuk has endured an alarming rate of accidental and violent death, and in most cases these deaths are related to alcohol use. Alakanuk's experience is not without precedent in rural Alaska in general and western Alaska in particular. High rates of alcoholism, child abuse, sexual assault, violent crime, and mental health care problems plague the region as a whole. During the last ten years, despite ANCSA and all the state-funded schools and projects, these rates have increased.

Although violent, self-inflicted death occurs elsewhere in the region as a whole, nothing comparable to the high rate of suicide seen in Alakanuk has occurred in the more traditional, tightly integrated coastal or tundra communities elsewhere in the region. Native residents within Alakanuk as well as throughout the region have repeatedly assessed the epidemic as a consequence of the conditions existing at the time. They maintain that although individuals are responsible for their own actions, they cannot be expected to act appropriately if they are not in control of their land, language, and life. This assessment implies that a sector of Alakanuk's population had lost such a sense of control. The recent economic recession only made the situation worse.

A 1987 study of violent deaths conducted among young adults in western Alaska villages both supports and refines the conclusion that social disruptions and the nontraditional character of the region were contributing factors in the suicide epidemic. Public Health Service clinical psychologists Barbara Doak and Barbara Nachmann attempted to determine how those who suffered violent deaths differed from a similar group matched for age, sex, and village of origin. After carefully examining sixteen items more frequently present in suicides and other violent deaths, they concluded that four items are particularly important: region of origin, evidence of family success, evidence of individual success, and alcohol use by the subject.

It seems possible . . . that in a region of disrupted cultural loyalties, bright and ambitious youth from families who have ventured most daringly into the socioeconomic arena might be the ones most exposed to painful pressures which, with the help of alcohol, could tip them into disaster.

Personal success was the one item which marked the suicide group as different from other violent deaths. This lends itself to the speculation that, given the pressures which we have assumed pushed all of them toward some violent extreme, these who were most striving for excellence might be the ones most likely to take deliberate self-destructive actions rather than careless, unplanned ones.[2]

Doak and Nachmann concluded that there is no single suicidal personality, and no particular set of circumstances can predict who will take their lives.[3] For example, alcohol use, an unstable income, and cultural disruption do not necessarily lead to suicide and violent death. However, these conditions can set the stage for desperate acts among some talented, energetic, young adults—primarily men—facing limited and frustrating social and economic opportunities. As Roger Lang, a former president of the Alaska Federation of Natives, once said, "These are the ones who try to cross the bridge with no one to greet them on the other side."[4]

Empowerment for the Future

We have to know our culture and ourselves before we can face the future.
—Joe Friday, Chevak, Alaska[5]

The people of Nelson Island have retained important aspects of their traditional beliefs, but increasingly, these beliefs are neither understood nor sufficiently valued by the outside world that increasingly influences their lives. Young Yupik men and women living in communities such as Alakanuk have left this past behind and, in some measure, have attempted to enter the modern world, but they have found themselves blocked at the starting gate.

Local Governance

Federal assimilation policies officially ended with the Indian Reorganization Act in the 1930s. However, less overt efforts to assimilate the Yupik people continue—as exemplified in the corporate systems set up under ANCSA, the policy of mainstreaming in public education, and ambiguous public policies on the tribal status of Alaska natives.

For most Yupik people, their identity as Alaska natives is still linked to their relationship with the land, and retaining control of that land is a major focus of political effort. Today they continue to test the limits of both corporations and tribal governments to accomplish this goal. Calista (the native corporation for western Alaska) is only recently beginning to develop effective means of fostering their members' Yupik identity. Reacting in part to corporate failures, whether real or perceived, some Yupiit have asserted native sovereignty (inherent powers of self-government) and have established tribal governance in the form of the Yupiit Nation, which represents nineteen coastal and Kuskokwim communities. Viewed narrowly, the sovereignty movement is a reaction against the ANCSA corporation model. More broadly, it represents a concerted effort to take back political and cultural control of village communities from outside influences and to assert Yupik cultural identity in a variety of positive ways.

Increased control of, along with increased accountability for, the institutions directly affecting their lives will be essential to Yupik cultural survival. Given resistance to such initiatives by state and federal authorities, as well as factional disputes within Yupik communities, it is unlikely that leaders of the sovereignty movement will be able to fulfill all their goals. Nevertheless, the debate over how to make government more responsive to the needs of Alaska natives in general and the Yupik in particular has been a positive process in itself, giving participants a voice in their future. The Yupiit continue to work for increased self-government through increased local control over schools, courts, land, and local resources.

Economic Policy

The mixed economy characteristic of western Alaska is not a phase in the ultimate assimilation of Yupik people but an economically necessary and culturally preferred form with which many Yupiit identify. Yupik people today seek to retain a voice in resource allocation and economic development that affects their communities. As village populations increase at the same time government spending declines, hunting and fishing remain important in western Alaska—both for what these activities produce nutritionally and as a focus for a preferred lifestyle and cultural identity. Comanagement of commercial and subsistence resources, by such arrangements as, for example, the Kuskokwim Salmon Working Group and the Waterfowl Conservation Committee, have been initiated to ensure fair resource allocation and provide a vehicle through which Yupik community members can simultaneously express and affirm their cultural identity.

Nelson Islanders, for example, have to date been successful in using the new economic means at their disposal to improve their own circumstances. At the same time, they are working to reevaluate their traditional rules for living. Nelson Islanders, however, are far from dismissing their rich tradition as being unimportant in their daily lives.

A fundamental difference between Yupik and non-native views on the meaning of subsistence harvesting activity remains largely unrecognized. Even when it is acknowledged—as in the debate between wildlife managers, who view the decline in geese as the result of overharvesting, and the Yupik elders, who contend that limited harvests insult the geese causing them to go elsewhere—unequal power relations favor the non-native point of view.

Increasingly Yupik community leaders are finding ways to express and defend their point of view. For example, in 1995, the region's nonprofit corporation the Association of Village Council Presidents declared a five-year moratorium on field research on migratory birds in the coastal wetlands. The resolution was as much an expression of local resistance to nonlocal control as it was concern over the appropriateness of geese research and management. Since then, an emphasis on cooperative management has developed, with biologists writing to village councils indicating their desire to work more closely with community members, and community leaders talking about allowing biological research to continue in their areas, but under strict local control.

Education: Learning What It Means to Be Yupik

Many Yupik recognize that education in western Alaska is not just a local business but a powerful industry tied to the needs and desires of the larger society. Who it employs, what and how they teach, and how they interact with the community are all of vital importance to Yupik cultural identity.

Today, many Yupik schools support active bilingual and bicultural programs. With the notable exception of Bethel's newly established Yupik immersion program, the majority of these programs do not seek to maintain the Yupik language on an equal footing with English, but rather to use Yupik instruction in the primary grades as part of an effort to mainstream students as quickly as possible. By the time students enter high school, instruction in the Yupik language can occupy as little as forty-five minutes of their day.

All students need more than technical knowledge to succeed in life. They need pride in their heritage and an understanding of who they are as well as the belief that they can make valuable contributions to their families and communities. Native American communities throughout the nation are striving to develop programs that provide practical knowledge without destroying personal identity. Education that reinforces the value of being Yupik may be important in reducing the disproportionately high dropout rate.

As long as uniformity, as opposed to cultural pluralism remains the goal of the educational systems, a disproportionate number of students will fail and emerge with low self-esteem and ambivalence toward the wider society. Conversely, pride in their Yupik heritage will carry students a long way toward a satisfying future.

Efforts to ensure that Yupik continues to be a living language are at the heart of current efforts being made to preserve. According to Yupik language specialists Osahito Miyaoka and Elise Mather, "Once the Yupik are culturally and linguistically deprived to the marrow of the bones, all Yupiks will be lost in the mosquito-like swarm of Kass'aqs [white people] and will be no more than additional few Kass'aqs even if they do not look white. The people's identity could be kept and consolidated more effectively through the language."[6] In 1979 the Central Alaska Yupik language was one of only a handful of Alaska native languages expected to survive into the twenty-first century, with 14,000 fluent speakers out of a total population of 17,000 in the Kuskokwim heartland.[7] Since then, the number of fluent speakers has been steadily shrinking, as elders pass away and, more critical to language survival, fewer and fewer children grow up speaking Yupik as their first language. Realizing what they stand to loose, recent efforts to combat this decline have intensified, including a Yupik immersion program in Bethel, an annual four-week bilingual teachers' institute for training and teaching-material development, and numerous recording projects and elders' conferences to ensure the passing on of traditional knowledge and experience. Though Yupik students are still taught primarily by non-native teachers, the number of certified Yupik teachers is increasing, which will provide both role models and increased increase local control.

All of these efforts have been threatened recently by proposed English-only legislation, as well as cuts and reallocations in statewide educational funding that would destroy bilingual and bicultural programs throughout the region. Such programs designed as a collaboration between professionals and the local community, with the latter, not the former, retaining control, are imperative for building positive Yupik identity.

High school junior Nick Williams, who lives in the tundra village of Nunapitchuk, told reporter Fern Greenbank, "We're just like you. We don't want to lose our language anymore than you'd want to lose yours."[8] Another student, Alice Tobeluk, spoke from the heart: "Our Native language helps maintain our culture. We believe that by preserving the language, we promote the bond between Native land and Native people. . . . To me, bilingual education is like having the key to the door of opportunity—self-esteem, confidence and a will to dedicate ourselves to future generations."[9]

More and more Yupik educators realize that the best cultural heritage programs are locally-developed programs that involve students in community-based projects that allow them to reflect on their surroundings rather than tell them what their surroundings are. Local groups need seed money to enable developers of successful programs to consult with local district personnel, to get their development efforts started, to field-test their programs, and to train teachers in program implementation. Without both recognition and the necessary startup funds, grassroots efforts stand little chance of reaching their potential.

Finally, Yupik educators recognize that it is critical to establish first-rate English language programs and technical training programs such as computer science courses to enable Yupik students to realize their potential fully. Too many Yupik students suffer less from a conflict between Yupik and non-native cultural values than from a lack of thorough grounding in either one. They are not fully functional in either their Yupik language or English, and they need to be competent in both. Western Alaska is not a backwater where the unskilled can survive, but it is home to a unique way of life requiring special skills. The ability to walk between two cultural and linguistic worlds is one of them.

FOOD FOR THOUGHT

Contemporary Yupik leaders, teachers, and community members seek to enhance their cultural identity as the work simultaneously to reduce their dependency. They strive to take responsibility and authority for local health, education, and political and economic organization. In a situation of rapid culture change, they selectively appropriate Western means according to their own practical purposes. The choices must be theirs if they are to retain control over their lives, and such control is an essential key to their continued survival as Yupik people.

When public monies declined in the 1990s, residents struggled to find solutions to village problems and ways to continue to live in their traditional homeland. Many Yupik still see themselves as living in a traditional relationship with the living resources of their environment, not merely surviving off them. Although it has dramatically declined in Yukon and Nushagak river communities, Central Yupik continues to be the primary language for most people living in coastal and tundra villages. Public housing programs have dictated the construction of single-family houses, yet elaborate patterns of sharing food and other goods between households, adoption of children, and hunting partnerships continue to nourish extended family relationships. People remain strongly committed to traditional harvesting activities and continue to share products of the hunt.

The passage of ANCSA and, more recently, heightened awareness of domestic problems have created a diffuse yet important cultural reformation in much of western Alaska. Consciousness-raising has concentrated contemporary Yupik efforts on maintaining control of land, resources, and local affairs; improving residents' health and sense of well-being; and adhering to cultural and linguistic traditions. This renaissance reflects a certain nostalgia for the "old ways" which, in political and economic terms, refer to times after many technological improvements had been introduced but before the Yupik people had experienced subordination to federal and state control and related dependency.

Signs of this reformation abound—in the Yupik Nation sovereignty movement the debate over subsistence rights, the revival of intra-and intervillage winter dance festivals, the hosting of local and regional elders' conferences, and the increased awareness of and concern for the preservation and use of the Yupik language and oral tradition. All these activities reveal the desire of many Yupik people to take control of their land and their lives and to assert their pride in being Yupik.

Finally, the situation in western Alaska at present is not a native problem for which non-natives must find a solution. The issues concern the entire state and society, and all Alaskans must work together to solve them. For the last 100 years, many have assumed that Alaska natives ultimately would lose their unique cultural identity and be assimilated into the dominant Anglo society, and that most small villages would die out. These predictions have not come to pass.

The increasing articulation of issues of native cultural identity and political control indicate a growing awareness of the value of being a Yupik person in the modern world. Increasingly men and women—teachers, elders, parents—dedicate their energies to communicate the Yupik view of the world to the younger generation. Their efforts reflect the desire of many Yupik people to gain recognition of their unique past, parts of which they hope to carry into the future.

Questions

1. In what ways do the lives of young people in Yupik communities today, differ from those of Yupik youth living in more traditional times?

2. What were the major outside influences affecting Yupik village life in the nineteenth century? How did those particular influences differ from those experienced by other native people living elsewhere in Alaska (e.g., the Aleuts or the Iñupiat)?

3. It is said that Yupik personal and community well-being can benefit from having "one's feet firmly grounded in the past when attempting to reach into the future." Why should this be so? Do you think this is a notion that applies to most other societies, or is it just applicable to only certain groups of people?

4. In what ways do Yupik attitudes and beliefs toward animals differ from your own? Does mainstream American society have anything to learn from the Yupiit as we struggle to protect our own natural environment?

5. Schools and various economic development initiatives aim to assist Yupiit to become assimilated into mainstream American society. Discuss the place subsistence hunting and fishing might occupy in the lives of Yupiit over the next twenty to thirty years.

NOTES

Portions of the material in this chapter are based on a Native policy paper that Fienup-Riordan prepared for the Institute of Social and Economic Research at the University of Alaska Anchorage in 1992.

1. Margaret Lantis, "American Arctic Populations: Their Survival Problem," in Henry P. Hansen, ed., *Arctic Biology* (Corvallis: Oregon State University Press, 1957), 126.

2. Barbara Doak and Barbara Nachman, *Violent Deaths among Young Adults in Southwest Alaska Villages: A Subgroup of Longitudinal Cohort Study* (Anchorage: Alaska Native Medical Center, 1987), 8.

3. Ibid., 10.

4. Ann Fienup-Riordan, "Culture Change and Identity among Alaska Natives: Retaining Control" (Anchorage: Institute of Social and Economic Research, University of Alaska, 1992), 11.

5. Ibid., 1.

6. Osahito Miyaoka and Elsie Mather, *Yup'ik Eskimo Orthography* (Bethel, Alaska: Yup'ik Language Center, 1979), 1.

7. Michael Krause, personal communication.

8. Fern Greenbank, "A Matter of Voice: Native Speakers Would Be Lost Without Their Language," *Anchorage Daily News*, 11 January 1998, forum 1.

9. David Ulen, "Silent Tongues as Alaska's Most Spoken Native Language Slips Away," *Anchorage Daily News*, 21 July 1991, A1.

RESOURCE GUIDE

Published Literature

Alaska Natives Commission. *Joint Federal-State Commission on Policies and Programs Affecting Alaska Natives.* Final Report, 3 vols. Anchorage, Alaska: Author, 1994.

Doak, Barbara, and Barbara Nachman. *Violent Deaths among Young Adults in Southwest Alaska Villages: A Subgroup of Longitudinal Cohort Study.* Anchorage: Alaska Native Medical Center, 1987.

Fienup-Riordan, Ann. *Eskimo Essays: Yup'ik Lives and How We See Them.* New Brunswick, N.J.: Rutgers University Press, 1990.

———. *The Real People and the Children of Thunder: The Yup'ik Eskimo Encounter with Moravian Missionaries John and Edith Kilbuck.* Norman: University of Oklahoma Press, 1991.

Krauss, Michael. *Alaska Native Languages: Past, Present, and Future.* Fairbanks: University of Alaska Native Language Center, 1980.

Lantis, Margaret. "American Arctic Populations: Their Survival Problems." In Henry P. Hansen, ed., *Arctic Biology,* 119–30. Corvallis: Oregon State University Press, 1957. (Revised and reprinted 1967, pp. 243–87)

Miyaoka, Osahito, and Elsie Mather. *Yup'ik Eskimo Orthography.* Bethel, Alaska: Yup'ik Language Center, 1979.

Films and Videos

Drum of Winter, 1989. Sarah Elder and Leonard Kamerling.
Every Day Choices, 1985. Sarah Elder.
We of the River, 1985. TV Station KYUK, Bethel, Alaska.
Yupiit Yuraryarait: A Dancing People, 1983. TV Station KYUK in Bethel, Alaska.

Index

About the Editor and Contributors

DAVID G. ANDERSON is an assistant professor of anthropology at the University of Alberta, Edmonton, Alberta, Canada.

HUGH BEACH is an associate professor in the Department of Cultural Anthropology and Ethnology at Uppsala University, Uppsala, Sweden.

BARBARA BODENHORN is an affiliated lecturer in the Department of Social Anthropology, Cambridge University, Cambridge, England.

RICHARD A. CAULFIELD is an associate professor of rural development in the Department of Alaska Native and Rural Development at the University of Alaska, Fairbanks.

HELEN D. CORBETT is a research associate at the Arctic Institute of North America, University of Calgary, Calgary, Alberta, Canada, and cofounder of the Amiq Institute, Canmore, Alberta, Canada.

HARVEY A. FEIT is a professor of anthropology at McMaster University, Hamilton, Ontario, Canada.

ANN FIENUP-RIORDAN is an anthropologist who has published widely on the Yupik Eskimos of Alaska.

MILTON M. R. FREEMAN is Henry Marshall Tory Professor of Anthropology at the University of Alberta, Edmonton, Alberta, Canada.

PATTY A. GRAY received her Ph.D. in cultural anthropology from the University of Wisconsin, Madison.

GRETE K. HOVELSRUD-BRODA is the general secretary of the North Atlantic Marine Mammal Commission at the University of Tromsø, Tromsø, Norway.

ARNE KALLAND is a professor of anthropology in the Department and Museum of Anthropology at the University of Oslo, Oslo, Norway.

JOHN MACDONALD is the coordinator of the Igloolik Research Center, Nunavut Research Institute, Igloolik, Nunavut, Canada.

PATRICK MOORE is a native language consultant with the Department of Education, Yukon, Canada.

LEAH OTAK is the operations manager of the Igloolik Research Center, Nunavut Research Institute, Igloolik, Nunavut, Canada.

RASMUS OLE RASMUSSEN is an associate professor of North Atlantic regional studies at Roskilde University, Roskilde, Denmark.

BRUCE RIGBY is the executive director of the Nunavut Research Institute of Nunavut Arctic College, Iqaluit, Nunavut Territory, Canada.

PETER P. SCHWEITZER is an associate professor of anthropology at the University of Alaska, Fairbanks.

SUSANNE M. SWIBOLD is a research associate at the Arctic Institute of North America, University of Calgary, Calgary, Alberta, Canada, and co-founder of the Amiq Institute, Canmore, Alberta, Canada.

ADRIAN TANNER is a professor of anthropology at Memorial University of Newfoundland, St. Johns, Newfoundland, Canada.